TRIBES, LAND, AND THE ENVIRONMENT

Law, Property and Society

Series Editor:
Robin Paul Malloy

The Law, Property and Society series examines property in terms of its ability to foster democratic forms of governance, and to advance social justice. The series explores the legal infrastructure of property in broad terms, encompassing concerns for real, personal, intangible, intellectual and cultural property, as well as looking at property related financial markets. The series is edited by Robin Paul Malloy, and book proposals are welcome from all interested authors.

Robin Paul Malloy is E.I. White Chair and Distinguished Professor of Law, and the Kauffman Professor of Entrepreneurship and Innovation at Syracuse University College of Law, USA. He is Director of the Center on Property, Citizenship, and Social Entrepreneurism. He is also Professor of Economics (by courtesy appointment) in the Maxwell School of Citizenship and Public Affairs, Syracuse University. Professor Malloy writes extensively on law and market theory and on real estate transactions and development. He has authored eight books (one now in its third edition and another in its second edition), and edited seven additional books. He has also written more than 30 scholarly articles, and contributed to 12 other books. His recent books include: LAW AND MARKET ECONOMY (2000, in English and translated into Spanish and Chinese); LAW IN A MARKET CONTEXT (2004); and REAL ESTATE TRANSACTIONS 3RD EDITION (with James C. Smith, 2007).

Tribes, Land, and the Environment

Edited by

SARAH KRAKOFF
University of Colorado Law School, USA

EZRA ROSSER
American University Washington College of Law, USA

Routledge
Taylor & Francis Group
LONDON AND NEW YORK

First published 2012 by Ashgate Publishing

Published 2016 by Routledge
2 Park Square, Milton Park, Abingdon, Oxfordshire OX14 4RN
711 Third Avenue, New York, NY 10017, USA

First issued in paperback 2016

Routledge is an imprint of the Taylor & Francis Group, an informa business

British Library Cataloguing in Publication Data
Tribes, land, and the environment. -- (Law, property and society)
1. Environmental law--United States. 2. Environmental justice--United States. 3. Indians of North America--Government relations. 4. Indians of North America--Politics and government. 5. Tribal government--United States.
I. Series II. Krakoff, Sarah. III. Rosser, Ezra.
344.7'3046'08997-dc23

Library of Congress Cataloging-in-Publication Data
Tribes, land, and the environment / [edited] by Sarah Krakoff and Ezra Rosser
p. cm. -- (Law, property and society)
Includes bibliographical references and index.
ISBN 978-1-4094-2062-0 (hardback)
1. Indians of North America--Land tenure. 2. Environmental law--United States. 3. Indians of North America--Legal status, laws, etc. 4. Property--United States. 5. Land tenure--Government policy--United States. I. Krakoff, Sarah. II. Rosser, Ezra.
KF5660.T75 2012
346.7304'3208997--dc23

2011043436

ISBN 13: 978-1-138-27465-5 (pbk)
ISBN 13: 978-1-4094-2062-0 (hbk)

Contents

This book is dedicated to the memory of David Getches

Introduction

Sarah A. Krakoff and Ezra Rosser[1]

Federal Indian law—the body of law that governs the relationship between the United States federal government and American Indian nations—originated in disputes about land. In *Johnson v. McIntosh*, Chief Justice John Marshall adopted the quasi-international law notion that legal title to indigenous peoples' lands vested in the federal government as inheritor of the so-called discovery rights of European nations.[2] With that swift blow, indigenous peoples' pre-contact claims to unitary rights in their aboriginal lands were reduced to rights of use and possession, unless formally recognized by the United States.[3] Several years later, *Worcester v. Georgia*'s holding was that state laws had no effect within the Cherokee Nation's boundaries,[4] but the conflict was driven by Georgia's ceaseless efforts to oust the Cherokee from those lands altogether. Ever since these and other foundational clashes, American Indian nations have struggled to maintain at least remnants of their aboriginal lands, notwithstanding various historic efforts to eradicate the presence of tribally held lands and resources. Today, in the era of American Indian Tribal Self Determination, approximately 56 million acres of land are held in trust by the federal government for American Indian tribes and individuals, and Alaska Native entities hold an additional 45 million acres. Many tribes also own some land in fee simple as a result of tribal land reacquisition programs. While all of this is but a tiny fraction of what aboriginal peoples formerly held (the entire continent, in pre-contact times), tribal lands and resources are nonetheless a crucible for many of the most controversial and fraught issues at the cross-roads of several fields of law, including but not limited to federal Indian law, property law, and environmental law. The chapters in this volume explore the sources of controversy, describe their effects, and attempt to map solutions.

Before summarizing these important contemporary contributions, another glance at the past will illuminate their context. One-hundred and forty years after *Johnson* and *Worcester* were decided, members of fishing tribes in the Northwest began to protest state restrictions on their treaty rights to fish at off-reservation

---

1 Sarah A. Krakoff is a Professor of Law and Wolf-Nichol Fellow at the University of Colorado Law School. Ezra Rosser is an Associate Professor at American University Washington College of Law.

2 21 U.S. (8 Wheat.) 543 (1823).

3 *See id.*

4 31 U.S. (6 Pet.) 515 (1832).

sites. In Oregon and Washington, competition for the dwindling populations of salmon prompted state officials to arrest tribal members for engaging in their ancient, traditional, and treaty-guaranteed practices. Putting up with state-imposed restrictions would not only have violated the tribes' legal rights, but also would have imposed a cost on tribes for a problem—the evisceration of the salmon runs—to which they did not contribute. In Washington, the United States sued the state on behalf of fourteen tribes. The tribes intervened in the litigation, represented by David Getches, who was then the director of the Native American Rights Fund. The tribes sought an interpretation of their treaty rights that entitled them to the opportunity to take up to 50 percent of the salmon and steelhead that passed through their off-reservation fishing sites.[5] If the tribes' interpretation prevailed, they would win more than the right to take fish. They would affirm the broader notion that nineteenth-century treaties, which guaranteed not just specific enumerated rights but also reserved general rights to self-governance, remained in full force.[6] The tribes won.[7] The federal district court affirmed the tribes' interpretation, a holding as controversial in its own time as it has proved to be important ever since.

David Getches, the determined young lawyer at NARF who represented the Washington tribes and went on to write some of the most important contemporary scholarship on federal Indian law, natural resources law, and water law,[8] recently passed away. We pay homage to his incalculable contributions here. Without the work of tribal leaders, like Billy Frank of the Nisqually Tribe, who put their bodies on the line, and their lawyers, like David Getches, who crafted modern arguments to breathe life into centuries-old promises, many of the issues described in this book would have unfolded very differently. Tribes govern their lands and strive

---

5 *See* Charles F. Wilkinson, Crossing the Next Meridian: Land, Water and the Future of the West 204–07 (1992) (describing the events leading up to the fishing rights litigation and the details of the case).

6 *See* Sarah Krakoff, *Mark the Plumber v. Tribal Empire, or Non-Indian Anxiety v. Tribal Sovereignty*, in Indian Law Stories 261 (Philip Frickey, Carole Goldberg & Kevin Washburn eds. 2011) (describing the backdrop of the fishing rights disputes as including larger questions about tribal resurgence).

7 *See* United States v. Washington, 348 F. Supp. 312 (W.D. Wash. 1974), *aff'd*, 520 F.2d 676 (9th cir. 1975). In subsequent parallel litigation, the Supreme Court affirmed the conclusion and reasoning. *See* Washington v. Washington State Commercial Passenger Fishing Vessel Association, 443 U.S. 658 (1979).

8 *See, e.g.*, David H. Getches et al., Cases and Materials on Federal Indian Law (6th ed. 2011); David H. Getches, Water Law in a Nutshell (4th ed. 2008); David H. Getches, *Beyond Indian Law: The Rehnquist Court's Pursuit of States' Rights, Color-Blind Justice, and Mainstream Values*, 86 Minn. L. Rev. 267 (2001); David H. Getches, *Conquering the Cultural Frontier: The New Subjectivism of the Supreme Court in Indian Law*, 84 Cal. L. Rev. 1573 (1996). This is a very incomplete list. Including all of David Getches's publications over the course of his prolific career would extend these footnotes unreasonably.

to manage their reservation environments because they persist as sovereigns, with unique status and rights under domestic law. None of that was, or is, a given. At every stage, tribes and their allies have had to bring the law to life. The window of opportunity that presented itself in the late 1960s and early 1970s was a crucial one. The spirit of the times, public and judicial, allowed for a reaffirmation of the treaty guarantees, and a renaissance of *de facto* exertions of tribal powers.

Times are different now than they were when David Getches started his career. Yet as the following chapters reveal, many of the sources of tension remain the same. The themes that ran through the Northwest fishing cases—conflicts between states and tribes, disparate imposition of regulatory burdens owing to natural resource scarcity, and questions about the vitality of ancient legal promises—run through the chapters below. Furthermore, the legal resolution of the Northwest tribal fishing rights cases helped to create the framework of contemporary Indian law, without which many of today's assertions of tribal rights to manage their lands and resources might not exist. We would do well to recall that there is precedent, factual and legal, for the liberatory potential of devoting a life's work to fighting for the rights of tribes to chart their own environmental destinies.

Chapter 1 addresses the theme of tribal environmental self-determination head on. In "Towards a Trust We Can Trust: The Role of the Trust Doctrine in the Management of Tribal Natural Resources," Alex Tallchief Skibine argues that the Indian trust doctrine should be decolonized. The trust doctrine governs the relationship the federal government has with tribes, and imposes on the federal government duties of protection and fair dealings. Most reservation land accordingly is held in joint trust by the federal government and by the particular Indian nation. Skibine argues that a decolonized trust would emphasize tribal sovereignty, limit congressional plenary power, and break from notions, rooted in the discovery doctrine, of ultimate federal title over tribal land. By introducing different conceptions of the trust doctrine and visions for the federal–tribal relationship, Chapter 1 makes a provocative argument and sets the doctrinal stage for many of the chapters that follow.

Blending theory and practice, James M. Grijalva explores the challenges of tribal management and oversight of energy development on reservations, and the public participation possibilities of facilitated stakeholder gatherings. Chapter 2, "Control and Accountability: The Twin Dimensions of Tribal Sovereignty Necessary to Achieve Environmental Justice for Native America," starts with an overview of the U.S. Environmental Protection Agency (EPA)'s pro-tribal sovereignty approach to environmental regulation of Indian lands. Grijalva argues that, as tribes increasingly exercise their authority to review environmentally damaging projects, new stresses will be placed on the EPA's approach. Tribal institutions for public participation must be both open and strong, given the threats to sovereignty posed by external reaction to tribal regulatory authority over off-reservation development, and the frequent intra-tribal disagreements over tribal environmental governance policies. Grijalva ends by describing public involvement processes that he participated in, which revealed schisms as well as areas of agreement between tribal governments and environmental organizations. He suggests that such processes could provide models for a way forward that could strengthen tribal self-governance as well as tribal environmental protection. Building on the theme of improving tribal institutions, in the following chapter, Dean B. Suagee provides an overview of the causes of climate change and suggests a number of ways in which Indian nations can participate in the global response. Chapter 3, "The Climate Crisis, the Renewable Energy Revolution, and Tribal Sovereignty," briefly reviews the causes of global warming, and then discusses various changes in our consumption patterns that can prevent catastrophic climate change impacts. The chapter serves as a primer on climate change and mitigation strategies, suggesting multiple ways for tribes to participate in the transition from fossil fuel dependence to energy efficiency and a renewable energy future.

In Chapter 4, "Application of Environmental Justice to Climate Change-Related Claims Brought by Native Nations," Elizabeth Ann Kronk argues that environmental justice is a necessary part of the consideration of climate change-related claims brought by Native nations. Native peoples are particularly vulnerable to global warming impacts, and Kronk begins by situating this vulnerability in the claims brought by the Native Village of Kivalina—a Native Alaskan community at risk of falling into the ocean as a result of rising sea levels—against many of the companies profiting from the global consumption of fossil fuels. Kronk then describes the rise of environmental justice as an area of concern. She outlines the ways in which environmental justice has distinctive contours in the Native nation context because of inherent tribal sovereignty, the U.S. federal trust responsibility, the unique connections that many Native nations have to land, and the potential application of the United Nations Declaration on the Rights of Indigenous Peoples. In Chapter 5, "The Promise and Perils of Renewable Energy on Tribal Lands," Sara C. Bronin highlights the environmental and legal attributes common to many reservations—relatively larger amounts of open space and relatively fewer land use regulations, for instance—that make them attractive for the siting of renewable energy facilities. Renewable energy projects could also serve tribal communities that, even today, lack access to the energy grid. Bronin's primary focus is the unfulfilled promise of the Indian Tribal Energy Development and Self-Determination Act of 2005 (ITEDSA) to promote tribal self-governance when it comes to energy development.

Chapter 6, "At the Margins: Border Tribes' Struggles to Protect Reservation Lands, Waters, and Communities," argues that the rights of border tribes—tribes located near the Mexican and Canadian borders—are being infringed by border policies that fail to recognize the sovereign interests of these tribes. Allison M. Dussias shows not only that the Boundary Waters Treaty and subsequent agreements between the United States and Canada failed to take into account tribal interests in the same resources, but also that tribes continue to be largely excluded from program implementation and decision-making. Similarly, the Tohono O'odham Nation's ability to meet the needs of tribal members is being severely impaired by the environmental and financial impacts of illegal immigrants crossing the tribe's 75 mile stretch of the United States–Mexico border. In its effort to stem the immigration flow, the U.S. government has failed to engage on a government-to-government basis with the Tohono O'odham Nation. Dussias highlights the efforts tribes have made in spite of these challenges and ends by calling upon the U.S. government to treat border tribes as full partners in endeavors to make progress on common goals. In the next chapter, Jacqueline Phelan Hand builds on these themes with a detailed account of the history of United States–Canada agreements involving the protection of the Great Lakes and the marginalization of Great Lakes tribes in the negotiations and resulting protection schemes. Chapter 7, "Co-operating to Protect the Shining Big Sea Water and its Siblings: Consultation with Native Peoples in Protecting the Great Lakes," illustrates the commitment of area tribes to protecting the Great Lakes and to participating alongside Canada, the United States, and the states and provinces bordering the Great Lakes. Almost immediately after being marginalized by an agreement process that did not include tribal representation, tribes met to protest their exclusion and insist upon their rights in the management of the Great Lakes. Hand, borrowing concepts from Canadian law, argues for a more robust consultation with tribes in the management of shared resources.

In Chapter 8, "Tribes as Conservation Easement Holders: Is a Partial Property Interest Better than None?" Jessica Owley argues that tribes should be cautious about jumping on the conservation easements bandwagon. The chapter introduces conservation easements, explains their purposes, and covers the legal bases—under state, tribal, and federal law—for tribes to be holders of conservation easements. Owley addresses why conservation easements may be an attractive property right for tribes, but also highlights some of their downsides. The heart of Owley's argument is that, contrary to the position of many environmentalists, conservation easements are not free of risks and may in fact ultimately promote a less environmentally protective understanding of property. Tribes, according to Owley, need to consider carefully the pros and cons of conservation easements before rushing into them to ensure that their goals align with the conservation easement framework. While Owley's concerns stem from the potential traps for tribes of buying into a property rights approach, the next chapter describes the limits and the potential for informal approaches to tribal rights in land. Chapter 9, "Natural Allies: Conservationists, Indian Tribes, and Protecting Native North America," tells the story of the efforts of the Indian Law Resource Center and the Traditional Seminoles to find and secure land for the tribe's annual ceremony. Traditional Seminoles live largely separate from non-Indian societies in the Florida everglades. They sought the assistance of the Center when development made the site they had been using for their ceremony inappropriate. As Kirsten Matoy Carlson and Robert T. Coulter describe, the hunt for a suitable replacement site was complicated by the Traditional Seminole belief that they should not own land, and by some environmental groups' resistance to the idea that limited human use of land could be consistent with conservation. Although the story illustrates many of the stumbling blocks that present themselves when tribes and environmentalists join forces, Carlson and Coulter's chapter offers an example and road map for how tribes and environmentalists ultimately can work together to pursue common interests.

Tribes, Land, and the Environment concludes with Chapter 10, "The Role of Indigenous Custom in Environmental Governance: Lessons from the Inter-American Human Rights System," in which Ghislain Otis provides an international law perspective on the land and resource rights of indigenous peoples. Otis gives a brief history of the rising attention to indigenous rights in international law before focusing on the work of the Inter-American Court of Human Rights. As described in the chapter, customary practices and behavior have become central elements of proof for indigenous peoples seeking to have their rights to land and resources recognized. Chapter 10 indicates the promise, and the limitations, of international law as a mechanism for the protection of indigenous peoples' rights to set their own path in the use of their land and resources.

As readers make their way through these diverse contributions, we encourage them to keep track of the common threads. In our view, they include but are not limited to: the difficulty of accommodating group rights, whether in the American Indian law or international law contexts, within a socio-legal culture committed to liberal individualism; the potential for tension between protecting tribal sovereignty and promoting environmental protection/stewardship; and the recurring risk that stereotypes (whether of the romantic or savage variety) will preclude constructive engagement with indigenous peoples about environmental and land protection. We hope that this book advances the reader's knowledge and understanding about these important matters.

Chapter 1

Towards a Trust We Can Trust: The Role of the Trust Doctrine in the Management of Tribal Natural Resources

Alex Tallchief Skibine[1]

The political relationship between the federal government and the American Indian nations located within the United States is said to be a trust relationship. Under this relationship, also known as the trust responsibility, the Indian nations surrendered some of their sovereignty and acknowledged their political dependence on the United States. In return, the United States undertook a trustee's duty to protect the tribal land base and guarantee the Indian nations' right to self-government within this land base.[2] Most scholars trace the beginning of the trust doctrine to Chief Justice Marshall's famous utterance in *Cherokee Nation v. Georgia* that the relationship between the United States and the tribes resembled that of a guardian to its ward.[3] Others, like Mary Wood, have argued that the trust doctrine emerged from the huge land transfers that took place between the United States and the tribes.[4] Yet others, like Robert Miller, agree that it originated from land transfers, but trace it to the land transfers that took place as a result of the doctrine of discovery according to which the United States obtained "ultimate title" to all Indian lands.[5] Whatever its origins, it seems to have had some pre-constitutional roots, given that the 1787 Northwest Ordinance contained these famous words: "The utmost good faith shall always be observed towards the Indians; their lands and property shall never be taken from them without their consent."[6]

---

1 S. J. Quinney Professor of Law, University of Utah S. J. Quinney College of Law.

2 Other more specific trust duties were also undertaken pursuant to specific treaties and Acts of Congress.

3 30 U.S. 1, 54 (1831).

4 Mary Christina Wood, *Indian Land and the Promise of Native Sovereignty: The Trust Doctrine Revisited*, 1994 Utah L. Rev. 1471 (1994) [hereinafter Wood, *Indian Land and the Promise of Native Sovereignty*].

5 Robert J. Miller, Native America, Discovered and Conquered 166 (2006).

6 *Reprinted in* Act of Aug. 7, 1789 (Northwest Ordinance), ch. 8, art. 2, 1 Stat. 50, 52. This Article also stated, however, that "just and lawful" wars against the Indians could be authorized by Congress. *Id.*

The trust doctrine's uncertain origins have been followed by a long and tortuous path through legal history, which in turn has generated very mixed feelings on behalf of Indian tribes. Thus it is not surprising that recently there have been suggestions from scholars such as Kevin Gover,[7] Stacy Leeds,[8] and Lincoln Davies,[9] among others, that the trust doctrine should be abandoned, or at least seriously modified, especially when it comes to control of Indian natural resources. These scholars take the position that, when it comes to management of the reservations' environment and control of tribal natural resources, the trust doctrine is anachronistic and a serious impediment to both tribal self-government and economic development. Other scholars, notably Mary Wood, take a much more conciliatory position and advocate the continued use of a vigorous trust doctrine as a means to protect the reservations' environment from deleterious federal policies and actions by federal officials.[10] Finally, others, like Reid Chambers, adopt a middle ground.[11] According to Chambers, the major problem with the trust doctrine is that it has been misunderstood. Properly conceived, the trust doctrine should only be viewed as a doctrine to protect and encourage tribal self-government.[12] This essay aligns with this latter view, but its main purpose is to lay the legal foundations for such a decolonized trust doctrine and explain its major doctrinal ramifications for the field of Federal Indian law.

One of the problems with the trust doctrine is that there are at least two major conceptions of it. The one first endorsed by Chief Justice Marshall was that the trust relationship between the tribes and the United States is there to protect the continuing existence of tribes as self-governing sovereign entities. Mary Wood has

---

7 Kevin Gover, *An Indian Trust for the Twenty-First Century*, 46 NAT. RESOURCES J. 217 (2006).

8 Stacy Leeds, *Moving towards Exclusive Tribal Autonomy over Lands and Natural Resources*, 46 NAT. RESOURCES J. 439 (2006).

9 Lincoln L. Davies, *Skull Valley Crossroads: Reconciling Native Sovereignty and the Federal Trust*, 68 MD. L. REV. 290 (2009).

10 Mary Christina Wood, *Protecting the Attributes of Sovereignty: A New Trust Paradigm for Federal Actions Affecting Tribal Lands and Resources*, 1995 UTAH L. REV. 109 (1995).

11 Reid Peyton Chambers, *Compatibility of the Federal Trust Responsibility with Self Determination of Indian Tribes: Reflections on Development of the Federal Trust Responsibility in the Twenty-First Century*, 2005 Rocky Mtn. Min. L. Found. Paper No. 13A (2005).

12 *Id.* at 22. Chambers gives three reasons while this version of the trust should be adopted. First, tribes are no longer really dependent on the United States. Second, the version of the trust that emerged during the allotment era was racist. Third, as a doctrine of federal common law, the trust doctrine should reflect the current policies of Congress and such policies currently endorse the promotion of tribal self-determination and self-government.

termed this version of the doctrine the "sovereign trust" branch.[13] She contrasted that version with one she called the "guardian ward" one. That second version developed during the plenary power or allotment era (about 1880–1930). Its main purpose was to give plenary power to the federal government over Indian land, natural resources, and people, after the treaty era was ended in 1871.[14] Through the years, Congress has used, and some may say abused, this power extensively to control and manage the tribes' natural resources.[15] Under this version of the doctrine, the trust arose out of necessity because Indian tribes and people were said to be "weak and defenseless." Indians as individuals became "wards" of the government because they were considered incompetent to manage their own personal affairs. During that era, the doctrine was transformed from one concerning the political relation between the tribes and the United States to one focusing on the relationship between the federal government and the Indians, as individual wards. The whole idea behind most of the allotment Acts was that the trust period was only temporary and would cease to exist when the wards became competent enough to be assimilated into the dominant mainstream society. This policy was officially abandoned with the enactment of the Indian Reorganization Act of 1934,[16] but many of the legal principles adopted during that period were never overturned.[17]

Because of this conflicting and confusing history, some scholars look at the trust as just a paternalistic doctrine with racist origins that can be and has been used to oppress Indian people. Others, however, make the opposite mistake: they tend to romanticize the trust in that they think that there is a general trust obligation permeating all tribal dealings with the United States and, therefore, the federal government should always be legally and morally bound to act for the benefit of the tribes. This essay does not agree with either version and rather attempts to demystify the trust doctrine by giving a frank evaluation of its usefulness and viability. It first discusses, from a tribal perspective, the pros and cons of the doctrine. It then explains what should be the correct understanding of the doctrine and the ramifications of this understanding concerning the power of Congress over the reservation environment.

---

13 *See* Wood, *Indian Land and the Promise of Native Sovereignty*, *supra* note 4, at 1496–1504.

14 *See* United States v. Kagama, 118 U.S. 375 (1886), Cherokee Nation v. Hitchcock, 187 U.S. 294 (1902).

15 *See* Judith Royster, *Practical Sovereignty, Political Sovereignty, and the Indian Tribal Energy Development and Self-Determination Act*, 12 Lewis & Clark L. Rev. 1065 (2008).

16 48 Stat. 984 (1934), 25 U.S.C. 461 et. seq.

17 *See* Judith Royster, *The Legacy of Allotment*, 27 Ariz. St. L. J. 1 (1995).

The Benefits and Drawbacks of the Doctrine for Tribes

The Benefits

I have identified the trust doctrine's eight major benefits to tribes. They are ranked here, albeit subjectively, in their order of importance:

1. Perhaps the most prominent benefit of the doctrine is that "Trust" lands cannot be taxed by the states. Some lands that were taken out of trust and are now owned by Indians in fee simple are being taxed by the states even though these lands are still in Indian ownership and located within Indian reservations.[18] Some Justices, like Justice Thomas, have taken the position that "alienability" means taxability when it comes to Indian land.[19]
2. Another equally important benefit of having land placed into trust is that Indian tribes retain jurisdiction over such lands even if they are located outside Indian reservations. Thus all lands held in trust are defined as being "Indian Country" for jurisdictional purposes.[20] The Indian Gaming Regulatory Act, for instance, allows tribes to conduct gaming on lands located outside Indian reservations only if such lands have been taken into trust.[21]
3. Another important benefit is that, because the trust doctrine somewhat enlarges the power of Congress over Indian Affairs under the Constitution,[22] it allows Congress more leeway to preempt state law. This is especially important in legislation preempting state law beyond the borders of Indian reservations.[23] Legislation such as the Indian Child Welfare Act is a prime example.[24]
4. The fourth benefit is political and not legal. The existence of a general trust relationship between the tribes and the United States can be used by tribes, at least as a moral argument, in their lobbying efforts to persuade Congress to enact legislation enforcing and funding this trust responsibility.

The following three benefits have important caveats that make them somewhat discountable.

---

18 *See* County of Yakima v. Confederated Tribes, 502 U.S. 251 (1992).

19 Cass County v. Leech Lake, 524 U.S. 103 (1998).

20 *See* 18 U.S.C. 1151.

21 25 U.S.C. 2719.

22 *See infra* notes 45–60 and accompanying text.

23 *See* Alex Tallchief Skibine, *Tribal Sovereign Interests Beyond the Reservation Borders*, 12 Lewis & Clark L. Rev. 1003, 1031–41 (2008).

24 *See* Matthew L.M. Fletcher, *ICWA and the Commerce Clause*, in The Indian Child Welfare Act at 30: Facing the Future 30 (Matthew L.M. Fletcher, Kathryn E. Fort & Wenona T. Singel eds. 2009).

5. Tribes and individual Indians can get damages from the United States under the Indian Tucker Act for breach of trust in cases of mismanagement of trust resources by the federal government.[25] The problem here is that, even though Congress, using the trust doctrine, has enacted legislation vesting a substantial amount of power to control tribal natural resources in federal officials, tribes and Indians do not generally get compensated for breach of trust unless there is an egregious violation of a specific statutory duty.[26]
6. Under the doctrine, the executive branch is supposed to consider its trust duties when implementing federal laws affecting the reservations' environment.[27] This played a role, for instance, in the EPA's adoption of its Indian Policy Statement in 1984 concerning implementation of environmental programs on Indian reservations.[28] However, courts have not forced the government to consider its general trust responsibility before making decisions and have only required that the government abide by specific trust duties delineated in each statute.[29] As a result, federal agencies faced with conflicts of interests between their trust duties and other statutory mandates often ignore their trust responsibilities towards the Indians.[30]
7. The trust doctrine is the basis for the Indian canon of statutory construction according to which both the executive branch and the judiciary have to interpret laws affecting Indians to the benefit of such Indians.[31] At times, the canon played a positive role in the interpretation of key environmental statutes such as the Indian sections of the Clean Water Act and the Clean

---

25 White Mountain v. United States, 537 U.S. 465 (2003), Cobell v. Kempthorne, 569 F. Supp.2d 233 (D.D.C. 2008).

26 *See* United States v. Navajo Nation, 537 U.S. 488 (2003).

27 *See* Mary Christina Wood, *The Indian Trust Responsibility: Protecting Tribal Lands and Resources Through Claims of Injunctive Relief Against Federal Agencies*, 39 Tulsa L. Rev. 355 (2003).

28 The EPA Indian policy, which emphasized the government to government relationship between the United States and each tribe can be seen as a strong endorsement of tribal self-government. *See* William D. Ruckelshaus, U.S. Envtl. Prot. Agency, EPA Policy for the Administration of Environmental Programs on Indian Reservations (1984), *available at* http://www.epa.gov/tribalportal/pdf/indian-policy-84.pdf.

29 *See* Curtis G. Berkey, *Rethinking the Role of the Federal Trust Responsibility in Protecting Indian Land and Resources*, 83 Denver U. L. Rev. 1069 (2006). *See also* United States v. Jicarilla Apache Nation 131 S. Ct. 2313 (2011), stating "When the Tribe cannot identify a specific, applicable, trust-creating statute or regulation that the government violated … neither the Government's 'control' over [Indian assets] nor common-law trust principles matter." *Id.* at 2325.

30 See Nevada v. United States, 463 U.S. 110 (1983). *See also* Ann C. Juliano, *Conflicted Justice: The Department of Justice's Conflict of Interest in Representing Native American Tribes*, 37 Ga. L. Rev. 1307 (2003).

31 Montana v. Blackfeet Tribe, 471 U.S. 759, 766 (1985).

Air Act.[32] The problem is that the Indian canon of statutory construction has not been used consistently by the lower courts and the executive department,[33] and has been basically ignored by the Supreme Court.[34]

8. The last "benefit" can also be considered a problem. It is what I call the "trust or bust" argument. It is the argument that the only alternative to a trust relationship is a return to the policy of "Termination."[35] Decisions such as *Native Village of Venetie v. Alaska* show that some courts may still buy into this argument.[36]

The Problems

1. Perhaps the biggest problem is that, as described above, there are various "conceptions" of what the trust doctrine is. The fact that the trust is ill-defined and vague has been responsible for its lack of enforcement in some areas, as identified with alleged benefits 5, 6, and 7 above.
2. Under one of the prevailing versions, the trust doctrine's primary function was to vest Congress with plenary power and control over tribal natural resources and Indian affairs generally. Congress has used this plenary power to delegate to the executive branch a substantial power to control the reservation environment. In its most recent decision, the Court has unfortunately reiterated this colonial concept, stating "Throughout the history of the Indian trust relationship, we have recognized that the organization and management of the trust is a sovereign function subject to the plenary authority of Congress."[37] Relatedly, the Supreme Court has never used the trust doctrine as a limit on Congressional power over Indian tribes.
3. The trust doctrine is full of racist baggage that seems to be permanently stuck to it.[38] This has led some to argue that, as long as we keep the trust doctrine, we will never move beyond paternalism nor arrive at a correct

---

32 *See* Montana v. United States, 137 F. 3d 1135 (9th cir. 1998), Arizona Public Service Co. v. EPA, 211 F.3d 1280 (D.C. Cir. 2001).

33 *See* Scott C. Hall, *The Indian Law Canon of Construction v. The Chevron Doctrine: Congressional Intent and the Unambiguous Answer to the Ambiguous Problem*, 37 Conn. L. Rev. 459 (2009).

34 *See* Chickasaw Nation v. United States, 534 U.S. 84 (2001).

35 The Termination policy was in effect from 1943 to 1961, see Charles F. Wilkinson & Eric R. Biggs, *The Evolution of the Termination Policy*, 5 Am. Indian L. Rev. 139 (1977).

36 522 U.S. 520 (1998) (holding that ANCSA terminated Indian Country in Alaska because is set aside land for Alaskan Native Tribes in fee rather than into trust status).

37 United States v. Jicarilla Apache Nation, 131 S.Ct. 2313, 2323 (2011).

38 *See, e.g.*, Sandoval v. United States, 231 U.S. 28, 39 (1913) (holding that the Pueblos of New Mexico qualified as Indians for the purposes of have a trust relationship with the federal government because they were "essentially a simple, uninformed, and inferior people").

understanding of what the proper place of tribes within the United States legal system should be.[39]

Towards a Trust We Can Trust

The ultimate question here is whether the trust doctrine can be "decolonized" or re-conceptualized so that it can reemerge as a useful and contemporary doctrine that can properly define the rightful place of tribes within the United States legal system.[40] The next section addresses the three major problems identified above and explains what a decolonized trust doctrine should look like.

1. The Trust Doctrine as Foremost a Federal Responsibility to Protect the Tribes' Right to Self-government

Perhaps the most important step towards a decolonized trust is the repudiation of the racist conception of the trust doctrine that emerged during the allotment or plenary power era. Properly understood, the trust doctrine should be considered a type of quasi-constitutional incorporation doctrine. It is the doctrine that incorporated Indian tribes as domestic dependent sovereigns within the United States political and legal system. In other words, upon incorporation into the United States, Indian tribes lost some of their sovereignty as fully independent nations, but in return, the United States was entrusted with the responsibility to protect the right of tribes as self-governing entities within the federal system. Furthermore, because the trust doctrine played a role in the Court's description of Indian tribes as domestic dependent nations under the Constitution,[41] and has been used to aggrandize the power Congress has under the Indian Commerce Clause,[42] this doctrine can fairly be described as a constitutional doctrine.

In her comprehensive work on the doctrine, Professor Wood identified four attributes of tribal sovereignty that the trust should protect: "A secure land base, a functioning economy, self-government, and cultural identity."[43] While

39 For a version of this argument see Robert Williams, Like A Loaded Weapon: The Rehnquist Court, Indian Rights, and the Legal History of Racism in American (2005) (arguing that many of the Court's Indian law precedents are full of racist imagery and language that has never been repudiated and, therefore, can be brought up again, like a loaded weapon, to support anti-tribal positions).

40 For one of the earliest attempt to comprehensively address this issue, see Robert N. Clinton, *Redressing the Legacy of Conquest: A Vision Quest for a Decolonized Federal Indian Law*, 46 Ark. L. Rev. 77 (1993). Interestingly, after noting the conceptual problems in dealing with the trust doctrine in a "decolonized" world, Professor Clinton did not advocate for the abolition of the doctrine. *Id.* at 134.

41 *See* Cherokee Nation v. Georgia, 30 U.S. 1 (1831).

42 *See infra* discussion at note 45.

43 *See* Wood, *Indian Land and the Promise of Native Sovereignty*, *supra* note 4, at 1474.

limiting sovereignty to these four attributes is reasonable, Wood ranks them, placing protection of the land base ahead of the others as "the linchpin to other attributes of sovereignty."[44] I disagree with this ranking. The linchpin of tribal sovereignty should be self-government. Instead of subjugating self-government to protection of a land base, it should be the other way around. In other words, while the tribal land base should be protected from external actors like the states, the federal government should not have any role in protecting the land base from tribal governments. Protecting the tribes from themselves amounts to re-inserting aspects of the guardian ward version of the trust into federal policies.

With land but no sovereignty or self-government, the tribes are nothing more than regular land owners. They would also be without power to implement policies preserving cultural traditions or the environment. In addition, protecting the land base at the expense of self-government is paternalistic and amounts to telling the tribes that they cannot be trusted to look after their own interest.

2. The Trust Doctrine and Congressional Power over Indian Affairs

Although the Congress's power over Indian tribes started out as relatively plenary, that was largely because the power to regulate commerce with the Indian tribes was boosted by the treaty power and the war power. During the late 1800s, when the Interstate Commerce power was narrowly construed, the Court conceded that Congress did not have plenary authority over Indian tribes pursuant to the Indian Commerce Clause.[45] However, the Court relied on the trust doctrine, the political question doctrine, and the fact that the United States had ultimate title to all Indian lands pursuant to the doctrine of discovery, to vest Congress with truly plenary authority over all Indian affairs.[46] During the modern era, roughly the 1970s to the present, the Court abandoned reliance on the political question doctrine,[47] but concluded that the Commerce Clause, along with the trust doctrine, still gave Congress plenary authority over Indian Affairs.[48] Under the modern view, "plenary" does not mean "absolute" power over tribal resources in that Congress cannot deny tribes their constitutional rights to vested property rights unless it is truly for their benefit.[49] Under the

44 *Id.*

45 *See* United States v. Kagama, 118 U.S. 375 (1886).

46 Lonewolf v. Hitchcock, 187 U.S. 553 (1903).

47 *See* Delaware Tribal Business Comm. v. Weeks, 430 U.S. 73 (1977).

48 *See* Morton v. Mancari, 417 U.S. 535 (1974). *See also* United States v. Jicarilla Apache Nation, 131 S. Ct. 2313, *supra* note 37.

49 *See* Sioux Nation v. United States, 448 U.S. 371, 415 (1980) (stating that "this power to control and manage is not absolute, while extending to all appropriate measures for protecting and advancing the tribe, it is subject to limitations inhering in … a guardianship and to pertinent constitutional restrictions").

modern view, the Court will decide whether such congressional legislation is truly for the benefit of the tribes and not assume that it is.

There are two main problems with the Court's contemporary plenary power approach. First, the power of Congress to regulate commerce with Indian tribes has no internal limitations. Its limits are only imposed externally by other provisions of the Constitution. The problem here is that the right to tribal self-government is not considered a constitutional right. This means that Congress can use the commerce power to regulate strictly internal tribal affairs even if such regulations severely interfere with tribal self-government and have nothing to do with commerce. The power of Congress to "regulate Commerce among the states" has changed throughout history. Justice Marshall, in *Gibbons v. Ogden*, thought the interstate commerce power was very broad and comprehensive.[50] Yet, from the late 1800s until 1937, it was narrowly construed.[51] The Court changed its mind during the New Deal and the Commerce power was considerably enlarged.[52] The Court restricted this power somewhat after 1990. By contrast, the power of Congress pursuant to the Indian Commerce power seems to be stuck in time as being plenary, with the Court arbitrarily and erroneously declaring that "the central function of the Indian commerce clause is to provide Congress with plenary power to legislate in the field of Indian Affairs."[53]

The word "commerce" is somewhat ill-defined and general. Thus viewing Congress's Commerce Clause power as capable of evolving to adapt to new situations is consistent with a theory of constitutional interpretation according to which the framers adopted a general constitutional framework along with principles such as separation of power and checks and balances, but left the details to be filled in by future generations of judges and legislators.[54] Condemning the power of Congress under the Indian Commerce Clause to being fixed and plenary forever does not conform to any theory of constitutional interpretation except perhaps the most extreme form of originalism. Yet, no one in the originalist camp has argued that the Indian Commerce Clause was meant to give plenary authority to Congress over Indian tribes.

The second problem with this view is that, even in cases where tribes may have protected constitutional rights, such as property rights in their natural resources, which cannot be taken without duc process or fair compensation, Congress can avoid these constitutional restrictions by pretending to act as a trustee. Some have argued that, in such instances, Congress should not be given any leeway in

50 22 U.S. 1 (1824).

51 *See* Hammer v. Dagenhart, 247 U.S. 251 (1918).

52 *See* United States v. Darby, 312 U.S. (100 1941) (overturning Hammer v. Dagenhart, 247 U.S. 251 (1918)).

53 *See* Cotton Petroleum v. New Mexico, 490 U.S. 163, 192 (1989).

54 *See* Jack M. Balkin, *Framework Originalism and the Living Constitution*, 103 Nw. U. L. Rev. 549 (2009).

determining what is in the best interests of the tribes.[55] Reid Chambers has argued that the trust doctrine should be construed to limit the power of Congress over Indian Affairs, and that the standard should be whether Congressional legislation is rationally tied to the fulfillment of Congress's role as a trustee for the tribes.[56] This standard is only useful, however, if one has a concrete and precise understanding of what is in the best interests of the tribes. The lack of a precise standard has led some, like Mary Wood, to presume too much.[57] Her proposal leaves open the possibility that federal interference with tribal self-governance might be justified if tribes are acting in ways that do not promote environmental protection. My argument is that, to be truly decolonized, the trust doctrine should never justify congressional legislation that interferes with tribes' right to self-government and self-determination, at least, not without the full consent and support of the affected Indian tribes. In other words, any such legislation lacking tribal consent should never be considered "rationally tied" to the fulfillment of the trust relationship.

Does this mean that Congress can never enact legislation interfering with tribal self-government? The simple answer is no. Congress can enact legislation pursuant to its normal power to "regulate Commerce with the Indian tribes." The catch here is that, while this power is indeed very broad, there are limits. The legislation has to be somehow connected to the regulation of commerce between the United States and the tribes. Commerce with Indian tribes goes beyond trade with the tribes. As Justice Marshall once stated, commerce is "intercourse,"[58] and as some scholars have noted, the original 1790 Trade and Intercourse Acts regulated much more than just "trade" with the Indians.[59]

There are many advantages to re-conceptualizing congressional power in this manner. For one thing, it would force Congress and the tribes to understand that there are two distinct types of powers Congress can use in the area of Indian Affairs, and that these powers have their own limits. In other words, Congress can wear two hats but not at the same time. Congress can act as a trustee or as a regulator. If it is acting as a trustee, the legislation can include areas beyond

---

55 *See* Nell Newton, *The Judicial Role in Fifth Amendment Takings of Indian Land: an Analysis of the Sioux Nation Rule*, 61 Ore. L. Rev. 245 (1982); *See also* Comment, *Federal Plenary Power in Indian Affairs after Weeks and Sioux Nation*, 131 U. Pa. L. Rev. 235 (1982).

56 *See* Chambers, *Trust Responsibility*, *supra* note 11, at 28.

57 *See* Ezra Rosser, *Ahistorical Indians and Reservation Resources*, 40 Envtl. L. 437, 513–18 (2011) (critiquing Mary Wood's enhanced conception of the trust doctrine as presented in her article, *A New Trust Paradigm*, *supra* note 10, because it empowers, and indeed may require, courts and federal administrative agencies to block projects approved by tribal governments if such projects are harmful to the environment).

58 Gibbons v. Ogden, 22 U.S. 1 (1824).

59 See Jack M. Balkin, *Commerce*, 109 Mich. L. Rev. 1, 24 (2010). Balkin also noted that the constitutional convention originally voted to give Congress power to regulate "affairs" with the Indians and there is no evidence "that the shift from 'affairs' to 'commerce' was thought to change the meaning or the scope of the powers granted." *Id.* at note 82.

"commerce" with Indian tribes but such legislation has to be truly for the benefit of the tribes, meaning that it is legislation that is supportive of tribal self-government and self-determination. Congress can also act as a regulator and, in such a case, the legislation can interfere with tribal self-government. However, such legislation has to be somewhat connected with "commerce with the Indian tribes."

3. Unmooring the Trust Doctrine from Some Aspects of the Doctrine of Discovery

As already mentioned, one of the problems with the Trust doctrine is that it is tied to the doctrine of discovery.[60] Under the doctrine of discovery as enunciated in *Johnson v. M'Intosh*,[61] upon discovery of this continent, the European discovering nations acquired the ultimate title to all Indian lands and the Indians only retained a right of occupancy, or aboriginal title. This right of occupancy was not constitutionally protected and could be taken by the United States by purchase or conquest.[62] While it is too late in the day to extricate the doctrine of discovery from all of American Indian law or undo everything that has been done in its name, I think it is time we rethink the idea that the United States acquired "ultimate title" to all Indian lands. Furthermore, renouncing that aspect of the discovery will eliminate one of the justifications for Congress's plenary authority over tribal natural resources, which is that the United States has "ultimate title" to such resources while the tribes only have beneficial title. Other countries have modified their initial common law under which aboriginal title was acquired by the discovering nation.[63] What Chief Justice Marshall actually meant by "absolute" or "ultimate" title is far from clear. A credible interpretation is that it was meant as a term of art that could be equated to ultimate political dominion coupled with the exclusive right to acquire the land from the tribes.[64]

The doctrine of discovery is still relevant today because it is the doctrine that incorporated the tribal territories within the geographical limits of the United States and it also played a role in politically incorporating the tribes within the

60 *See supra* note 5 and accompanying text.

61 21 U.S. 543 (1823).

62 For a relatively modern application of the doctrine, see Tee-Hit-Ton Indians v. United States, 348 U.S. 272 (1955).

63 *See*, for instance, Mabo v. Queensland, 107 A.L.R. 1 (1992) where the Australian High Court abandoned the theory of *Terra Nulius* under which Australian aborigines had no right whatsoever to the lands they were occupying at the time of discovery and stating "it is imperative in today's world that the common law should neither be nor be seen to be frozen in an age of racial discrimination." *Id.* at 41.

64 Professor Robert Clinton, for instance, takes the position that the term was probably derived from English usage where the courts wanted to assign to the New World a system of land tenure akin to the one existing in England according to which the ultimate title to all land was originally in the Crown and thus all land titles were ultimately derived from the Crown. Presentation of Robert Clinton at conference, Treaty to Trust to Carcieri, held at Arizona State University on April 28–29, 2011.

legal system of the United States as domestic dependent nations.[65] I have argued elsewhere that this tie between the doctrine of discovery and the trust doctrine is important because it makes the trust a doctrine of constitutional incorporation.[66]

Practical Consequences of a Decolonized Trust Doctrine

1. Controlling Congressional Power

Most importantly, the re-conceptualization of the trust doctrine as described above would mean that Congress could no longer act as a "conqueror" when legislating in the area of Indian affairs. Declaring that Congress has plenary power without any elaboration, as the Court has done in the past, allows Congress to enact laws that have nothing to do with its role as trustee or with the regulation of "commerce," even if very broadly construed. This plenary power doctrine in federal Indian law is not a constitutional doctrine, it is a doctrine of conquest. It is a doctrine that makes all issues related to the legitimacy of congressional power under the Indian Commerce Clause political questions. It allows Congress to still act as a conqueror in the field of Indian Affairs. It should be repudiated.

2. Clarification Concerning the Duty of the Executive Branch and the Courts to Take the Trust Doctrine into Consideration

Re-conceptualizing the trust doctrine, as suggested above, would also clarify the doctrine's role in statutory construction and in guiding the actions of executive branch officials. For instance, the decolonized trust approach could prevent miscommunications that result in poor outcomes for tribes, such as those between the Navajo Nation and the United States when Secretary of the Interior Hodel approved a lease that had been negotiated between the Navajo Nation and Peabody Coal Corporation after concealing key information from the Navajo Nation.[67] The Navajos sued the United States for breach of fiduciary duties, arguing that a reasonable trustee would not have approved the lease because it was detrimental to the interests of the Navajo Nation. The Supreme Court denied the claim, holding that, when Secretary Hodel approved the lease, he was not in breach of specific statutory trust duties. Implicit in this holding was that the Secretary was not acting as a trustee for the tribe when he approved the lease.

To this holding one may have reacted by asking: if not pursuant to the trust, in what capacity was he acting? Why was he given the power to approve the lease in the first place if not pursuant to his powers as trustee? Under current law, there

65 *See* Cherokee Nation v. Georgia, 30 U.S. 1 (1831).

66 *See* Alex Tallchief Skibine, *Integrating the Indian Trust Doctrine into the Constitution*, 39 Tulsa L. Rev. 247 (2003–2004).

67 *See* United States v. Navajo Nation, 537 U.S. 488 (2003).

was no way to answer that question adequately. The Secretary could have been acting as the ultimate "owner" of the resource being leased. Or he could have been acting as a trustee for the Indians. Certainly, the Navajos thought this was what he was doing. Or he could have been acting just as a regulator, which is what the Court determined. Under the theory being proposed here, the result would have been clear from the start. The Secretary could no longer be considered the ultimate owner of tribal resources. He could also no longer be considered to be acting as a trustee since giving him such approval power here may not have been supportive of tribal self-government. Thus there is only one alternative left: he could "regulate" such commercial transactions between the tribe and non-Indians under his regular Indian commerce power. While the outcome in the lawsuit may have been the same, at least the Navajos would have been on notice that the Secretary may not have been acting with their best interests in mind. Furthermore, the decolonized version of the doctrine should force concerned parties to re-consider why the Secretary has that approval power in the first place, and whether he should keep having it. *United States v. Jicarilla Apache Nation* represents the latest example of the confusion that arises from the many roles the United States assumes in administering the Indian trust. The Court there held that the tribe could not invoke the fiduciary exception to the attorney client privilege in its attempt to discover certain documents because the United States' role as trustee for the tribe could not be equated with that of a private trustee under the common law. Key to this holding was the Court's finding that, in administering the Indian trust, the United States is looking more after its own interests as a sovereign than after the interests of the tribes.[68] Concerning statutory interpretation, it has already been mentioned that the Indian canon of statutory construction is used inconsistently by the lower courts and basically ignored by the Supreme Court.[69] The debate has generally centered on whether the Indian canon is a substantive rule of statutory construction or a discretionary grammatical-type canon like all the Latin canons.[70] Although the Court has at times held that the canon is rooted in the trust doctrine,[71] it has also at other times stated that the Indian canon was developed because Indian tribes were rendered weak and defenseless as a result of policies adopted by the United States towards them. If this is the normative explanation for the Indian canon, the easy retort is that, since Indian tribes are no longer weak and defenseless, the canon should no longer be used. However, as explained by the editors of the leading treatise on federal Indian law:

---

68 131 S. Ct. 2313 (2011). After stating "[t]he Government has often structured the trust relationship to pursue its own policy goals." *Id.*, at 2324, the Court remarked that in many cases "while it was formally acting as a trustee, the Government was in fact asserting its own sovereign interest in the disposition of Indian lands." *Id.*

69 *See supra* notes 31–34 and accompanying text.

70 Such as, for instance, *Expressio unius*, *Ejusdem generis*, or *Noscitur socis* just to name three.

71 *See* Montana v. Blackfeet tribe, 471 U.S. 759, 766 (1985).

> Chief Justice Marshall grounded the Indian law canons in the value of structural sovereignty, not judicial solicitude for powerless minorities … The consequence of understanding the Indian canons as fostering structural and constitutive purposes are quite significant. The implementation and force of the canons do not turn on the ebb and flow of judicial solicitude for powerless minorities, but instead on an understanding that the canons protect important structural features of our system of governance.[72]

As further explained by Philip Frickey, Marshall first used the Indian law canons in interpreting treaties made with Indian nations because he viewed these treaties as quasi-constitutional documents since they were the primary documents incorporating Indian nations into the political system of the United States.[73] According to Frickey, Marshall devised this interpretive methodology because he knew that, at the time, the United States' power over Indian tribes could not be meaningfully challenged in the courts. Thus, the Indian canons can be viewed as an antidote to soften the plenary power of Congress in Indian affairs.

In Marshall's time, Congress's plenary power over Indian tribes was achieved through the treaty power, the war power and the Commerce Clause. Today, the treaty and war powers are no longer used in the field of Indian affairs but, as this chapter has explained, the congressional power is still described as plenary as a by-product of the trust doctrine and the commerce power. Under the methodology set forth in this chapter, the Indian canon would have to be used whenever Congress enacted legislation as a trustee but not when it enacted legislation as a "regulator" pursuant to its power to regulate commerce with the Indian tribes. To be sure, at times, deciding in what capacity Congress was acting when it enacted legislation affecting Indians may be difficult. Thus, in some statutes, Congress may have enacted some sections as a trustee and others as a regulator.[74] The deciding factor should be whether the ambiguity is contained in a section that, as a whole, is consistent with the concepts of tribal self-government and self-determination or goes against such principles.

The only caveat is that there are many Acts of Congress that were not enacted with the best interests of the Indians in mind, but these Acts also go beyond the regulation of commerce with the Indian tribes. I have in mind the many acts that terminated Indian tribes during the termination era, disestablished Indian reservations during the allotment era, or plainly go beyond the regulation

72 Cohen's Handbook of Federal Indian Law 123 (Nell Jessup Newton et al. eds. 2005).

73 Philip P. Frickey, *Marshalling Past and Present: Colonialism, Constitutionalism and Interpretation in Federal Indian Law*, 107 Harv. L. Rev. 381, 408–11 (1993).

74 For how such an analysis is to be conducted in the context of the Indian Gaming Regulatory Act, see Alex Tallchief Skibine. *Indian Gaming and Cooperative Federalism*, 42 Ariz. St. L. J. 253, 268 (2010).

of commerce.[75] Although under my theory, such acts should be considered unconstitutional because Congress is acting as a Conqueror, the Supreme Court has, unfortunately, decided otherwise and has upheld their constitutionality based on various notions of congressional plenary power depending on what period of history such cases were decided. Needless to say, the Indian canon should apply to such legislation. The reason for this is that the only possible explanation or legitimate reason for such legislation is that Congress was assumed to have acted as a trustee for the benefit of the tribes. Thus, legislation allotting Indian reservations or even "terminating" Indian tribes should be liberally construed with ambiguities resolved to the benefit of the Indians.[76]

3. The Problem of State Taxation of Indian Lands

Some may argue that it is only because the United States is considered to have acquired ultimate title to all Indian lands under the doctrine of discovery that tribal treaty lands are now considered to be held in trust by the United States and therefore cannot be taxed by the states. One response to this argument is that, in making treaties with the tribes, Congress has specifically acted to confirm title to the tribes, granting tax-free status to such lands.[77] The counter argument is that what makes these lands immune from taxation is their restriction against alienation,[78] and under the conception of the trust doctrine and congressional power presented above, Congress may no longer have the power to restrict alienation of Indian lands. In other words, legislation such as the Trade and Intercourse Acts might be unconstitutional.[79] This flows from the fact that the United States would no longer have ultimate title to all Indian land, and since Congress could no longer enact legislation that is not supportive of tribal self-government or self-determination, it could no longer enact legislation that would restrict the right of Indians to alienate their own lands.

There are two arguments that can be leveled to rebut this contention. First, contrary to what the Supreme Court stated in some cases, alienability does not have

75 P.L. 280 would be such an example. Act of August 15, 1953, ch. 505, Pub. L. No. 83-280, 67 Stat. 588.

76 *See, e.g.*, Menominee Tribe v. United States, 391 U.S. 404 (1968).

77 How tribal treaty lands came to be considered to be held in trust is somewhat of an enigma. The more likely explanation is that it just happened as a result of administrative fiat. Having treaty land considered to be held in trust has been questioned by scholars. *See, e.g.*, Tim Coulter, Native Land project, Draft General Principles of Law Relating to Native Lands and Natural Resources, Indian Law Resource Center, ch. IV, at 55–77 (2010). *See also* Robert Clinton, pp. 429–38 of material prepared for conference, Treaty to Trust to Carcieri, held at Arizona State University Sandra O'Connor College of Law, April 28–29, 2011.

78 *See* Cass County v. Leech Lake Band, 524 U.S. 103 (1998).

79 25 U.S.C. 77.

to mean taxability.[80] Secondly, even if alienability means taxability, Congress can still restrict the sale or lease of such Indian lands to non-members under its regular commerce power. There is no question that this activity relates to commerce with Indian tribes. It is part of "trade and intercourse" between non-tribal members and Indian tribes.[81] Under my theory, however, Congress could no longer, without tribal consent, restrict the sale of treaty lands to members of the same tribe since such sale cannot be considered to be part of commerce between the tribe and the United States.

Conclusion

The problem with abandoning the trust doctrine from an Indian perspective is that I do not see the Court abandoning the notion that Congress has plenary authority over the affairs *of* the Indians instead of just over the affairs *with* the Indians. Furthermore, there is no likelihood that Congress will quickly repeal all the statutes enacted over the last 200 years that have given broad powers over Indian reservations to federal officials. In addition, abandoning the trust should mean that it would have to be replaced by something besides another termination policy, and there is no guarantee as to what this might be. Properly conceived, the trust doctrine should be viewed as a quasi-constitutional doctrine incorporating tribes as political sovereigns within the greater political system of the United States. Right now, there is a risk that, without any firm understanding as to the place of tribes within the federal system, tribes are becoming viewed and incorporated not as governments but as economic actors, like corporations with quasi-public functions such as public utilities and the like. The real danger presented by this trend is that the special doctrines that have defined the rights of Indians, including the trust doctrine, will disappear and federal Indian law will slowly but surely be merged or mainstreamed into the rest of American public law.[82] Should this happen, there is a strong possibility that the survival of Indian tribes, as culturally distinct sovereign governments, will be threatened.

80 *See* Cass County v. Leech Lake Band, 524 U.S. 103 (1998).

81 There is a possibility that, even if authorized under the Commerce power, placing such restrictions against alienation on tribal treaty lands may amount to a taking of property without fair compensation, see Babbitt v. Youpee, 519 U.S. 234 (1997), Keystone Bituminous Coal v. DeBenedictis, 480 U.S. 470 (1987), Andrus v. Allard, 444 U.S. 51 (1979). Of course, the tribes could always agree to such restrictions in order to guarantee their constitutionality.

82 *See* Philip P. Frickey, *(Native) American Exceptionalism in Federal Public Law*, 119 Harv. L. Rev. 431 (2005).

Tribal Sovereignty and Environmental Impacts

Chapter 2
Control and Accountability: The Twin Dimensions of Tribal Sovereignty Necessary to Achieve Environmental Justice for Native America

James M. Grijalva[1]

For three decades or more, perhaps the most pressing environmental justice issue in Indian country has been the need for effective, fully operational environmental programs capable of regulating non-Indian facilities on tribal and fee lands. The U.S. Environmental Protection Agency (EPA) has long conceptualized a government-to-government relationship with Indian tribes premised on tribal sovereignty as the best means for addressing that challenge. Important progress has been made toward actualizing the EPA's policy commitment to tribal environmental self-determination, although much work remains to achieve comprehensive environmental protection for Native America.

The new energy economy is sparking another self-determination era seemingly in tension with tribal environmental sovereignty. Tribal governments are increasingly seeking energy justice by taking control of natural resource extraction and related businesses in Indian country. Effectively regulating the environmental impacts of expanded development under the federal model requires the opening of administrative procedures to public observation and comment, which is prompting a new Indian country environmental justice issue. The emerging question is whether tribes can adapt the federal model of public participation in culturally relevant ways that preserve the environment as well as the political and cultural legitimacy of tribal governments. Initial positive indications from a creative EPA initiative on collaborative problem solving suggest that this important goal may be attainable.

This chapter traces the evolution of the EPA's sovereignty-based approach to Indian country environmental justice, and explores its challenges and promise. A key obstacle to building fully functioning environmental regulatory programs is the chilling effect of repeated non-Indian legal challenges to the EPA's policy actions and tribes' claims of regulatory jurisdiction. A fundamental challenge to

1 Friedman Professor of Law and Director, Tribal Environmental Law Project, University of North Dakota School of Law.

creating culturally relevant public participation processes is a not uncommon schism created between tribal governments and their citizens as a result of colonization and historic federal control. The best hope for overcoming these limitations and achieving true environmental justice for Native America turns on tribal sovereignty, understood in this context to mean the right of indigenous peoples to self-determine whether and how Western legal constructs can be adapted in culturally relevant and useful ways.

Self-determining Environmental Justice for Native America: Independent Tribal Regulatory Programs

Popular and academic commentary may never settle on whether indigenous peoples were the first environmentalists or share a universal land ethic, yet it seems beyond serious debate that their cultures are intrinsically land- and place-based in ways that differ from those of most non-Native communities. Thus, while they share some environmental concerns, indigenous communities face human health and welfare risks from environmental degradation that are different from those of their neighbors. For example, a low level of mercury contamination in fish tissue may present little risk to the average American, but significant risk to a Salish Indian whose culture and diet revolve around salmon fishing.[2] What should environmental justice for Native America mean in this context? Perhaps the least ethnocentric way to define it is to let indigenous peoples determine the relationship they desire with the natural environment. Environmental justice, then, would mean achieving a level of environmental quality adequate for indigenous peoples to practice and maintain their self-defined cultural relation to the land and natural environment.

From the perspective of positive law, indigenous self-determination is invariably linked with inherent governmental sovereignty. The United Nations Declaration on the Rights of Indigenous Peoples treats indigenous self-determination as an individual human right and as a collective political right to self-government.[3] As applied to American Indian tribes in the United States, the concept of tribal self-determination has been the guiding policy principle of the federal government since 1970, the so-called "Year of the Environment," in which Congress launched the modern environmental regulatory state. Federal Indian law views self-determination through its conceptions of tribal sovereignty, the inherent governmental status and power of Indian tribes that pre-existed the United States, but which has been subjected to control by Congress and the Supreme Court.

2 *See* Catherine A. O'Neill, *Environmental Justice in the Tribal Context: A Madness to EPAs Method*, 38 Envtl L. 495 (2008).

3 G.A. Res. 61/295, U.N. GAOR, 61st Sess., 107th plen. mtg., U.N. Doc. A/RES/61/295 (Sept. 13, 2007).

The long and turbulent course of federal Indian control begat historical legacies that today constrain tribal governments from exercising full sovereignty independent of the federal government. Colonization and assimilation eradicated many tribes' traditional forms of governance. Indian Reorganization substituted Western models of government, and termination then attacked them. Even in the current self-determination era, patent federal expectations that tribes mimic state governmental processes and requirements for federal approval of tribal actions undermine the legitimacy and effectiveness of tribal self-government, particularly for complex matters like environmental management.

The enduring legacy of allotment is another obstacle to independent tribal environmental management. The federal government's misguided turn of the century campaign to open Indian country to non-Native immigrants manifests today in a crazy-quilt checkerboard of Indian and non-Indian lands used by a significant population of non-Indians whose allegiance, if any, typically favors state over federal government, and certainly does not favor tribal government.

The Supreme Court seems myopically sympathetic to the non-Indian refrain that tribal jurisdiction over them amounts to unfair taxation without representation, a patently hypocritical complaint from those who have benefitted, and continue to benefit, from the federal government's unilateral assertion of control over Indian lands and tribes.[4] Modern Court decisions reflect an unprincipled and unpredictable trend of restricting exercises of tribal sovereignty that affect non-Indian Americans within tribal territories in a variety of non-environmental cases.[5] Uncertainty over whether the Court would tolerate independent tribal regulation of the environmentally damaging activities of non-Indians within Indian country is perhaps the biggest challenge to comprehensive tribal protection. A second threat lies outside Indian country, where federal Indian law offers tribes no prospect of claiming jurisdiction over non-Indians; the migratory nature of air and water pollution means that industrial activities undertaken outside tribal territories may cause extraterritorial impacts inside. For these and other reasons, there are few examples of tribes enacting and implementing significant environmental regulatory schemes apart from federal programs. Yet, as discussed in the next section, that does not mean that tribes are powerless to preserve their land-based culture.

Environmental Self-determination within a Cooperative Federalist System: Federally Approved Tribal Regulatory Programs

Beyond vexing legal and administrative challenges, any separate tribal environmental law would be forced to coexist with pervasive federal environmental law.

4 *See* Philip P. Frickey, *A Common Law for Our Age of Colonialism: The Judicial Divestiture of Indian Tribal Authority Over Nonmembers*, 109 Yale L.J. 1 (1999).

5 *See* David H. Getches, *Conquering The Cultural Frontier: The New Subjectivism of the Supreme Court in Indian Law*, 84 Cal. L. Rev. 1573 (1996).

America's environmental regulatory state seeks a relatively uniform level of environmental quality nationwide through implementation of federally prescribed minimum standards in every state. Although Congress initially crafted the major environmental statutes without considering Indian country, and only later added disparate provisions piecemeal, federal courts have had little trouble applying federal environmental programs there, following the Supreme Court's consistently broad endorsement of federal authority over Indian affairs.[6]

Increased federal authority and the elevated prominence of national interests also distinguish modern environmental laws from earlier days when protection of human health and regulation of environmental degradation were left almost wholly to states' general powers over public welfare. Congress conferred on the EPA broad and potentially preemptive powers, but they were designed for use in concert with local regulation. The key feature of this "cooperative federalism" model was a federal–state partnership where the EPA supervised the state government as it implemented federal programs adapted to its needs and priorities within federally specified parameters.

Coincidentally, America's modern environmental paradigm accords nicely with the nation's current Indian policy aspiration of replacing unilateral federal control of Indian country with federal–tribal partnerships grounded in tribal self-determination. Congress has amended nearly all of the major environmental statutes so that the EPA has clear authority to work with tribal governments in essentially the same fashion that it works with state governments. These so-called "treatment-as-a-state" provisions offer tribes varying regulatory roles within the federal system, like making policy decisions, monitoring environmental quality, setting environmental standards, issuing pollution permits, and taking enforcement actions. Within certain federal parameters, the system is a means for translating indigenous environmental values into federally enforceable regulatory requirements.[7]

Respect for tribal sovereignty has been the guiding principle of the EPA's Indian program since shortly after the agency's creation in 1970. The EPA quickly realized that Congress had not accounted for Indian country's unique circumstances in its initial design of the new environmental regimes. Concerned about potential regulatory gaps, in the mid-1970s the EPA administratively created

6 *See* Davis v. Morton, 469 F.2d 593 (10th cir. 1972) (applying the National Environmental Policy Act to Indian country despite its silence on the question). *See also* Atlantic States Legal Foundation v. Salt River Pima-Maricopa Indian Community, 827 F.Supp. 608 (D. Ariz. 1993) (holding that the Clean Water Act abrogated Indian tribes' sovereign immunity); Blue Legs v. Bureau of Indian Affairs, 867 F.2d 1094 (8th cir. 1989) (holding that the Resource Conservation and Recovery Act abrogated Indian tribes' sovereign immunity).

7 For a more detailed description and analysis of EPA's nearly 40-year-old Indian program, and the litigation it has spawned, *see* James M. Grijalva, Closing the Circle: Environmental Justice in Indian County (2008).

several tribal regulatory roles similar to those played by states. On the heels of those program-specific actions, in 1984 the EPA adopted a broad, cross-program Indian Policy promising special consideration for Indian interests and government-to-government relationships with tribes in the management of environmental programs in Indian country. Congress's treatment-as-a-state amendments, enacted in the late 1980s and 1990, were a clear outgrowth of the EPA's work under the Indian Policy.

A few years later, the general environmental justice movement coalesced and demanded communities of color and low income not be forced to suffer disproportionate environmental impacts as a result of unfair or inadequate regulatory implementation. In Indian country, the stage was already set for the EPA's response. Its prior Indian program actions had been motivated by a parallel concern that Congress's inadvertent regulatory gaps would leave the Indian country environment less protected than other areas of the nation. The solution, the EPA had said, was delegating implementation responsibility to tribal governments. The EPA's first environmental justice strategy, as well as its first race-based environmental risk report, followed suit in recognizing that unequal environmental impacts in Indian country were best addressed through tribal sovereignty.[8]

To those familiar with environmental justice outside Indian country, the agency's focus on building tribes' governmental infrastructure might seem misplaced. The archetypal complaint of environmental injustice is usually that the government is administering the law in ways that unfairly impact communities of color or low income, for example, by issuing permits with less stringent conditions or imposing less significant penalties for non-compliance in those communities. Such substantive denials of justice are invariably linked to the government's lack of awareness and/or sensitivity to certain communities' health and welfare interests, so the EPA's institutional responses are often aimed at achieving meaningful citizen participation in various phases of the government's administrative processes.[9]

Until very recently, that has not been the approach in Indian country. Rather than reach out to affected indigenous peoples and their grassroots organizations, the EPA has identified the community of reference as the legal and political entity called an Indian tribe, and engaged it (more or less) in government-to-government dialogues about implementing federal programs.[10]

---

8 U.S. EPA, EPA's Environmental Justice Strategy (1995); U.S. EPA, Tribes At Risk: The Wisconsin Tribes Comparative Risk Project (1992).

9 EPA defines environmental justice as the "fair treatment and meaningful involvement of all people regardless of race, color, national origin, or income with respect to the development, implementation, and enforcement of environmental laws, regulations, and policies." Office of Environmental Justice, U.S. EPA, Frequently Asked Questions, http://www.epa.gov/compliance/environmentaljustice/resources/faqs/index.html (last visited May 22, 2011) (follow hyperlink *How Does EPA Define Environmental Justice?*).

10 *See* EPA Policy for the Administration of Environmental Programs on Indian Reservations (Nov. 8, 1984).

The reasons for the different approach derive from the intersection of federal Indian law and environmental law. The fundamental principle that Indian tribes retained aspects of their inherent sovereignty despite incorporation within the United States made tribes eligible for governmental regulatory roles that other communities of color and low income simply could not play. In addition, long-maintained political relations between sovereign tribes and the federal government potentially skewed states' otherwise comprehensive health and welfare powers in those portions of states that federal law calls "Indian country." Uncertainty over states' legal authority to administer federal environmental programs in Indian country was the genesis of the EPA's original conclusion that there was a regulatory hole in nationwide environmental protection.[11] Therefore, somewhat ironically, tribal sovereignty appeared central to understanding both the cause of the Indian country regulatory gap and its potential solution.

In the vocabulary of contemporary environmental justice, Indian country's lack of operating programs threatened indigenous peoples with disproportionate environmental risks and excluded them from meaningful involvement in developing solutions. The EPA's initial response of directly implementing critical program components in Indian country when necessary—like issuing permits to companies whose operations would otherwise be unlawful—addressed some of the more troubling human health risks. However, permit programs are often predicated on value judgments that Congress left to local governments. For example, pollution discharge permits issued by the EPA under the Clean Water Act must include conditions adequate for protecting the levels of water quality specified by state and tribal governments as necessary for preserving their desired uses of particular water bodies. The absence of applicable water quality standards makes determining adequate permit conditions difficult. In theory, the EPA's direct implementation authority could fill such voids, but because Congress designed federal authority as a backup to states' primary roles, it is less adaptable to site-specific conditions or priorities.

Federal inflexibility is particularly vexing in Indian country where achieving environmental justice requires more than just avoiding the same human health risks that the majority society faces. Indigenous peoples' ancient cultural connections to the natural environment present contemporary human health risks that are different in degree and kind from those of the majority society. Beyond bare health concerns, environmental degradation of Indian country potentially threatens a variety of general welfare interests. Destruction of sacred plants or animals may not directly cause indigenous peoples physical injury, but may nonetheless harm their cultural and spiritual identity and survival.[12] The EPA long ago recognized that indigenous respect for the earth, combined with the historical shrinkage of tribal land bases,

11 EPA Policy for Program Implementation on Indian Lands 3 (Dec. 19, 1980).

12 *See* National Environmental Justice Advisory Council, U.S. EPA, Fish Consumption and Environmental Justice 2–18 (2001); U.S. EPA, Tribes At Risk, *supra* note 8, at 6, 18, 32–4.

means that tribes see environmental degradation of Indian country as an attack on tribal territory and pollution prevention as an act of self-preservation.[13]

The significant regulatory roles available to tribes in the cooperative federalist system address many of these legal and practical shortcomings. At the most basic level, tribal implementation helps fill the Indian country regulatory gap with operating programs capable of reducing environmental risks. Just as important, the resulting programs are oriented by the tribe's conclusions about the unique interests at stake and the environmental criteria necessary for their protection. Statutory provisions protecting states' similar decisions from second-guessing by the EPA also ensure respect for tribes' value judgments when challenged by regulated entities or states.[14]

Articulating indigenous environmental values through federal program parameters is surely not true tribal environmental self-determination, yet the approach yields very significant legal consequences. Perhaps most notable is the opportunity for influencing environmentally harmful activities adjacent to but *outside* of Indian country. Federal courts have consistently validated the EPA approvals of tribal standards and classifications more stringent than those of adjacent states,[15] triggering federal expectations that pollution permits issued within the states be conditioned on compliance with the downwind and downstream tribes' value judgments. While the Supreme Court has not yet ruled on this issue, it has been highly skeptical of tribal authority over non-Indians in the *absence* of federal delegation, even in situations that did not involve extraterritorial jurisdiction.[16] However, by partnering with the EPA, tribes may receive a measure

13 U.S. EPA, Federal, Tribal and State Roles in the Protection and Regulation of Reservation Environments 1 (July 10, 1991).

14 Arizona v. U.S. EPA, 151 F.3d 1205 (9th cir. 1998) (affirming EPA's rejection of the state's demand that the Yavapai–Apache Tribe evaluate more extensively the possible consequences of its proposed reservation air quality redesignation).

15 *Id.* (affirming EPA's approval of the Yavapai-Apache Tribe's air quality redesignation to a classification more stringent than the state's for the surrounding airshed); Albuquerque v. Browner, 97 F.3d 415 (10th cir. 1996) (affirming EPA's approval of the Pueblo of Isleta's water quality standards that were more stringent than the state's standards for the same river upstream of the Pueblo), *cert. denied*, 522 U.S. 965 (1997); Nance v. U.S. EPA, 645 F.2d 701 (9th cir. 1981) (affirming EPA's approval of the Northern Cheyenne Tribe's air quality redesignation to a classification more stringent than the state's for the surrounding airshed), *cert. denied*, 454 U.S. 1081 (1981).

16 *See* Plains Commerce Bank v. Long Family Land and Cattle Co., 554 U.S. 316 (2008) (denying tribal court jurisdiction over non-Indian bank conducting business on reservation); Nevada v. Hicks, 533 U.S. 353 (2001) (denying tribal court jurisdiction over tort committed by a non-Indian state official on reservation); Atkinson Trading Co., Inc. v. Shirley, 532 U.S. 645 (2001) (denying tribal tax authority over non-Indian company conducting business on reservation); Strate v. A-1 Contractors, 520 U.S. 438 (1997) (denying tribal court jurisdiction over non-Indian parties to a civil tort action arising on reservation); South Dakota v. Bourland, 508 U.S. 679 (1993) (denying tribal regulatory

of insulation from the Court's increasingly narrow view of inherent sovereignty because of the deference often paid by courts to administrative agencies charged by Congress with implementing federal programs. Lower courts have deferred multiple times to the EPA's conclusions on how best to apply environmental law to Indian country,[17] the roles tribes might play,[18] and the means for testing tribes' environmental jurisdiction over non-Indians.[19] The Supreme Court has declined

authority over non-Indians hunting and fishing on reservation); Brendale v. Confederated Tribes and Bands of Yakima Indian Nation, 492 U.S. 408 (1989) (plurality decision denying tribal zoning authority over non-Indian land use within one portion of the reservation, but upholding tribal zoning authority over non-Indian land use in a different portion of the reservation); United States v. Montana, 450 U.S. 544, 566 (1981) (denying tribal regulatory authority over non-Indians hunting and fishing on reservation). *But see* U.S. v. Mazurie, 419 U.S. 544 (1975) (noting with approval a congressional delegation to tribes of authority over non-Indian alcohol distributors within Indian reservations).

17 HRI, Inc. v. U.S. EPA, 198 F.3d 1224 (10th cir. 2000) (upholding the EPA's direct implementation of the Safe Drinking Water Act Underground Injection Control Program on lands whose Indian country status was disputed by the Navajo Nation and New Mexico); Phillips Petroleum Co. v. U.S. EPA, 803 F.2d 545 (10th cir. 1986) (upholding the EPA's direct implementation of the Safe Drinking Water Act Underground Injection Control Program on the Osage Indian Mineral Reserve despite the then Act's silence on Indian country implementation); Washington Dep't of Ecology v. U.S. EPA, 752 F.2d 1465 (9th cir. 1985) (affirming the EPA's rejection of a state's application for hazardous waste regulatory authority over Indian reservations on its conclusion that the Resource Conservation and Recovery Act's express preference for state regulation combined with its silence on Indian country implementation did not amount to congressional authorization for state regulation). *But see* State of Michigan v. EPA, 268 F.3d 1075 (D.C. Cir. 2001) (finding that the EPA's decision to directly implement the Clean Air Act operating permit program on reservation lands whenever it deemed their Indian country status was in question, but without any obligation for resolving the question created the prospect of permanent federal jurisdiction at odds with the Act's express preference for tribal implementation in Indian country and state implementation outside Indian country); Arizona v. U.S. EPA, 151 F.3d at 1212–13 (invalidating the EPA's federal implementation plan promulgated to give effect to the Yavapai–Apache Tribe's air quality redesignation because the Clean Air Act specifically authorized tribal implementation plans).

18 Nance, 645 F.2d at 712–14 (affirming the EPA's authorization of the Northern Cheyenne Tribe's air quality redesignation despite the Clean Air Act's then silence on Indian country implementation). *But see* Backcountry Against Dumps v. EPA, 100 F.3d 147 (D.C. Cir. 1996) (invalidating the EPA's approval of the Campo Band of Mission Indians' landfill program because the Resource Conservation and Recovery Act defines Indian tribes as municipalities that are not eligible for program delegation).

19 Arizona Public Service Co. v. EPA, 211 F.3d 1280 (D.C. Cir. 2000) (affirming the EPA's interpretation of the Clean Air Act as a congressional delegation to Indian tribes of authority over non-Indian air polluters within reservations, thereby obviating any need for tribes to show inherent sovereignty over them), *cert. denied*, 532 U.S. 970 (2001); Montana v. U.S. EPA, 137 F.3d 1135 (9th cir. 1998) (finding that the EPA's determination that the Salish and Kootenai Tribes demonstrated their jurisdiction over non-Indian water polluters

every opportunity presented for reviewing those Indian program challenges, but tribes and the EPA are cautiously optimistic that its apparent fears of unfair or discriminatory tribal regulation can be mitigated by the extensive federal supervision and constraints intrinsic to the EPA's regulatory systems.

Nonetheless, that external threat to tribal sovereignty has been and remains the most potent obstacle to accomplishing the EPA's objective of building effective tribal programs to fill the Indian country regulatory void. For tribes that manage to overcome that obstacle, a new risk—this one internal and thus perhaps more pernicious—confronts them, as discussed below.

Federal Public Participation Process as a Tribal Flashpoint: Internal Attacks on Tribal Sovereignty

By definition, tribal implementation of federal environmental law necessarily creates genuine opportunities for incorporating indigenous interests into program design and operation. Yet, while it is appropriate and preferable that tribes rather than federal agencies identify and articulate those interests, the voice heard comes from tribal governance institutions and not tribal citizens *per se*.

Like generalizing one universal indigenous environmental ethic shared by every tribe, it is presumptuous to assume that all members of a particular tribal community would uniformly define the environmental cultural values and the best means for protecting them. The possibility of dissonance between the people and the government is likely to be heightened when the relevant tribal institutions are modeled on the representative democratic forms foisted on tribes by the United States following the Indian Reorganization Act of 1934.[20] The model assumes, of course, that tribal councils and tribal administrative agencies, regardless of their consistency with traditional norms of governance, legitimately speak for and on behalf of their citizens. The troubling frequency of intra-tribal disputes over the political legitimacy of modern tribal governments, however, often suggests otherwise.

In the recent past, environmental conflicts between tribal governments and their citizens has typically arisen in the context of development undertaken in Indian country by non-Indian firms at the behest of the self-appointed trustee of tribal natural resources.[21] The federal government had the final say in whether and how projects would be carried out, so more often than not the tribal government's

---

within the Flathead Reservation was consistent with the Supreme Court's jurisprudence on inherent tribal sovereignty), *cert. denied*, 525 U.S. 921 (1998).

20 Pub. L. No. 383, 48 Stat. 984 (codified as amended at 25 U.S.C. §§ 461–479 (2011)).

21 *See* Report on Reservation and Resource Development and Protection, Task Force Seven: Reservation and Resource Development and Protection, Final Report to the American Indian Policy Review Commission (1976).

participation in decision-making was limited. In some cases the tribal government and its citizens were united by and in their opposition to federal plans. In others, the tribal government supported federal proposals, and some tribal citizens accused it of sacrificing long-held cultural values for short-term revenue and jobs.

Conflicts over who is the authentic indigenous voice arise today within a new constellation of players and powers as tribal self-determination becomes the animating principle of Indian country's new energy economy and new environmental protection regime. Increasingly, proponents of major Indian country projects are the tribes themselves, sometimes working alone and other times joining with non-Indian firms in true business partnerships. Where federal environmental law requires approval for proposed development, state-like tribal regulatory roles take on heightened importance: now it is possible that the terms and conditions under which the tribe's project moves forward will be determined in the first instance by a tribal, not federal, agency. The ostensible conflict of interest (which of course also exists for every project proposed by the federal and state governments outside of Indian country) amplifies an emerging environmental justice issue. The question is whether and how tribal administrative *agencies* will ensure the implementation of federal regulatory programs provides environmental justice for tribal *citizens*.

A key flashpoint for intra-tribal environmental justice conflicts is the administrative process for public participation required by federal environmental laws. The EPA, and tribes running delegated EPA programs, must allow and consider citizen input at key points in the regulatory scheme. Tribal business deals are usually struck in private, so regulatory hearings and agency meetings are often where tribal citizens first learn officially of the scope of proposed development projects and have their first opportunity to voice concerns or objections.

Timing is just one challenge to applying the federal public participation process to Indian country. Tribal citizens with past negative experiences of federal agency processes for public input might naturally be skeptical of a tribal agency process that mimics a federal one. Suspicion can grow into feelings of disempowerment when an agency approves a project or issues a permit following meetings where citizens urged rejection outright, mistakenly believing that the risks of environmental impacts were legal grounds for refusal rather than simply the basis for determining the conditions of the permissions. Misunderstandings over the complexities of federal environmental law are certainly not limited to Indian country, but in that unique context they contribute to any preexisting sense the environmental programs are culturally incongruous or insensitive, and therefore illegitimate.

The EPA's National Environmental Justice Advisory Council has flagged several potential threats that federally required public participation processes portend for the political legitimacy of tribal environmental sovereignty. One risk arises when federal agencies treat tribal governments like any other interested party in conventional public participation activities. Another crops up where the EPA responds to public concerns raised by individual residents of Indian country without adequately consulting the tribal government. The Advisory Council has cautioned the EPA to conduct its Indian country environmental justice activities in ways that are respectful of tribal sovereignty.[22]

An additional risk to tribal program legitimacy arises from the fact that federal participation procedures are grounded in Western conceptions of due process that may or may not harmonize with traditional indigenous views of equity and justice. The Advisory Council has noted that due process is not a new concept for indigenous peoples, who have traditionally valued honesty, integrity and an opportunity to speak before collective decisions are made. The Council urged the EPA, however, to respect "tribal sovereignty in action" by allowing tribes to articulate the cultural and social norms of due process relevant to their communities and traditions.[23]

One challenge for tribes implementing federal environmental programs, then, is to develop public participation processes that are culturally relevant to tribal citizens as well as legally adequate under federal requirements. The goal should be adapting federal programs to the cultural context so that tribal sovereignty and full inclusion of individual citizen voices become mutually reinforcing. A recent EPA initiative sheds light on how feasible and beneficial attaining that goal might be.

The EPA's programmatic environmental justice work began officially in 1994 when it opened the Office of Environmental Justice (OEJ). That same year the EPA also created the American Indian Environmental Office (AIEO) to coordinate the hard work of implementing the treatment-as-a-state provisions. One year later, OEJ's first official strategy treated Indian country issues separately, indicating that unequal environmental impacts in Indian country were best addressed through tribal sovereignty. The AIEO would take the lead for government-to-government relations facilitating tribal assumption of federal environmental programs, while the OEJ would work with tribal citizens and grassroots organizations to ensure their fair treatment and meaningful involvement.

The OEJ's most significant programmatic effort in Indian country was supporting the Indigenous Peoples Subcommittee of the National Environmental Justice Advisory Council in the early 2000s. The Council issued important reports on consulting with tribal governments and public participation in Indian country.[24]

---

22 National Environmental Justice Advisory Council & Indigenous Peoples Subcommittee, U.S. EPA, Guide on Consultation and Collaboration with Indian Tribal Governments and the Public Participation of Indigenous Groups and Tribal Members in Environmental Decision Making 22 (2000).

23 National Environmental Justice Advisory Council, U.S. EPA, Meaningful Involvement and Fair Treatment by Tribal Environmental Regulatory Programs 3 (2004).

24 While these reports acknowledged environmental justice issues related to tribal governments' treatment of their own citizens, the reports' clear impetus and overriding concern centered on risks posed by non-Indian objections to tribal regulation. Although outside the scope of this chapter, how tribes treat non-Indians within their environmental public participation processes also raises important questions of tribal governmental

Some of the ideas generated there took root outside Indian country in a new OEJ initiative training citizen groups in collaborative methods of solving environmental conflicts. A participant in one of five regional workshops happened to be a tribal citizen, who commented on an evaluation form that the program's emphasis on alternative dispute resolution seemed appropriate for Indian country environmental conflicts. Within a few years, the OEJ had reconfigured its collaborative training program for the unique circumstances of Indian country and rolled out a pilot project at the Navajo Nation, as explained in the next section.

Collaborative and Culturally Relevant Public Participation: Sovereign Solutions

Several factors supported holding the first Indian country workshop in Navajoland. The Navajo Nation's environmental program is long-running and extensive, with legal and regulatory programs covering air and water pollution, solid waste, drinking water systems, underground storage tanks, pesticides, hazardous substance releases and development-related impacts. These programs are administered by the Navajo Nation Environmental Protection Agency, an experienced administrative agency whose actions are governed by separately established uniform procedures that among other things prescribe methods for notifying the public of proposed actions and taking public comment.

The citizen and grassroots network at Navajo is also extensive and experienced, with eight or more established environmental organizations and citizens who have been on the front lines of Indian country protection since the beginning of modern environmental law in the United States. Key players in those organizations, as well as in the Navajo EPA, were members of the National Environmental Justice Advisory Council, and had established working relations with OEJ staff. Against a backdrop of past disputes between the environmental organizations and Navajo EPA, tension mounted over pending regulatory approvals for construction of a 1500 megawatt coal-fired power plant proposed by the Navajo Nation and its multi-national business partner, and expected to spew thousands of tons of regulated air pollutants into the Navajo environment annually. One tribal environmental organization would soon establish a protest camp at the proposed site.[25]

Several Navajo environmental groups urged the OEJ to respond by bringing in its collaborative problem-solving workshop. Navajo EPA was receptive to participating. The OEJ agreed and assembled a planning team of grassroots and agency representatives, which began tailoring the OEJ's model for its new application to Indian country.

---

legitimacy. *See* Dean B. Suagee & John P. Lowndes, *Due Process and Public Participation in Tribal Environmental Programs*, 13 Tulane L. Rev. 1 (1999).

25 For a detailed account of this conflict and its practical and theoretical implications, *see* Ezra Rosser, *Ahistorical Indians and Reservation Resources*, 40 Envtl. L. 437 (2010).

The planning team realized at the outset that its chances of success would be diminished if participants perceived the effort as simply another federally conceived and directed initiative. Therefore, while OEJ's funding made the workshop possible, it was officially co-sponsored by three Navajo environmental organizations,[26] Navajo EPA and the OEJ, and was conducted primarily by an independent facilitator with extensive experience in alternative dispute resolution and Indian country. The planning team paired the facilitator with a Navajo peace-maker to reflect its express attempt at building cross-cultural bridges. I served as a second independent trainer, focusing on the legal issues arising from the intersection of federal and Navajo environmental law. The Director of the Indigenous Environmental Network served as a technical advisor.

The deliberate inclusion of representatives from Navajo EPA and other key tribal governmental institutions was a significant planning decision. The OEJ's prior regional workshops had focused on disaffected community groups and not the governmental agencies they were seeking to engage. The Navajo planning team adapted the model to their needs, believing a multi-stakeholder approach—where parties with past or current conflicts cooperatively explored culturally relevant means of resolving them—would be more productive. The team identified and invited representatives from each Navajo EPA program and the agency's Director, two Tribal Council members, one chapter president, two lawyers from the Tribe's Department of Justice, and staff from eight Navajo governmental offices. Approximately the same number of representatives was invited from seven Navajo environmental organizations.[27]

About 40 people attended the two-and-a-half-day workshop on Alternative Dispute Resolution and Environmental Law at the Navajo Nation Museum in Window Rock, Arizona. The planning team consciously incorporated appropriate local customs into the meeting's structure, beginning with an opening prayer in a traditional hogan on the Museum grounds, followed by a two-hour listening circle within which each person shared her or his reasons for participating. Talking head presentations were given on interest-based negotiation, Navajo peace-making and tribal environmental self-determination, but the wisdom in the room came from discussion among the participants, often in the Navajo language.

The workshop's primary thrust was using appropriate and culturally relevant dispute resolution tools to establish ground rules for resolving a hypothetical intra-tribal environmental conflict over a proposed air pollution permit. Participants broke into small groups and role-played from unfamiliar perspectives: environmental activists became industry officials or EPA employees; tribal governmental staff became leaders of concerned citizen groups. The players then negotiated for their

26 Diné Care, Black Mesa Water Coalition, and Eastern Navajo Diné Against Uranium Mining.

27 Participants attended from Big Mountain, Black Mesa Trust, Black Mesa Water Coalition, C'Aquifer, Diné Care, Dooda Desert Rock, and Eastern Navajo Diné Against Uranium Mining. A Navajo representative from the local Sierra Club chapter also attended.

clients' respective interests with a clearer sense of their cultural responsibilities to the other parties' integrity and interests. The small groups reported their experiences, and all participants discussed the general themes revealed by comparing concessions gained, demands unfulfilled and insights gained.

Speaking strictly as an observer outside the community and culture, I thought that the synergy between Western mediation and Navajo peace-making was apparent, and striking. It also seemed to me directly applicable to the public participation processes required under federal and Navajo environmental law. Some of the key participants shared that view, and a series of follow-up conference calls after the workshop concentrated on principles that workshop participants had initially agreed might improve communication between Navajo environmental organizations and Navajo EPA. When the OEJ found resources to support a follow-up meeting, nearly all of the original participants committed to reconvene.

The second meeting occurred within three months of the initial workshop. This time the location was Farmington, New Mexico, on the eastern edge of the Navajo Reservation, selected to take advantage of another meeting that the Navajo environmental organizations were attending, but also because the first workshop had been in the seat of Navajo government. The preliminaries having been established in the first workshop, the participants began immediately to identify principles for more productive relations between Navajo environmental organizations and Navajo EPA. By the end of the meeting,[28] the parties had reached an agreement in principle, which was finalized two months later at a second follow-up meeting sponsored by a Navajo peace-makers group. At Navajo EPA's annual public conference in April 2007, the parties officially announced the Protocols for Communication and Collaboration between Navajo Grassroots Organizations and Navajo EPA.

Practically, the Protocols sought better and earlier communication between Navajo EPA and the environmental organizations, and enhanced cooperation in addressing difficult challenges. Symbolically, the Protocols envisioned a community of spirit, premised expressly on the fundamental laws of the Diné people, as codified in the Navajo Nation Code. Navajo law embraces *Beenahaz'aanii* (life comes from it) and recognizes a sacred Diné obligation to respect and protect the elements of life. The Protocols acknowledged the sacred duty, and incorporated *A'hil nahata* (to reason together) and *Al'gha'dino't aah* (agree with each other) into ground rules for communication and dialogue.

Two years later, the EPA reassembled the workshop team on the Wind River Reservation in western Wyoming, home of the Northern Arapaho and Eastern Shoshone Indian Tribes. The director of the community organization Wind River Alliance had recently been appointed to the National Environmental Justice Advisory Council and had participated in the OEJ's original Indian country

28 Exploiting their sense of common purpose sparked by the meetings with Navajo EPA, the Navajo environmental organizations stayed in Farmington following the meeting for a day-long discussion of coalition-building principles.

workshop in Window Rock. She suggested that a similar event might help address growing concerns over coalbed methane development rapidly expanding in the region and repair strained relations with the Tribes' Environmental Quality Commission. The Commission's director had also just been appointed to the Advisory Council, and was amenable to the plan.

The workshop was structured similarly to the Navajo training, with representatives from the tribal government and the tribal environmental organization, as well as several non-Indian residents of the reservation. The substantive legal information and related role-play materials were changed to reflect the community's interest in underground injection of hazardous wastes and protection of drinking water supplies and systems.

For resource reasons and others, the workshop was scaled back somewhat in terms of advance planning and overall training time. Unfortunately, that precluded the participation of a traditional Arapaho or Shoshone peace-maker, so any direct connections with traditional dispute resolution methods were not as patent as had been the case at Navajo. It also meant that realistically there was little chance for developing sophisticated protocols for the future, although the parties did come to agreement on a written set of ideas generated at the end of the workshop for improving communication between the parties on various water quality issues.

As grassroots environmental organizations around Indian country heard about the initial, positive results of the Navajo and Wind River workshops, interest mounted in additional training opportunities. In 2010, the OEJ expanded the initiative beyond single reservations by inviting multiple tribes and environmental organizations to participate in two regional workshops. One was held for Ojibway tribes in Wisconsin and upper Michigan; the second meeting involved a number of Minnesota Chippewa bands.

The workshop team was the same, as was the overall thrust of the meeting, but the dynamic was quite different. Although both tribal agency staff and environmental organization members attended in roughly equal numbers, the regional aspect resulted in a lack of parity: some reservations had only government representatives appear, while other reservations had only environmental groups present. That alignment of participants reduced tensions in the meeting room appreciably, and led perhaps to more objective and productive discussions, but it also decreased opportunities for making real headway on improving current relations between tribal agencies and the organizations they work with regularly. It also practically precluded any chance of establishing ground rules for parties' future communications. Nonetheless, participants' evaluations of the regional meetings reflected the nearly unanimous agreement of the prior reservation-specific workshops as to their value in blending public participation processes and traditional cultural values in ways that could help avoid or resolve intra-tribal environmental conflicts.

Conclusion

Emerging within the larger and unprecedented context of a truly global marketplace responsible for changing the entire planet's climate, the dawning era of tribal energy and environmental self-determination raises unique environmental justice challenges for Native America. Tribal sovereignty will increasingly come to mean natural resource development undertaken by tribal governments under environmental terms and conditions set by tribal agencies. Practical considerations make it likely that tribes' economic and environmental activities will be undertaken pursuant to federal programs and policies rather than apart from them, although a long history teaches that federal influences can affect tribal citizens' perceptions as to the political legitimacy of tribal governmental institutions. History also shows that environmental conflicts will arise regardless of governmental or cultural forms, and yet, the particular cultural relevance of environmental preservation for indigenous peoples may raise uniquely fundamental questions over the cultural legitimacy of tribal governments.

For nearly 40 years, inherent tribal sovereignty and government-to-government relations with tribes have been fundamental cornerstones of the EPA's Indian program, and more recently have informed the agency's environmental justice strategies for Indian country. Tribes' regulatory roles in implementing federal environmental law offer the possibility of comprehensive operating programs providing effective public health protection in Indian country. Sovereignty in this context means the authority of tribal governmental agencies to adapt the federal programs to incorporate and protect indigenous cultural values. Tribes' value judgments then animate federally enforceable standards, applicable to tribal projects as well as non-Indian development activities in Indian country despite the Supreme Court's dim view of tribal regulatory authority over non-Indians. The federal force is particularly dramatic where the EPA constrains non-Indian actors *outside* tribal territories in order to ensure compliance with comparatively more stringent tribal environmental criteria.

Many tribes have taken significant steps toward achieving environmental justice in their territories as a result of the EPA's long-standing policy commitment to tribal sovereignty. However, those gains are far from comprehensive,[29] and

29 Timely and accurate data on EPA-approved tribal programs is notoriously difficult to obtain. EPA's Tribal Compliance Assistance Portal, last updated October 16, 2008, reports that the EPA has approved approximately 30 tribes for operating pesticide certification or enforcement programs under the Federal Insecticide, Fungicide and Rodenticide Act, five tribes for undefined programs under the Clean Air Act, one tribe for primacy under the Safe Drinking Water Act, and 27 tribes for the Clean Water Act's water quality standards program. *See* http://www.epa.gov/tribalcompliance/pubsafety/psregsdrill.html (last visited May 22, 2011). The EPA's Water Program reports that, as of May 9, 2011, it has approved the water quality standards for 37 tribes. *See* http://water.epa.gov/scitech/swguidance/standards/wqslibrary/approvtable.cfm (last visited May 22, 2011).

their limited extent makes them more visible and thus more vulnerable to states and non-Indians desirous of getting the EPA's pro-sovereignty policy before the Supreme Court. Without question, the prospect of non-Indian attacks on the legal legitimacy of tribal environmental programs has substantially retarded their growth and expansion to date.

A parallel risk is the prospect of internal attacks on tribal governments by their own citizens as a result of the federally required public participation processes within tribal environmental programs. In the highly charged atmosphere of environmental conflicts, any perceived or assumed discord between those processes and culturally appropriate ones can and often does become a rallying call that challenges not only substantive aspects of the tribal environmental program, but also the political legitimacy of the tribe's sovereignty. Ironically, that sovereignty threat may be addressed best by what the National Environmental Justice Advisory Council called "tribal sovereignty in action," that is, tribes articulating for themselves the cultural and social norms and traditions relevant to resolving community conflict.

It remains to be seen whether the OEJ's Indian country initiative for solving environmental problems collaboratively was a constructive step in that direction. One training surely cannot bridge the chasm wrought for some tribes by a long and torturous history of federal control. Yet it does seem clear that the initiative showed that the process of developing culturally relevant means for resolving intra-tribal environmental conflicts could itself be an important community-building enterprise that reinforces common cultural values. When conflicts do arise, the previously developed principles could provide a culturally relevant, consensus framework for working cooperatively toward maintaining community harmony. In this way, tribal sovereignty is central to both control and accountability—to environmental program development and the full inclusion of tribal citizens in programmatic decisions—thus making possible genuine environmental justice for Native America.

Chapter 3

The Climate Crisis, the Renewable Energy Revolution, and Tribal Sovereignty

Dean B. Suagee[1]

Introduction

Like the other indigenous peoples of the world, American Indian and Alaska Native tribes will suffer, and are suffering, from the impacts of climate change in ways that are different from the cosmopolitan peoples who inhabit most of the centers of political and economic power. Impacts will be experienced differently, in large part, because the material cultures of indigenous peoples tend to be woven into the ecosystems where they live and because their religious cultures also tend to be rooted in the particular places where they live. The roots of their cultural identities reach back into mythic time, with countless generations of traditional ecological knowledge. The kinds of impacts that we expect global warming to bring, the kinds of impacts that we are already witnessing, will stress indigenous cultures in ways that will threaten their survival as distinct peoples.[2] As the plant and animal communities on which indigenous cultures depend drastically change, it will be increasingly difficult for indigenous peoples to maintain their ways of life. The traditional knowledge of the elders will seem less and less relevant in the lives of children and younger adults.

Have these kinds of impacts become inevitable? If there is still hope for avoiding the worst, is such hope beyond the control of the tribes? Is the fate of

---

1 Of Counsel, Hobbs, Straus, Dean & Walker, LLP, Washington, D.C. J.D. University of North Carolina (1976), LL.M. American University Washington College of Law (1989). The author thanks Beth A. Baldwin, J.D. Candidate, 2012, University of Colorado Law School, for her exceptional assistance in finishing this chapter. Portions of this chapter are adapted from several earlier works by the author, including: *Going "Code Green" in Indian Country*, 23:4 Nat. Res. & Env't 55 (2009); *Tribal Self-Determination in a Low-Carbon Economy*, 24:3 Nat. Res. & Env't 58 (2010); *The Climate Crisis, the Green Energy Revolution, and Tribal Sovereignty*, Sovereignty Symposium XXII (Oklahoma City, June 3–4, 2009); and *Solar Energy: Let's Get Passive!*, 26:1 Nat. Res. & Env't 54 (Fall 2011).

2 Rebecca A. Tsosie, *Indigenous People and Environmental Justice: The Impact of Climate Change*, 78 U. Colo. L. Rev. 1625, 1628 (2007); Daniel Cordalis & Dean B. Suagee, *The Effects of Climate Change on American Indian and Alaska Native Tribes*, 22 Nat. Res. & Env't 45 (2007–2008).

indigenous peoples in the hands, so to speak, of the industrialized countries? Are there strategies that Indian tribes in the United States themselves could undertake to, in effect, participate in changing the course of world history?

Global warming is being caused, for the most part, by human activities that consume fossil fuels, releasing carbon dioxide (CO_2) into the atmosphere.[3] Since roughly 1850, the early part of the industrial revolution, the CO_2 level in the atmosphere has increased from about 280 parts per million (ppm) to about 380 ppm, a 36 percent increase; in that same time frame, the mean surface temperature of the Earth has risen 0.7°C (1.3°F), and, if we stopped burning fossil fuels today, the Earth's surface temperature would continue to rise another 0.5°C (0.9°F) until it reaches a state of thermal equilibrium.[4] Climate scientist James Hansen warned in December 2005 that, if we do not start changing the trend, we may pass a tipping point beyond which "it will be impossible to avoid climate change with far ranging undesirable consequences."[5] Dr Hansen predicted that continuing on a "Business-as-usual" scenario would yield "additional warming of 2 or 3°C this century and *imply changes that constitute practically a different planet*."[6]

Strategies to cope with the impacts of climate change—commonly referred to as "adaptation"—are necessary, and Indian tribes will need to be engaged in adaptation programs. This chapter, however, is not about adaptation. Rather, this

---

3 *See generally* Intergovernmental Panel on Climate Change, Climate Change 2007: The Physical Science Basis; Summary for Policymakers (2007), *available at* http://www.ipcc.ch/pdf/assessment-report/ar4/wg1/ar4-wg1-spm.pdf [hereinafter IPCC Physical Science Summary]. In addition to burning fossil fuels, another significant source of increased concentrations of carbon dioxide (CO_2) in the atmosphere is the pattern of land use changes that take trees and other kinds of plants out of ecosystems, thus eliminating their capacity for capturing CO_2 from the atmosphere. *Id.* at 2. In addition to CO_2, there are also greenhouse effects associated with other anthropogenic gases, including methane and nitrous oxide. *Id.* at 3.

4 American Solar Energy Society, Tackling Climate Change in the U.S.: Potential Carbon Emissions Reductions from Energy Efficiency and Renewable Energy by 2030, at 166 (Charles F. Kutscher ed. 2007), *available at* http://www.ases.org/images/stories/file/ASES/climate_change.pdf [hereinafter ASES Report].

5 James E. Hansen, *Is There Still Time to Avoid 'Dangerous Anthropogenic Interference' with Global Climate?: A Tribute to Charles David Keeling*, Presentation on Dec. 6, 2005 at the American Geophysical Union, San Francisco, CA., *available at* http://www.columbia.edu/~jeh1/2005/Keeling_20051206.pdf [hereinafter Hansen, *Dangerous Anthropogenic Interference*]. In a more recent publication, Dr Hansen has concluded that an initial objective of reducing atmospheric CO_2 to 350 ppm must be pursued within decades because "today's CO_2, about 385 ppm, is already too high to maintain the climate to which humanity, wildlife, and the rest of the biosphere are adapted." James E. Hansen et al., *Target Atmospheric CO_2: Where Should Humanity Aim?*, 2 Open Atmos. Sci. J. 217, 230 (2008) [hereinafter Hansen, *Target Atmospheric CO_2*].

6 Hansen, *Dangerous Anthropogenic Interference*, *supra* note 5, at 1 (emphasis added).

chapter is about strategies for reducing emissions of carbon dioxide. If we are to have any hope of avoiding the more catastrophic impacts of climate change, we need to start reducing emissions of carbon dioxide and other greenhouse gases. In the lexicon of climate change, such strategies are often referred to as "mitigation." Given that global warming is mostly driven by emissions of carbon dioxide from combustion of fossil fuels, reducing carbon dioxide emissions will require us to achieve much greater efficiency in our use of energy and replace much of our consumption of fossils fuels with renewable energy resources (including solar, wind, biomass and geothermal).[7] Of course, we are not going to stop burning fossil fuels tomorrow or next year, but we do need to start changing our ways. Soon. And dramatically.

To achieve reductions in carbon dioxide emissions on the scale needed will require action at all levels of government: federal, state, local, and tribal. Although we are now in the fourth decade of the Self-Determination era of federal Indian policy, when most people talk about "all levels of government," they typically include federal, state, and local and overlook Indian tribes.[8] This may help to explain why the literature on governmental actions to address climate change generally overlooks possible roles for tribal governments. This chapter offers a step toward rectifying this oversight, offering suggestions on what tribes might do rather than examples of what particular tribes are doing.

This chapter focuses on how Indian tribal governments can help to bring about the transition to the energy economy of the future, an economic order in which energy will be used efficiently and most of our needs will be met with renewable resources. The emphasis is on strategies that tribes can employ through the use of their sovereign powers as governments. There is also some discussion of how tribes can participate in programs created by the federal government and the states. A number of states are already providing leadership in making this transition happen, and tribes can become engaged in state programs. There may eventually be a comprehensive federal program—while prospects for action by Congress seem unlikely at present, the Executive Branch is moving ahead under existing authority. Tribes are engaged in many federal programs, and should be involved in many others, but this chapter does not attempt to catalogue relevant federal programs. Rather, the objective of this chapter is to suggest some strategies that tribal governments can pursue on their own, as sovereigns. Another objective of this chapter is to offer tribal leaders a source for talking

---

7 Intergovernmental Panel on Climate Change, IPCC Special Report on Renewable Energy Sources and Climate Change Mitigation: Summary for Policymakers (2011), *available at* http://www.ipcc.ch/news_and_events/docs/ipcc33/SRREN_FD_SPM_final.pdf [hereinafter IPCC, IPCC Special Report on Renewable Energy Sources and Climate Change Mitigation].

8 *See, e.g.*, Global Climate Change and U.S. Law (Michael B. Gerrard ed. 2007) (including chapters on regional, state, and local government initiatives, but no discussion of tribal governments).

points that they can draw upon in their contributions to the national dialogue on the climate crisis and energy policy.

Toward a Post Fossil Fuels Economy

The global climate crisis provides a compelling reason to shift to an economic order that uses energy efficiently and meets most of our needs for energy services with renewable resources.[9] There are other good reasons, as well. Meeting our energy demands through efficiency and renewables will also reduce our dependence on imported oil, reduce the demand for energy resources that cause major environmental impacts other than global warming,[10] and create the kinds of jobs that are not readily outsourced to other countries.[11] We will have "cleaner air and water, more efficient products, more workers trained in the next great global industry, higher energy prices but lower bills, greater productivity, healthier people, and an export industry in clean power products that people across the world will want to buy."[12] We might also help ourselves to many kinds of amenities that add up to an enhanced quality of life—sunspaces in passive solar homes, daylighting in public buildings, more bike paths, walkable mixed-use neighborhoods clustered in transit-oriented development, organic vegetables from local farms and greenhouses attached to homes, less land paved over, and more land left for the plants and creatures that make up the web of life.

---

9 *See, e.g.*, IPCC, IPCC Special Report on Renewable Energy Sources and Climate Change Mitigation, *supra* note 7; Pew Center on Global Climate Change, Climate Change 101: Understanding and Responding to Global Climate Change 4 (2011), *available at* http://www.pewclimate.org/docUploads/climate101-fullbook_0.pdf; Union of Concerned Scientists , Climate 2030: A National Blueprint for a Clean Energy Economy (2009), *available at* http://www.ucsusa.org/publications.

10 *See generally* National Academy of Sciences, Hidden Costs of Energy: Unpriced Consequences of Energy Production and Use (2010) [hereinafter NAS, Hidden Costs of Energy]. As stated in this report, "In aggregate, the damage estimates presented in this report for various external effects are substantial. Just the damages from external effects the committee was able to quantify add up to more than $120 billion for the year 2005." *Id.* at 15. These are the costs of environmental and health impacts, not including climate change impacts. The two major categories of sources are coal-fired power plants, at $62 billion annually, and motor vehicles, at $56 billion annually. *Id.* at 6, 12.

11 American Solar Energy Society, Estimating the Jobs Impacts of Tackling Climate Change 2 (2009), *available at* http://www.ases.org/pdf/ASES_TCCJobs_FullReport.pdf; Presidential Remarks on the Economy and Clean Energy, Daily Comp. Pres. Docs., 2010 DCPD No. 12 (Jan. 8, 2010). ("Building a robust clean energy sector is how we will create the jobs of the future, jobs that pay well and can't be outsourced.")

12 Thomas L. Friedman, Hot, Flat, and Crowded: Why We Need a Green Revolution and How It Can Renew America 174 (2008).

For reasons such as these, the Obama Administration has promoted energy efficiency and renewable energy in legislation and administrative initiatives, including more that $90 billion appropriated for existing programs through the American Recovery and Reinvestment Act (Recovery Act)[13] and an Executive order.[14] The Obama Administration has put forth the proposition that America should step up and lead the world in the revolution to an energy future that emphasizes efficiency and renewables and other low-carbon sources of energy.[15]

While President Obama and some leaders in Congress use the term "clean" energy[16] to describe low-carbon forms of energy, I prefer the term "green" energy, which means energy efficiency and environmentally acceptable renewable energy facilities.[17] We can call it "clean" or "green" or get somewhat more specific and use the term "renewable," but whatever words we use, some fundamental changes are coming as we move toward a post-fossil fuels economy. American Indian and Alaska Native tribes need to be part of making the transition to a green energy future happen.

---

13 *Securing American Energy*, The White House, http://www.whitehouse.gov/energy/securing-american-energy (last visited July 7, 2011).

14 Exec. Order No. 13,514, 74 Fed. Reg. 52117 (Oct. 8, 2009) (requiring Federal agencies to set a 2020 greenhouse gas emissions reduction target within 90 days; increase energy efficiency; reduce fleet petroleum consumption; conserve water; reduce waste; support sustainable communities; and leverage Federal purchasing power to promote environmentally responsible products and technologies); Presidential Memorandum on Federal Fleet Performance, Daily Comp. Pres. Docs., 2011 DCPD No. 386 (May 24, 2011) (encouraging agencies to "leverag[e] Federal purchasing dollars to build manufacturing capacity for more alternative fueled vehicles"); Presidential Memorandum on Improving Energy Security, American Competitiveness and Job Creation, and Environmental Protection Through a Transformation of Our Nation's Fleet of Cars and Trucks, Daily Comp. Pres. Docs., 2010 DCPD No. 409 (May 21, 2010).

15 Presidential Remarks on Energy, Daily Comp. Pres. Docs., 2009 DCPD No. 517 (June 29, 2009) ("We can remain the world's leading importer of oil, or we can become the world's leading exporter of clean energy. We can allow climate change to wreak unnatural havoc, or we can create jobs utilizing low carbon technologies to prevent its worst effects. We can cede the race for the 21st century, or we can embrace the reality that our competitors already have: The nation that leads the world in creating a new clean energy economy will be the nation that leads the 21st century global economy.")

16 *E.g.*, American Clean Energy and Security Act, H.R. 2998, passed by the House, June 26, 2009; Cong. Rec. H7471 (June 26, 2009).

17 As I understand it, the word "clean" is intended to emphasize the reduction or avoidance of carbon dioxide emissions, but even if carbon dioxide can successfully be captured and sequestered from coal-fired power plants, unless one overlooks the impacts of mining, it strikes me as a misnomer to call coal "clean" or "green." Much the same could be said of mining uranium for nuclear power, which also produces waste that will remain toxic for a span of time comparable to the time span that human beings have been the species that we are today.

Global Warming and the Wedges Strategy

While there is consensus that we need to change course, there is some uncertainty regarding what the target should be for atmospheric CO_2 levels. Many analysts have proposed that if we can stabilize CO_2 levels in a range from 450 to 500 ppm, followed by actual reductions in CO_2 levels over the long term, we might be able to escape the more catastrophic impacts of global warming.[18] More recently, Dr Hansen has argued that, for long-term stabilization of the climate, our target should be 350 ppm,[19] a concentration level that we have already exceeded. While we may not yet have consensus on what the target should be,[20] we have a good idea of the scale of the needed emissions reductions, and we know that we have no time to waste.

Stabilization Wedges

In order to stabilize CO_2 levels in the atmosphere, we need to dramatically reduce our emissions. In 2004, two Princeton University professors, Robert Socolow and Stephen Pacala, published an article in which they proposed the concept of "stabilization wedges" as a strategy for changing the trend.[21] The concept of wedges is based on the graph that is used to show the increasing amounts of CO_2 emissions worldwide over time, with time on the *x*-axis and CO_2 emissions on the *y*-axis. Worldwide CO_2 emissions in 2006 amounted to seven billion tons per year, which, under a business as usual scenario would double to fourteen billion tons by 2056; the corresponding amounts for the United States are about 1.6 billion tons and 2.7 billion tons.[22] The basic idea is that first we need to stop the line on the

18 ASES Report, *supra* note 4, at 169 (noting Hansen's recommendation of stabilizing CO_2 at 475 ppm, and the Pacala and Sacalow recommended target of 500 ppm). A report published by the World Wildlife Fund (WWF) says that we should be working toward keeping the overall increase in average global temperature to no more than 2°C over pre-industrial levels, and that if we can stabilize the concentrations of greenhouses gases in the atmosphere at 400 ppm by about 2100 after hitting a peak of 475 ppm toward the middle of this century, we would bring the probability of exceeding the 2°C average global increase down to where it would be "unlikely." Karl Mallon, Greg Bourne & Richard Mott, Climate Solutions: WWF's Vision for 2050, at 3–4 (2007), *available at* http://www.worldwildlife.org/climate/Publications/WWFBinaryitem4911.pdf.

19 Hansen, *Target Atmospheric CO_2*, *supra* note 5.

20 *See generally* National Research Council, Climate Stabilization Targets: Emissions, Concentrations, and Impacts over Decades to Millennia (2011).

21 Stephen W. Pacala & Robert H. Socolow, *Stabilization Wedges: Solving the Climate Problem for the Next 50 Years with Current Technologies*, 305 Science 968 (2004); *see also* Robert H. Socolow & Stephen W. Pacala, *A Plan to Keep Carbon in Check*, Scientific American, Sept. 2006, at 50 [hereinafter Socolow & Pacala, *A Plan to Keep Carbon in Check*].

22 Socolow & Pacala, *A Plan to Keep Carbon in Check*, *supra* note 21, at 52, 57.

graph from going up and then start bringing it down. The "wedges" are the various ways in which reductions in CO_2 emissions can be achieved. Socolow and Pacala call for holding the curve flat over the next 50 years using existing technologies, and then bringing it down.

To hold the curve flat, Socolow and Pacala divide up the reductions in emissions needed into seven wedges, each of which represents one billion tons of CO_2 that would otherwise be emitted 50 years from now. Assuming a straight-line increase under the business as usual scenario, each wedge represents a total of 25 billion tons of CO_2 (that is, zero per year at present, 0.5 billion tons per year in 25 years, one billion tons per year in 50 years).

One of the key points that the wedges concept conveys is that there is no single solution to the problem; rather, the solution must consist of a mix of solutions. Socolow and Pacala divide up the aggregate reduction needed into seven wedges for the convenience of using the one billion tons per year reduction target figure, in order to "make the task of reducing emissions vivid."[23] They also identify fifteen different ways of accomplishing one of the seven wedges, divided into five categories: end user efficiency and conservation; power generation; carbon capture and storage (CCS); alternative energy sources; and agriculture and forestry.[24]

While Socolow and Pacala's wedges strategy features energy efficiency and renewable energy, their list of options also includes measures such as expanding nuclear power and carbon sequestration. Is it possible that we could get all the wedges that we need from energy efficiency and renewable energy?

Renewable Energy and Energy Efficiency Wedges

To what extent can we rely on efficiency and renewables to provide for our energy needs and achieve reductions of CO_2 emissions on the scale needed? One of the more detailed sets of answers is set out in a collection of studies commissioned by the American Solar Energy Society (ASES), captioned TACKLING CLIMATE CHANGE IN THE U.S. (hereinafter "*ASES Report*").[25] The studies indicate that it is possible for us to get the reductions in CO_2 emissions that we need by choosing energy efficiency and renewable energy technologies.

The ASES Report adopts the wedges approach, analyzing the potential contributions of energy efficiency and a variety of renewable energy technologies for reducing carbon emissions in the United States by 2030, to put us on a path to achieve emissions reductions by mid-century in the range of 60 to 80 percent below 2005 levels.[26] The ASES Report focuses on what can be accomplished now

---

23 *Id.* at 52–53.

24 *Id.* at 54.

25 ASES Report, *supra* note 4.

26 ASES report, *supra* note 4, at 170. The scope and time frame of the ASES Report are different from the scope and time frame of the Socolow and Pacala articles—the United States over 25 years vs the world over 50 years. Given these differences, comparison of the

and in the mid-term, relying on existing technologies, rather than assuming there will be technological breakthroughs. The nine wedges in the ASES Report are: overall energy efficiency, buildings, plug-in hybrid electric vehicles, concentrating solar power, photovoltaics, wind power, biomass, biofuels, and geothermal power.[27]

The ASES Report suggests that we can get there from here. Or at least it is a realistic possibility. By moving ahead with energy efficiency and renewables, we can change the trend line on the graph from an upward slope to a downward slope. Whether we can change the trend fast enough to stabilize the atmosphere before climate-related catastrophes become commonplace, time will tell.

Energy Marketplaces and Governmental Policies

The kinds of markets in which energy is bought and sold can be described in different ways. For electricity, there are both retail and wholesale markets. At the retail level, consumers generally buy from utilities and at the wholesale level, utilities trade among themselves, or buy from independent producers. For energy consumed in operating buildings, many of the energy choices are made by developers within frameworks set by building codes. Energy consumption choices for appliances, motors, heating and cooling equipment are made in a wide range of settings; to some extent the range of choices has been limited by energy efficiency standards imposed through regulations. Energy for motor vehicles is generally sold in filling stations, but the consumption choices are framed by fuel economy standards, land use planning, public investments in roads, and the relative lack of public investment in public transportation. For the wide range of investments that can be generically categorized as energy efficiency improvements, there is no single market and no single way of tracking these kinds of investments. (The term "investment" seems generally more accurate than "expenditure" since money spent on energy efficiency yields returns in the form of recurrent reductions in operating costs.)

In the markets in which energy goods and services are bought and sold, there are many factors that contribute to decisions that keep us moving along the status

---

projections in the ASES report to the needed reductions as set out by Socolow and Pacala requires some attention to detail, and only a few points of comparison are offered here. Since the ASES reductions are projected to be achieved in a 25 year time frame, over a 50 year time frame their projected carbon reductions can be estimated to be about (or at least) twice that much, or about 2.4 billion tons. So, the ASES projection of carbon reductions for the U.S. from a range of energy efficiency and renewable energy technologies amounts to about one-third of what Socolow and Pacala say we need to achieve worldwide to stabilize the climate. It is probably a reasonable assumption that, through a similar combination of energy efficiency and renewable energy technologies, the rest of the world could achieve twice the carbon reductions that we achieve in the United States.

27 ASES Report, *supra* note 4, at 33.

quo, the upward trend of carbon dioxide emissions. In many ways, regulatory policies and governmental subsidies send price signals to consumers that are contrary to the public interest in reducing emissions. Many decisions reflect short-term costs rather than life-cycle costs, sometimes because the person who makes the choice is someone other than the person who pays the operating costs and sometimes because the person paying out the money cannot afford the up-front cost of the investment and financing is either not available or is not convenient. Many decisions are made based on factors that have nothing to do with energy, such as style, convenience, and habit. Some decisions reflect the fact that having a grasp on the choices available and how to evaluate them requires information and knowledge that most consumers just do not have or are too busy to seek. Programs like Energy Star labeling on appliances help consumers in this regard by providing at least enough information to evaluate the projected operating costs.

Given the many ways in which energy from fossil fuels is imbedded in our national economy, there are many ways in which governmental policy tools can be brought to bear to facilitate the transition to the energy economy of the future. In a general sense, these policy tools establish the rules for various energy marketplaces or provide incentives or subsidies for certain kinds of investments. Some policy tools can be wielded at the federal level, some at the state level, and some the local level.

In the American system of government, tribal governments are conceptually similar to states, in that they are distinct from the federal government and exercise their own inherent sovereignty, and may also exercise delegated federal authority.[28] Tribes are generally not subject to the lawmaking authority of the states, and so, the kinds of laws that are typically enacted by states, or by local governments acting pursuant to state sovereignty, are not presumptively valid on trust lands in Indian country.[29] However, in many ways, the attributes of tribal sovereignty differ from the attributes of state sovereignty. Some of the differences include limits on the exercise of tribal powers imposed by federal courts applying the approach often called "implicit divestiture."[30] On a practical level, implicit divestiture means that, when tribal governments enact laws that apply to lands that are no longer in federal Indian trust or restricted status, or to persons who are not tribal members, they may well have to defend their tribal laws in federal court.

Although conceptually like states, as a practical matter, most tribes tend to be more comparable to local governments in the range of governmental programs and services that they administer, as well as in the relative size of their service populations. In the transition to the renewable energy future, some policy tools

28 *See generally* COHEN'S HANDBOOK OF FEDERAL INDIAN LAW §§ 4.01, 4.03 (Nell Jessup Newton et al. eds. 2005).

29 *See generally* COHEN'S HANDBOOK OF FEDERAL INDIAN LAW § 6.02[1] (2005 ed.). State laws may be valid on non-trust lands and with respect to the conduct of non-members. *Id.* at § 6.02[1].

30 *See* COHEN'S HANDBOOK OF FEDERAL INDIAN LAW *Id.* at § 4.02[3].

wielded at the state or federal level are largely beyond the reach of most tribal governments. Nevertheless, it is important for tribal leaders to be aware of how these policy tools are shaping energy marketplaces, among other reasons, so that tribal enterprises can participate in those marketplaces.

In using governmental policy tools for reducing CO_2 emissions, it warrants emphasis that consumers do not shop for units of energy in the abstract, but rather they shop for the services that various forms of energy provide, and for goods that require energy to make and/or to operate. As Amory Lovins has said, "Customers don't want lumps of coal, raw kilowatt-hours, or barrels of sticky goo. Rather, they want the services that energy provides: hot showers and cold beer, mobility and comfort, spinning shafts and energized microchips, baked bread and smelted aluminum."[31] If one form of energy can be replaced with another, the end user may not really care, or, if concerned about global warming, the end user may care a great deal.

Legacies of Historic Policies and Market Distortions

Governmental strategies to reduce greenhouse gas emissions cannot be written on a blank slate but, rather, must take into account the legacy of more than a century of laws and regulations, at federal, state, and local levels. While some hold the view that energy purchases and investments take place in "free" markets with decisions made by people acting rationally in their own self-interests, in fact, governmental policies have been distorting these marketplaces over many decades, and many of the policy-driven distortions operate counter to what we need to be doing to cope with global warming.[32]

As professor David Hodas has said, "Climate change presents the classic problem of externalities and the global commons."[33] Law and economics theory suggests that, as long as the global, long-term harms of climate change are not internalized into present-day transactions, rational actors can be expected to maximize their own self interest, by burning fossil fuels and dumping greenhouse gases into the atmosphere, at least until the other costs associated with the price of fossil fuels rise enough to make the alternatives cost-effective.[34] As the British government's Stern Review Report on the Economics of Climate Change

31 Amory B. Lovins & L. Hunter Lovins, *Mobilizing Energy Solutions*, American Prospect, Jan. 2002, at 18.

32 *See generally* Roberta Mann, *Subsidies, Tax Policy, and Technological Innovation*, in GLOBAL CLIMATE CHANGE AND U.S. LAW, *supra* note 8, at 576–83.

33 David Hodas, *State Initiatives*, *in* GLOBAL CLIMATE CHANGE AND U.S. LAW, *supra* note 8, at 344.

34 *Id.*

succinctly states, "Climate change presents a unique challenge for economics: it is the greatest and widest-ranging market failure ever seen."[35]

Externalities can be internalized through a variety of governmental policy tools, including command-and-control regulation (requiring sources of emissions to adopt reduction measures, the costs of which can be passed on to consumers of goods and services) and tax policies (which can provide both incentives and disincentives). At a macroeconomic level, a basic step in the transition to a low-carbon future could be to make the prices paid in energy marketplaces incorporate the costs associated with global warming, or at least drive the prices of fossil fuel inputs high enough that purchasers and investors choose efficiency and renewables on a grand scale. A tax on carbon would be one way to accomplish that. A "cap-and-trade" regime is another approach, in which there is an overall regulatory limit on greenhouse gas emissions, with a limited number of "allowances" or permits to pollute, and a market is created in which allowances are traded. As the cap is ratcheted down over time, market forces drive the transition to efficiency and renewables.[36] In the current political climate, raising the price of fossil fuels to internalize the costs of carbon emissions seems unlikely, but there are other tools that can be used.

Federal- and State-level Policy Tools

Governmental policies to internalize the externalities of greenhouse gas emissions would be adopted against a background of two bodies of existing law: environmental law and energy law.[37] Each of these bodies of law includes a variety of statutes and regulations at federal and state levels. Some aspects of our energy economy are regulated by federal agencies, and some are regulated at the state or local level. Federal and state tax policies are also major factors in shaping energy marketplaces.[38] A number of states have enacted laws or have otherwise launched initiatives that address aspects of the climate crisis.[39] The electric utility industry

35 Nicholas Stern, The Economics of Climate Change: The Stern Review, at Exec. Summary 1 (2007), *available at* www.hm-treasury.gov.uk/independent_reviews/stern_review_economics_climate_change/stern_review_report.cfm.

36 One such cap-and-trade regime is set out in the American Clean Energy and Security Act, which the U.S. House of Representatives passed in 2009 but which died in the Senate. H.R. 2998, as passed by the House, June 26, 2009; Cong. Rec. H7471 (June 26, 2009). This bill was designated H.R. 2454 when it was introduced; and is commonly referred to as the "Waxman–Markey" bill, after the names of its main sponsors.

37 *See generally* John C. Dernbach, *U.S. Policy*, in Global Climate Change and U.S. Law, *supra* note 8, at 61, 65–72.

38 *See* Jerome L. Garciano, *Green Energy Tax Policies: State and Federal Tax Policies for Renewable Energy and Energy Efficiency*, 25:4 Nat. Res & Env't 12 (Spring 2011); Roberta Mann, *Subsidies, Tax Policy, and Technological Innovation*, in Global Climate Change and U.S. Law, *supra* note 8, at 565.

39 Hodas, *supra* note 33, at 344–45.

is largely regulated at the state level,[40] and one of the main regulatory drivers for the deployment of utility-scale renewable energy projects has been renewable portfolio standards adopted by a majority of the states.[41] While historically, the reservations of many of tribes have been sources of fossil fuels for the national economy, tribes as law-making sovereigns have not had much direct influence on the system of laws that regulate energy marketplaces.

Macroeconomic issues, and governmental policy tools designed to work at the macroeconomic level, are mostly beyond the reach of tribal governments. While the scope of this chapter is the range of actions that tribal governments can take through the exercise of tribal sovereignty and in delivering governmental services, tribal policy-makers must be aware of the ways in which federal and state policies shape the markets in which reservation economies operate. It should also be noted that, in our current energy marketplaces, prices for fossil fuels, and for energy goods and services with fossil fuels imbedded in them, generally do not reflect the full costs of adverse impacts on the environment and public health, or the costs associated with global warming.[42] How long will the failure to internalize such costs continue? I hesitate to speculate. National political leaders who have a sense of responsibility to future generations might succeed in changing at least some of the rules that govern energy marketplaces. Some tribal political leaders might contribute to making such changes happen. In the meantime, there are policy tools available to tribal governments that operate at a scale below the macroeconomic level.

Policy Tools That Tribal Governments Can Use

Tribal governments could step up and assume leadership roles in moving us toward an efficient and renewable energy future, by using their sovereign powers to enact and implement various kinds of policy tools. Some of the governmental policy tools that can be brought to bear on greenhouse gas emissions operate at the national or international level and, as such, are largely beyond the control of tribes, except in the sense that tribal governments can engage in advocacy when these

40 *See generally* Walter R. Hall II, *et al.*, *History, Objectives, and Mechanics of Competitive Electricity Markets*, *in* Capturing the Power of Electric Restructuring 1 (Joey Lee Miranda ed. 2009).

41 Some 32 states have enacted a renewable portfolio standard or target of some kind. Information is available the Department of Energy website including the Database of State Energy Incentives for Renewables and Efficiency (DSIRE) at www.dsireusa.org. *See also* Stephen C. Braverman, *State Renewable Portfolio Standards and the Commerce Clause*, 25:4 Nat. Res. & Env't 15 (Spring 2011); Hodas, *supra* note 33, at 355–59. A national renewable energy standard could be enacted through federal legislation, but to date this is a policy tool that has only been used at the state level.

42 *See* NAS, Hidden Costs of Energy, *supra* note 10.

tools are being formulated and can learn how to work within the frameworks that are put in place. Some policy tools are available to state and local governments, and some of these could also be used by tribal governments. Advocates of energy efficiency and renewables tend to overlook how tribes could fit into the policy development framework, which should not be surprising, given the general lack of awareness in the American public regarding the status of tribes as sovereign governments. Tribal governments could emerge in leadership roles, but it looks like it will take some initiative from Indian country for this to happen.

This section looks at some of the options that tribes could pursue. One starting point is to look at the big picture of carbon dioxide emissions. The ASES Report uses a three-part breakdown for end-use energy consumption, for which it allocates CO_2 emissions as follows: buildings—43 percent; transportation—32 percent; and industry—25 percent.[43] In light of this breakdown, the discussion that follows emphasizes reducing emissions associated with buildings and transportation. Since renewable energy will largely be brought to market in the form of electricity, there is also some discussion of the electric power industry.

The range of actions that tribes can pursue is framed, at least in part, by federal statutes, regulations, the ways in which federal agencies administer assistance programs, and rulings by federal courts. So some discussion of federal law is included. Within this scope, this chapter is by no means comprehensive. The list of options suggested here is not intended to be exhaustive. Comprehensive analysis would require book-length treatment.

Showcase Communities and Climate Action Plans

The U.S. Environmental Protection Agency administers a Climate Showcase Communities program,[44] and a few tribes have received grants through this program.[45] Each of these tribal programs includes measures to reduce greenhouse gas emissions through energy efficiency and renewable energy. As such, these tribal programs could serve as models for other tribes.

If a tribal government wants to take a comprehensive approach to analyzing options and setting priorities, and to engage the tribal community in the project, it could develop a Tribal Climate Action Plan. How would a tribe develop

---

43 ASES Report, *supra* note 4, at 53. The 43 percent buildings slice is divided into three parts, as follows: 21 percent residential; 17 percent commercial; and 5 percent industrial.

44 *See* U.S. Envtl. Prot. Agency's Climate Showcase Communities Program web page, www.epa.gov/statelocalclimate/local/showcase/.

45 Climate showcase tribes include Choctaw Nation of Oklahoma, Confederated Tribes of Siletz Indians, Gila River Indian Community, Northern Cheyenne Tribe, and Santa Ynez Band of Chumash Indians. The intertribal organization Tanana Chiefs Conference, which represents a number of Alaska Native tribes, has also received assistance through this program. *Id.*

such a plan? A guidance document for cities, the Climate Action Handbook ("Handbook"),[46] was developed for the U.S. Conference of Mayors. There is, as yet, no guidance document for tribal governments. The Handbook starts with the question, "What can local governments do?" The short answer is quite a lot. Local governments have substantial power over some of the main sources of greenhouse gas emissions, including energy consumption in buildings and transportation. Local government operations and capital investments are themselves typically substantial sources of emissions and, as such, offer opportunities for reductions through implementing improvements or "best practices." Such changes in operations and capital investments also provide opportunities to lead by example.

The Handbook suggests that one of the first steps should be to adopt a resolution affirming the city's commitment to reducing global warming pollution. Tribal governments, of course, are familiar with the practice of adopting resolutions. A resolution could set out the process for developing a tribal climate action plan, which should include opportunities for the tribal community to become engaged in the process. Community education should be seen as of vital importance in developing and carrying out the plan. After all, most transactions involving the purchase of energy good and services take place in the private sector.

As envisioned by the Handbook, there are five milestones in a local government climate action campaign: (1) conduct a baseline inventory of global warming pollutants; (2) establish a target for emissions reductions; (3) develop a local climate action plan that includes actions to reduce emissions; (4) implement the climate action plan; and (5) measure, verify, and report the performance. The Handbook suggests that the climate action plan (milestone 3) should include eight categories of actions: (1) land use management and urban forestry; (2) transportation planning; (3) green (renewable) electric power; (4) energy efficiency; (5) green building; (6) water and waste management; (7) recycling and waste reduction; and (8) education and outreach. Within each of these categories, the Handbook suggests measures for the government and measures for the community (some of which would be voluntary, educational measures and some of which would be enacted as local laws). Measures are also categorized as short-term or long-term.

The Handbook also offers a wide range of examples of "best practices" that have been adopted by particular municipalities, organized according to the eight categories of actions. As an alternative or short-cut version of developing a tribal climate action plan, tribes could take actions drawn from these examples. If there were a handbook tailored to tribes, it should include such examples of leadership by particular tribes. Tribes need not wait for a handbook, of course, to start taking action to reduce greenhouse gas emissions. A tribal program could emphasize

46 ICLEI – Local Governments for Sustainability, U.S. Mayors' Climate Action Handbook (2008), *available at* http://www.iclei.org/documents/USA/documents/CCP/Climate_Action_Handbook-0906.pdf. *See also* Natural Capitalism Solutions, Climate Protection Manual for Cities (2007), *available at* http://www.climatemanual.org/Cities/downloads/ClimateProtectionManual_Cities.pdf.

energy efficiency and renewables as a strategy for community development, without trying to establish a baseline and measuring reductions. The Department of Energy offers training for tribes on this approach for community development.[47] Another step that tribes can take short of a climate action plan would be to consistently raise climate change issues in the review of proposed federal actions pursuant to the National Environmental Policy Act[48] and National Historic Preservation Act.[49] Tribes can also take a case-by-case approach to proposed projects that involve emissions above thresholds subject to regulation under the Clean Air Act.[50]

The Building Sector

More than 40 percent of greenhouse gas emissions in America are associated with energy consumption in buildings.[51] We know how to design buildings so that their consumption of non-renewable energy is net zero, and so the building sector offers an enormous opportunity for reducing emissions. The organization Architecture 2030 has issued a challenge to make net-zero energy the standard practice in new construction and major renovations by 2030.[52]

In Indian country, the built environment is largely financed by the federal government, with most residential units funded by the Department of Housing and Urban Development. Much of the existing housing stock is inadequate (e.g. about one-fifth of homes lack indoor plumbing), and the estimated need

47 *Tribal Energy Program: Tribal Community Development and Project Development*, U.S. Dep't of Energy, http://apps1.eere.energy.gov/tribalenergy/community.cfm (last visited July 12, 2011).

48 42 U.S.C. § 4332; 40 C.F.R. parts 1500–508; *see* Council on Environmental Quality, *Draft NEPA Guidance on Consideration of the Effects of Climate Change and Greenhouse Gas Emissions* (Feb. 18, 2010), *available at* http://ceq.hss.doe.gov/current_developments/new_ceq_nepa_guidance.html.

49 16 U.S.C. § 470f; 36 C.F.R. part 800; *see* Dean B. Suagee, *Consulting with Tribes for Off-Reservation Projects*, 25:1 Nat. Res. & Env't 54 (2010).

50 42 U.S.C. §§ 7401 to 7671q. As amended in 1990, the Act authorizes the Environmental Protection Agency to treat tribes like states. Pub. L. No. 101-549, §§ 107(d), 108(j) (codified at 42 U.S.C. §§ 7601(d), 7410(o)). *See generally* Dean B. Suagee, *Indian Country Environmental Law*, Ch. 15A, §§ 15A.02[2][c], 15A.05[1][b], in Environmental Law Practice Guide (Michael B. Gerrard, general ed. 2008 ed.). Tribes that do not choose to be treated like states can nevertheless influence Clean Air Act permits, including a range of options under the Federal Implementation Plan for Indian country. *See* Environmental Protection Agency, Review of New Sources and Modifications in Indian Country: Final Rule, 76 Fed. Reg, 38,748 (July 1, 2011) (to be coifed in various provisions of 40 C.F.R. parts 49 and 51).

51 *See* Architecture 2030 website at http://www.architecture2030.org/current_situation/building_sector.html.

52 Architecture 2030 website at http://www.architecture2030.org/2030_challenge/the_2030_challenge.

for housing is 200,000 units.[53] Given the large unmet needs for decent homes in much of Indian country, one might think that the federal government would have a strong interest in helping tribal housing programs build energy-efficient homes, which would be more affordable for Indian families to heat and cool. The Energy Independence and Security Act of 2007 requires that most federally subsidized new housing conform to the standards in the 2006 version of the International Energy Conservation Code,[54] but this requirement does not apply to federally subsidized Indian housing funded by the Department of Housing and Urban Development pursuant to the Native American Housing and Self-Determination Act (NAHASDA).[55] For housing built with NAHASDA, while energy efficiency investments are allowable, there is a countervailing regulatory requirement to keep the construction coats within a prescribed limit.[56] With a long waiting list for new homes, there may be local political pressure not to exceed the assigned cost limit, since doing so would be likely to mean fewer new homes.

Building codes One governmental policy tool that could be used by tribes to make new homes energy efficient would be to enact and enforce building codes that include energy efficiency standards. Since the Energy Policy Act of 1992,[57] the Department of Energy has been authorized to provide assistance to states and local governments to ratchet up the energy efficiency standards in their building codes, but this assistance program has never been available to tribal governments. The existing law[58] provides that, whenever the International Code Council revises its International Energy Conservation Code (IECC) for residential buildings, and whenever the American Society of Heating, Refrigeration, and Air Conditioning Engineers (ASHRAE) revises its commercial building standards, the Secretary of Energy will make a determination as to whether the code revisions will improve the energy efficiency of buildings. If the Secretary makes such a determination, then each state shall review its buildings codes in light of the revised standards and determine whether or not to revise its codes accordingly. The current law provides for the Department of Energy to provide technical assistance to states and

53 Roberta Youmans, *Federal Housing Finance Board, Native American Housing Needs & Proposed Recommendations*, Background Paper for the Millennial Housing Commission (April 2000).

54 Pub. L. No. 110-140, § 481 (codified at 42 U.S.C. § 12709).

55 25 U.S.C. §§ 4101– 4243.

56 The NAHASDA regulations emphasize the upfront costs of home construction by establishing a "total development cost" for each tribe, 24 C.F.R. § 1000.158, not the lower operating costs that could be achieved through energy efficiency.

57 Pub. L. No. 102-486, § 101(a)(2); 106 Stat. 2783 (codified at 42 U.S.C. § 6833).

58 The existing statutory language, sometimes referred to as section 304 of the Energy Conservation and Production Act [of 1976], was enacted by the Energy Policy Act of 1992 and was substantially amended by the Energy Policy Act of 2005. Pub. L. No. 109-58, § 128.

incentive funding for states to implement the enhanced codes. In states without a statewide building code, local governments are eligible for the incentive funding.

The existing statutory language does not mention tribal governments, and tribes have been left out for most of the two decades that this federal assistance program has been authorized. While this has not been a large federal assistance program, there never has been any justification for leaving tribal governments out. Most likely, the drafters of the original legislative language just did not think about Indian tribes as governments with the authority to enact and enforce building codes. Under traditional principles of federal Indian law, on lands within tribal jurisdiction, tribal governments have the inherent sovereign authority to enact and enforce building codes, and the existing statutory language does not affect this aspect of tribal sovereignty, nor does it grant authority to states to impose their building codes on lands within tribal jurisdiction. Fortunately, there have been some indications that this program is beginning to reach out to include tribal governments.[59]

The climate change bill that was passed by the House in June 2009[60] would have replaced the statutory language[61] with new language intended to put us on a path so that by 2030, the net energy consumption of new residential and commercial buildings would be close to zero.[62] In other words, the bill endorsed the Architecture 2030 challenge. If there eventually is federal legislation to move toward a net-zero energy standard for new construction, tribes should be included, but even without federal legislation, tribes could endorse the Architecture 2030 challenge.[63]

Passive solar design Realistically, how do we get to net-zero energy? In addition to energy efficiency, we should be promoting much wider adoption of the collection of techniques known as passive solar design. "Passive" solar heating systems generally capture sunlight, store it as heat, and move the heat to where

59 Presentation by staff of Pacific Northwest National Laboratory at the national workshop "Renewable Energy for Tribal Community Development," Denver, CO, June 28–30, 2011. For information on the DOE Energy Codes program, see U.S. Dep't of Energy's Building Energy Codes Program web page, http://www.energycodes.gov.

60 American Clean Energy and Security Act, H.R. 2998, § 201, *supra* note 36. Section 201 as passed by the House did include some references to tribes, but the treatment of tribes was not really consistent with their sovereign status.

61 Currently codified at 42 U.S.C. § 6833.

62 This basic concept was incorporated into the House-passed American Clean Energy and Security Act, H.R. 2998, § 201, *supra* note 36. That bill used the 2006 version of the International Code Council (ICC) Residential Energy Code (REC) as the baseline for homes, with incremental reductions in energy consumption pegged to that baseline, moving toward net-zero energy by 2030.

63 A list of states, local governments, and others that have endorsed the Architecture 2030 challenge is *available at* http://architecture2030.org/2030_challenge/adopters.

it is needed without mechanical inputs such as pumps and fans.[64] Passive solar is sometimes distinguished from "active" solar, in which fans and pumps are used, although this distinction may not be not all that significant; "hybrid" solar heating systems use both passive and active features.

Passive solar design techniques can meet a substantial part of the space heating load in most regions, although passive design has not been prominently featured in the green building movement.[65] In all passive solar space heating systems, there are two essential elements: aperture (south-facing glass or some other glazing material) to let the sunlight in, and thermal mass (e.g., masonry, concrete) to absorb sunlight and store it as heat. These two elements are relatively easy to incorporate into new construction without adding much to cost, but generally not so easy to do in retrofit. Orientation has to be done correctly from the start—south-facing glass requires a south-facing wall. (And west-facing windows should be kept to a minimum—by adding to cooling loads, they increase the demand for power and can be said to cause power plants.) Similarly, if you do not have enough mass on the inside of a building, adding some later presents a challenge. There are many nuances in passive design. Design options can be evaluated with software such as "Energy 10" (for buildings of 10,000 square feet or less), which was developed by the National Renewable Energy Laboratory (NREL).[66]

What can be done to rectify the neglect of passive solar? One step would be to re-tool land use planning laws to facilitate building orientation for solar design. The other obvious governmental policy tool is building codes. Here is one idea about how to incorporate passive solar into building codes. Consider the Architecture 2030 challenge. To achieve net-zero energy as the standard practice for new construction and major renovations by 2030, Architecture 2030 calls for a set of interim targets: all new buildings should be designed to consume 60 percent less fossil fuel energy than the current regional average for that building type. The targets are ratcheted to 70 percent less in 2015, 80 percent less in 2020, 90 percent less in 2025, and carbon neutral by 2030.

Building codes could include a performance-based standard that makes incremental targets such as those specified in by Architecture 2030 legal

---

64 *See generally* Edward Mazria, The Passive Solar Energy Book (1979). *See also* U.S. Department of Energy's Passive Solar Home Design web page, http://www.energysavers.gov/your_home/designing_remodeling/index.cfm/mytopic=10250.

65 *E.g.*, The Law of Green Buildings: Regulatory and Legal Issues in Design, Construction, Operations, and Financing (J. Cullen Howe & Michael B. Gerrard eds. 2010), contains but a single reference to passive solar, in Michael J. Zimmer and Jennifer M. Rohlender, *Green Building Financing*, *id.* at 103, 106 (noting that the installation of active and passive solar technologies is eligible for the energy efficient mortgage program administered by the Federal Housing Administration).

66 Energy 10 is available from the Sustainable Buildings Industries Council, see http://www.sbicouncil.org/energy-10-software. Energy 10 can be used to analyze and choose among the various options, including daylighting, passive cooling and ventilation, solar hot water, and photovoltaics.

requirements. For each building permit, a similar building that conforms to the IECC could be the baseline or reference case. A design tool such as the Energy 10 software could be used to refine the proposed building design, adding passive and other energy saving features, until it achieves the required target for energy consumption. Under this approach, no specific passive techniques would be required; rather, the permit applicant could choose the mix of techniques. Tribal governments could enact such codes. A variation on this idea would be for the governmental agency charged with administering the building code to help applicants for building permits meet the prescribed energy savings increments, in effect, treating code compliance as providing a public service. Tribal housing authorities, and tribally designated housing entities, could also provide such assistance. Passive design features could be integrated into new community buildings such as schools, clinics, and government offices. Showcasing passive solar in this way could build demand for passive solar in homes and other private buildings.

Retrofitting existing buildings Energy efficiency in new buildings is a big part of the solution, but we also need to be sure that federal assistance programs for retrofitting existing homes include tribal governments in appropriate ways. What should a program to retrofit existing buildings in Indian country look like and how much federal funding would be needed? There are a few existing models, but the best plan would be for the federal government to fund a network of regional assistance programs, designed in consultation with tribal governments, inter-tribal organizations, and tribal colleges, with engagement of all the relevant federal agencies and with input from the State Energy Program offices, national laboratories, and interested institutions of higher education.

One of the existing home retrofit programs, the Department of Energy's Weatherization Assistance Program, which is administered by the states, includes a mandate that low-income members of Indian tribes receive assistance equal to that provided to other low-income persons in each state.[67] In practice, the process in the regulations for tribes to receive direct funding has not worked—only a few tribes administer this program. In addition to making the Weatherization program work better in Indian country, there is a need for a retrofit program with a broader scope. One existing authorized program that could be useful in developing a broader building retrofit program is the Energy Efficiency and Conservation Block Grant (EECBG), which was authorized in 2007.[68] The tribal part of this program ought to be funded on a recurrent basis to help tribes maintain energy efficiency offices.

67 42 U.S.C. § 6863(d); *see also* 10 C.F.R. §§ 440.12, 440.13.

68 Energy Independence and Security Act, Pub. L. No. 110-140, §§ 542–545 (42 U.S.C. §§ 17152–17155) (including a 2 percent set-aside for Indian tribes). The range of activities that tribes can carry out under the EECBG program makes it somewhat comparable to the State Energy Program, 10 C.F.R. part 420, through which states provide a wide range of energy assistance. The State Energy Program has been authorized

Transportation and Land Use Planning

Transportation accounts for about 28 percent of energy consumption in America, and contributes 33 percent of our current CO_2 emissions.[69] There are essentially three main ways of reducing CO_2 emissions associated with transportation: make motor vehicles more efficient (thus reducing emissions per mile traveled); shift from petroleum to renewable energy (biofuels and/or electric and hybrid electric cars powered by renewable energy); and reduce the amount of travel we do in private motor vehicles. The third option includes making public transportation more widely available and reducing the need to use our cars by changing our approach to land use regulation.

Setting efficiency standards for motor vehicles has been treated as a matter of federal law[70] and is a matter that is largely beyond the reach of tribes as governments, as are the ultimate technology choices we make in shifting away from petroleum as our main fuel source for motor vehicles. Tribes can, of course, demonstrate leadership in the choices they make for their own vehicle fleets, and tribal leaders could become engaged in public discourse about these policy issues. If the next great technology for automobiles turns out to be plug-in hybrid electric vehicles (PHEVs) that are increasingly powered with renewable electricity, then tribal governments should be part of making that happen. This would include making sure that Indian country is not left out of the deployment of the smart grid for distribution of electric power, since it is the smart grid that enables PHEVs to become "rolling energy storage units," to use a term coined by Thomas Friedman.[71]

We need not wait for the next great transport technology, however, to reduce emissions from the transportation sector. We can start by reducing the need for motor vehicle travel through land use planning. This involves a set of policy tools that are within the realm of state and local governments. As a matter of principle, this should be within the scope of authority of tribal governments, although as a matter of case law, there are some impediments to land use planning by tribes on reservations in which lands have been removed from Indian trust or restricted title status.[72]

---

for more than 30 years. 42 U.S.C. § 6321. There has never been a comparable program for tribal governments.

69 *U.S. Energy Consumption by the Transportation Sector*, Bureau of Transp. Statistics, U.S. Dep't of Transp. (Oct. 2010), http://www.bts.gov/publications/national_transportation_statistics/html/table_04_04.html; *Inventory of U.S. Greenhouse Gas Emissions and Sinks: 1990–2009* at ES-8, U.S. Envtl. Prot. Agency (April 2011), http://www.epa.gov/climatechange/emissions/downloads10/US-GHGInventory-2010_Report.pdf.

70 49 U.S.C. 32901 et seq.; 49 C.F.R. parts 531 (automobiles) and 533 (light trucks).

71 Friedman, *supra* note 12, at 225.

72 Brendale v. Confederated Tribes & Bands of Yakima Nation, 492 U.S. 408 (1989) (holding that the Tribe had authority to impose its zoning law on fee lands within the so-

Unfortunately, land use regulation as it has been practiced in the United States throughout most of the twentieth century is a big part of the problem. The basic approach of "zoning"—separating industrial, commercial, and residential districts from each other—made a certain amount of sense when industrial zones were dominated by smokestack industries. When combined with federal and state subsidies for road construction and federal tax incentives for single-family housing, the traditional zoning approach to land use regulation has promoted sprawl.[73] Sprawl has been described as consisting of five basic components: housing subdivisions that are exclusively residential, shopping centers, office and business parks, civic institutions, and roadways.[74] The net effect of having four components for different daily activities connected by roadways is that people spend an inordinate amount of time and money moving from one component to another, emitting CO_2 all the way.

In response to a host of problems associated with sprawl, new approaches to land use planning have emerged, including "smart growth"[75] and "new urbanism."[76] These terms are not mutually exclusive but, rather, overlap quite a bit in content. Smart growth is a term with roots in land use regulation that generally emphasizes restoring center cities and older suburbs. New urbanism is a term that describes a school of thought among professionals of various disciplines, a school of thought that emphasizes mixed-use (residential and commercial), walkable neighborhoods, in which basic daily needs can be satisfied without automobile trips, and in which civic buildings (schools, government offices) and public spaces are convenient and contribute to a sense of community.[77]

Recognizing sprawl as a problem is a necessary step in curbing our greenhouse gas emissions. An important step in controlling sprawl is to become aware that there are alternative approaches to land use planning, approaches that, in addition to reducing the need for motor vehicle travel, also render communities more enjoyable places in which to live.

In their efforts to engage in land use planning, tribal government officials could draw upon the lessons of the smart growth movement and new urbanism. Although these approaches to planning arose in the context of urban and suburban America and the challenges of planning are different in rural settings common to

---

called "closed" area of the Reservation but not on fee lands within the "open" area). *See* Cohen's Handbook of Federal Indian Law, *supra* note 28 at § 4.02[3][c][1].

73 Andres Duaney et al., Suburban Nation: The Rise Of Sprawl And The Decline Of The American Dream 5–12 (2000); Robert H. Freilich, From Sprawl To Smart Growth: Successful Legal, Planning, And Environmental Systems 3–9 (1999).

74 Duaney et al., *supra* note 73 at 5–7.

75 *See* Freilich, *supra* note 73. *See also* Smart Growth Network's website, http://www.smartgrowth.org.

76 *See* Duaney et al., *supra* note 73. *See also* New Urbanism website, http://www.newurbanism.org/.

77 Duaney et al., *supra* note 73, at 183–212.

many Indian reservations, some aspects of these new approaches are nevertheless transferable. After all, reliance on motor vehicles is at least as problematic in Indian country as in suburbia. Although there are limits, to be sure, on tribal regulatory authority over fee lands, tribes do have quite a lot of practical authority for land use planning, including their ability to decide where to locate major community buildings such as schools, clinics, and government offices. Such location decisions can serve to promote walking and bicycling as practical alternatives to driving. Land use planning can also facilitate net-zero energy in buildings by designing subdivisions and lots so as to maximize orientation for solar design.

Electric power The electric utility industry is especially important in making the transition to the renewable energy future, because to a large extent, renewable energy will be brought to market in the form of electricity. As it currently exists, this industry is a big part of the problem of global warming. Generating electricity accounts for 42 percent of the U.S. share of CO_2 emissions, and the United States, with 5 percent of the world's population, is responsible for 23 percent of the world's CO_2 emissions.[78] This means that 10 percent of all the CO_2 emissions worldwide come from electric power plants in the United States. This hopefully will change as the electric power industry evolves into a big part of the solution to global warming.

The electric utility industry has historically been a highly regulated industry, subject to a complex mix of federal and state laws.[79] Tribes as sovereign governments have the power to create and regulate electric utilities to serve lands under their jurisdiction, and a small number of tribes have done so.[80] For most tribes, it will probably be more likely that they will interact with the electric power industry as owners of, or joint venture partners in, utility-scale renewable energy projects. Doing so will require detailed knowledge of the regulatory framework governing the utilities with which the tribe has dealings.

Much of the basic regulatory framework for the electric power industry was fashioned in the early twentieth century, long before the self-determination era of federal Indian policy, when the sovereign status of Indian tribes was not given much thought in the national consciousness. The regulatory framework has evolved quite a lot in the past three decades. There are two broad trends in

78 ASES Report, *supra* note 4, at 168–69. *See also* Chuck Kutscher, *Confronting the Climate Change Crisis: What is the Evidence, and What Can We Do About It?*, in Solar Today, July/Aug. 2006, at 28, 31 (with attribution to the U.S. Energy Information Administration).

79 U.S. Energy Information Administration, Electric Power Industry Overview, http://www.eia.doe.gov/cneaf/electricity/page/prim2/toc2.html [hereinafter EIA Overview].

80 A non-exhaustive list of tribes that have established electric utilities includes the Confederated Salish and Kootenai Tribes, Fort Mojave Indian Tribe, Gila River Indian Community, Metlakatla Indian Community, Navajo Nation, Tohono O'odham Nation, and Yakama Nation.

this evolution.[81] One trend has been restructuring, with movement toward more competition, and the other trend is a growing role for the federal government.[82] This section provides an overview of the regulatory framework and the trends in its evolution.

Overview of the electric utility industry The electric power industry has existed for more than a century, and a number different models have evolved for how electric utilities can be created, operated, and regulated. The range of models includes: investor-owned utilities (IOUs); publicly owned utilities (municipal power companies, public power districts, state power authorities); rural electric cooperatives; and federal power authorities.[83] According to the Energy Information Administration (EIA), an agency within the U.S. Department of Energy (DOE), there are more than 3170 electric utilities in the United States, including 210 IOUs, 2009 publicly owned utilities, 883 consumer-owned rural cooperatives, and nine federal utilities.[84] There are also a small number of electric utilities that have been created by tribal governments, although these tend to be ignored in federal and industry statistics.[85]

---

81 Jeffery S. Dennis, *Twenty-Five Years of Electricity Law, Policy, and Regulation: A Look Back*, 25:1 NAT. RES. & ENV'T 33 (2010).

82 *Id.*

83 *See generally* STEVEN FERREY, LAW OF INDEPENDENT POWER: DEVELOPMENT COGENERATION UTILITY REGULATION §§ 5:1 to 5:3 (1989). It should be noted that the terms used in this paper to describe these categories of utilities, while widely used, are not universal. Investor-owned utilities, for example, are sometimes referred to as "public" utilities, in part because their stock is publicly traded, and many IOUs have the words "public service" in their company name. This usage of the word "public," however, should be distinguished from utilities created and operated by cities and other units of local government, which are owned not by shareholders but rather by the citizens living and voting within the jurisdiction of a local government. The term "publicly owned" is sometimes used to describe both municipals and state power authorities. Sometimes the rural cooperatives are also included in this term, although that is not really accurate since they are private, non-profit membership organizations.

84 EIA Overview, *supra* note 78. *See also* American Public Power Association (APPA)'s website, http://www.publicpower.org/; National Rural Electric Cooperative Association (NRECA)'s website, http://www.nreca.coop; Edison Electric Institute (EEI)'s website, http://www.eei.org/ (EEI is the association of IOUs).

85 *E.g.*, the EIA Overview, *supra* note 79, does not expressly mention tribal electric utilities, although on close examination of the data on the EIA website it appears that tribal electric utilities are included in the publicly owned category. FERREY, *supra* note 83, includes some discussion of tribal electric utilities, at § 5:4, and cites U.S. Department of Energy testimony before the Senate Committee on Indian Affairs on February 25, 2004, that there were, as of that date, four full service tribal utilities. *Id.* There are also a few Indian reservations where the U.S. Bureau of Indian Affairs operates an electric utility. *See* 25 C.F.R. part 175. The EIA Overview includes the BIA as one of ten federal electric utilities.

In some ways the industry still reflects some of the basic public policy decisions that were made nearly a century ago. Some of those historic policy decisions involve the fundamental issue of whether electric power is a commodity to be sold for profit or as a public service to promote community development. As the industry has evolved in the United States, the resolution of this basic policy issue is that electricity is *both* a commodity and a public service, with some models for operating in this industry emphasizing one view over the other. The IOUs tend to emphasize profits while publicly owned utilities tend to put more emphasis on service.

Historically, the electric utility industry has been seen as performing three basic functions: generation of electric power, transmission of power over high-voltage lines, and distribution of power to consumers.[86] Throughout most of the twentieth century, many electric utilities were vertically integrated, in that they performed all three of these functions. In the early decades of the twentieth century, federal and state laws were enacted that treated the retail distribution of electricity as a "natural monopoly." In the absence of a competitive marketplace, IOUs were made subject to regulation by state regulatory agencies commonly known as "public utility commissions" (PUCs),[87] which set the rates that IOUs charge their retail customers. The federal government regulates the transmission of power in interstate commerce through the Federal Energy Regulatory Commission (FERC).[88] The involvement of the federal government in the electric power industry has continued to grow.[89]

Non-utility generation Some of the most dramatic changes in the electric power industry over the last three decades or so have to do with the development of generating facilities that are not owned by electric utilities.[90] The rise of non-utility generation has resulted from a number of factors, including federal support for technological development using renewable resources. In addition to direct federal funding, a range of federal and state tax credits have been enacted to encourage investments in renewable energy technologies.

One of the key regulatory developments that contributed to the rise of non-utility power was the enactment in 1978 of the Public Utilities Regulatory Policies

86 A fourth basic kind of function might be considered to include billing, metering, administrative tasks, and customer service. Walter R. Hall II et al., *supra* note 40. This function will become more important as we implement the smart grid. *See infra* text accompanying notes 106–110.

87 *See* Ferrey, *supra* note 83, at § 5:2.

88 Congress gave the FPC this authority in response to a U.S. Supreme Court ruling that it was contrary to the Commerce Clause of the Constitution for a state PUC to regulate of the sale of power from a utility in one state to a utility in another state. Public Utilities Commission of Rhode Island v. Attleboro Steam & Electric Co., 273 U.S. 83 (1927).

89 *See* Dennis, *supra* note 81.

90 As of 2007, there were some 1730 non-utility generators. EIA Overview, *supra* note 79.

Act (PURPA),[91] which included provisions relating to the interconnection of IOUs and "qualifying facilities" (QFs),[92] a term that includes small power producers using renewable resources (solar, wind, biomass, and geothermal) and cogeneration facilities (which produce both electricity and heat that is put to use rather than wasted). Not all non-utility producers are QFs, because they are larger than the size limits specified in PURPA, because they do not use renewable resources, or because they are not cogenerators in that they do not make use of their waste heat. The term "independent power producers" (IPPs) is used to describe non-utility projects that use renewable energy but which are not QFs. The EIA uses the term "nonutility power producers" as a term that includes QFs, cogenerators (whether or not they are QFs), IPPs, and Exempt Wholesale Generators.[93] The growth of non-utility renewable energy in the last decade or so has been driven, in large part, by "renewable portfolio standards" (RPS) imposed at the state level.[94] An RPS

91 Pub. L. No. 95-617, title II.

92 Pub. L. No. 95-617, § 210 (codified as amended at 16 U.S.C. § 824a-3). The statutory mandate for interconnection of QFs was modified in the Energy Policy Act of 2005. Pub. L. No. 109-58, § 1253, 119 Stat. 594 (2005). FERC was directed to determine whether the marketplace is sufficiently competitive such that the QF is able to sell its power; if so, then utilities are relieved of the obligation to buy it. FERC issued a final rule to implement this amendment to PURPA. Federal Energy Regulatory Commission, New PURPA Section 210(m) Regulations Applicable to Small Power Production and Cogeneration Facilities, Final Rule, Order on Rehearing, Docket No. RM06-10-001, Order No. 688-A (June 22, 2007), revising Order No. 688, 71 Fed. Reg. 64,342 (Nov. 1, 2006), FERC Stats. & Regs. ¶ 31,233 (2006) (Final Rule) (to be codified at 18 C.F.R. part 292). Pursuant to this rule there is a rebuttable presumption in some regions that QFs do have non-discriminatory access to markets, except that, for QFs of 20 MW or less, there is a rebuttable presumption that they do not. FERC has also published a final rule implementing related amendments to PURPA, including a change in the criteria for cogeneration facilities to be treated as QFs by requiring that the energy output be used in a beneficial and productive manner. Federal Energy Regulatory Commission, Revised Regulations Governing Small Power Production and Cogeneration Facilities: Final Rule, 71 Fed. Reg. 7,852 (Feb. 15, 2006); same, final order on rehearing, 71 Fed. Reg. 30,585 (May 30, 2006).

93 The category of exempt wholesale generators (EWG) was authorized by the Energy Policy Act of 1992. Pub. L. No. 102-486, 106 Stat. 2776 (1993) (formerly codified at 15 U.S.C. § 79z-5a, but that section was repealed by The Energy Policy Act of 2005, Pub. L. No. 109-58, 119 Stat. 974 (Aug. 8, 2005) and recodified at 42 U.S.C. § 16451). Unlike QFs, these EWGs are not required to use renewable fuels, and IOUs are not required to buy power from them. The main legal benefit given to them is that they are not regulated as electric utilities.

94 *See* Hodas, *supra* note 33, at 355–59; *see also* Donald S. McCauley, et al., *Renewable Portfolio Standards*, *in* Capturing the Power of Electric Restructuring 175 (Joey Lee Miranda ed. 2009).

requires each covered utility to include a certain amount of renewable electricity in its energy supply by a certain date.[95]

Competition and "unbundling" electric utilities During the 1990s, many state legislatures and PUCs adopted policies to promote competition in retail markets for electricity, generally based on the rationale that such competition would help to hold down the prices charged to consumers.[96] The shift toward promoting competition was accompanied by relaxing or eliminating mandates that had previously been imposed on IOUs to establish programs to help consumers adopt energy conservation measures,[97] although more recently IOUs are increasingly engaged in energy efficiency programs.

Competition in the utility industry has also been promoted through rules issued by FERC, including a rule to "unbundle" the sale of electricity at wholesale from the transmission of electricity,[98] and a rule to ensure open access to transmission facilities.[99] The unbundling of generation from transmission has led to the creation of independent system operators (ISOs), entities that manage transmission systems but have no financial stake in generating facilities.[100] In 1999, FERC issued an order on Regional Transmission Organizations,[101] a term that includes both non-profit ISOs and for profit entities.[102] FERC has issued several other decisions and rules relevant to the restructuring of the electric utility industry, including a rule codifying and revising its standards for "market-based rates" for wholesale sales of electric energy by public utilities.[103]

---

95 Stephen C. Braverman, *State Renewable Portfolio Standards and the Commerce Clause*, 25:4 Nat. Res. & Env't 15 (2011) (noting that as of September 2010, 32 states had adopted some type of RPS). The Database of State Energy Incentives for Renewables and Efficiency (DSIRE) provides information on state RPS policies at www.dsireusa.org.

96 *See generally* Walter R. Hall II et al., *supra* note 40.

97 *See* National Action Plan for Energy Efficiency, at Ch. 2 (2006), *available at* http://www.epa.gov/cleanenergy/documents/suca/napee_report.pdf.

98 FERC, Promoting Wholesale Competition Through Open Access Non-Discriminatory Transmission Services by Public Utilities; Recovery of Stranded Costs by Public Utilities and Transmitting Utilities; Order No. 888, FERC Stats. & Regs. ¶ 31,036 (1996).

99 Open Access Same-Time Information System and Standards of Conduct, Order No. 889, FERC Stats. & Regs. ¶ 31,035 (1996).

100 *See generally* Ferrey, *supra* note 83, at § 10:87.

101 Regional Transmission Organizations, Docket No. RM99-2-000, 89 FERC ¶ 61,285 (12-20-99).

102 *See generally* Ferrey, *supra* note 83, at § 10:91.

103 Market-Based Rates For Wholesale Sales of Electric Energy, Capacity and Ancillary Services, Docket No. RM. 04-7-000, Order No. 697 (June 21, 2007) (to be codified at 18 C.F.R. part 35).

The grid The "grid" is the network of transmission and distribution wires and other facilities that connect electric power generators and end users. The grid is currently evolving into the "smart grid," in which information technology is becoming integrated into the electric power infrastructure.[104] By integrating real-time, two-way communication with the delivery and use of electric power, the smart grid will yield a wide range of benefits. Of particular importance for renewable energy development, the smart grid will enable major improvements in the integration of distributed generation and storage options. For example, with the smart grid, a homeowner whose photovoltaic array helps a utility meet its peak demand could be paid accordingly. "Net metering" is a step in this direction, but the smart grid allows for much more precision in pricing. The smart grid will also enable plug-in hybrid electric vehicles to be used as "rolling energy storage units,"[105] in which their batteries provide storage and back-up capacity for intermittent wind and solar sources.

Of course, the smart grid is not really *evolving*. Rather this transition is being driven by proactive decisions and investments by many actors: utilities, regulators, lawmakers, and others. The extent to which Indian country helps lead the way or lags behind will turn, in large part, on the extent to which tribal leaders become engaged in making this transition happen.

As the grid becomes smarter, we must also deal with issues relating to the high-voltage transmission part of the grid, such as how to allocate the costs of upgrading existing lines and building new ones, and how to decide where new lines will be built.[106] One of the issues is what to emphasize in the future for the transmission part of the grid. One camp in the debate advocates a "nationwide 'backbone' system of extra-high voltage (EHV) lines to move power over great distances" which would facilitate "large-scale renewable generators."[107] The other camp advocates an emphasis on "a more localized grid, aimed at facilitating the development of local generation sources."[108] The localized emphasis would facilitate rooftop photovoltaics and community-scale wind and biomass generators. This is not necessarily an "either–or" issue; rather, incremental decisions may seek to balance the recommendations of both camps. Different tribes may find their interests aligned with either side in this debate. For example, Great Plains tribes with wind resources[109] may favor the "backbone" approach, while others

104 *See* U.S. Department of Energy, Smart Grid System Report (2009), *available at* http://www.oe.energy.gov/DocumentsandMedia/SGSRMain_090707_lowres.pdf.

105 *See* Friedman, *supra* note 12, at 225.

106 *See* John R. Norris & Jeffery S. Dennis, *Electric Transmission Infrastructure: A Key Piece of the Energy Puzzle*, 25:4 Nat. Res. & Env't 3 (2011).

107 *Id.*

108 *Id.* at 6.

109 Robert Gough, *Tribal Wind Power Development in the Northern Great Plains*, 19:2 Nat. Res. & Env't 57 (2004). *See also* Michael L. Connolly, *Commercial Scale Wind Industry on the Campo Indian Reservation*, 23:1 Nat. Res. & Env't 25 (2008).

may emphasize the localized approach. In any case, tribes should be aware of and engage in discussions regarding these issues. It should be noted that tribes have authority to control the use of their trust lands for transmission lines.[110] This authority is not only the power to block transmission lines but also the power to facilitate them, depending on a range of issues relating to off-reservation routes.

What can tribal governments do? In a subject matter that has largely been regulated by states and in which possible roles for tribal governments have been largely overlooked, how should tribes fit into this picture? What roles should tribal governments perform in helping to shape the evolution of the industry? One approach is to create a tribal electric utility, as a small number of tribes have done.[111] This approach seems particularly useful if the tribal government is mostly concerned with the distribution part of electric power service. There are different ways in which a tribal electric utility can be structured, a subject not discussed in this chapter, except to note that its governance structure should be somewhat insulated from politics and, if a governmental entity, it will need to have a limited waiver of the tribe's sovereign immunity so that it can enter into contracts. The municipal model in non-Indian America seems like a generally appropriate model to draw upon.

A tribal electric utility, of course, need not be limited to distribution but might also include other facets of the industry as well, such as providing energy efficiency services for customers or developing utility-scale renewable generating plants. A tribal utility could become innovative in providing energy-related services, perhaps looking to innovative utilities,[112] for example, and perhaps being innovative in its

110 25 C.F.R. § 169.3. *See* U.S. Department of Energy & U.S. Department of the Interior, Energy Policy Act of 2005,Section 1813 Indian Land Rights-of-Way Study: Report to Congress (2007), *available at* http://www.oe.energy.gov/DocumentsandMedia/EPAct_1813_Final.pdf.

111 *See supra* note 83 and accompanying text.

112 *E.g.*, Sacramento's municipal utility (known as SMUD) offers sub-meter installation and discounted rates for plug-in electric vehicle charging stations; a Cool Roof program which provides an incentive to homeowners to install roofing products that meet SMUD's solar reflectivity and emissivity standards; free shade trees for homes with eastern, western or southern exposures; a Carbon Offset program which funds local carbon-reduction projects like a methane-gas digester for a local dairy farm; and a Greenergy program, through which SMUD meets up to 100 percent of electricity usage with power generated from renewable resources, and uses Greenergy contributions to build more local, renewable energy sources. *Quick Guide to SMUD Programs and Services*, Sacramento Municipal Utility District, http://www.smud.org/en/about/Pages/programs-services.aspx (last visited July 26, 2011). Austin, TX's municipal utility, Austin Energy, offers a GreenChoice renewable energy program that provides customers with a fixed rate charge instead of a traditional fuel charge while buying energy produced from 100 percent renewable sources; rebates to customers who install solar water heaters, solar photovoltaics, and plug-in electric vehicle charging stations; and one of the nation's oldest

own right. A few ideas for the kinds of services that might be provided include: providing solar design services for new and existing buildings; making the arrangements (technical and financial) to install photovoltaic arrays on rooftops and parking lot shade structures; implementing the smart grid in tribal communities, with the realm of possibilities that will open up; and promoting the deployment of plug-in hybrid electric vehicles such as by owning and servicing the battery packs in tribal government vehicle fleets. By providing services that customers want, a tribal utility might be able to establish unchallenged governmental authority through the "consensual relations" exception to the general proposition, as stated in *Montana v. United States*, that tribes have been implicitly divested of regulatory jurisdiction over non-Indians on fee lands within their reservations.[113]

A tribal electric utility could have a subsidiary charged with developing utility-scale renewable energy projects, including negotiating power purchase agreements and managing the complex venture structures that seem to be necessary to attract private investment capital. Given that tribal governments are non-taxable entities, they need taxable equity partners to be able to use tax credits, and one way of doing this is a "partnership flip" arrangement in which the tribal entity does not hold much equity until the tax benefits have been exhausted.[114] A tribal electric

---

Green Building programs, which is responsible for implementing the City of Austin's energy code and rating buildings for sustainability. *Environmental Initiatives*, Austin Energy, http://www.austinenergy.com/About%20Us/Environmental%20Initiatives/index.htm (last visited July 26, 2011).

113 Montana v. United States, 450 U.S. 544, 565–66 (1981). *See* Cohen's Handbook of Federal Indian Law, *supra* note 28 at § 4.02[3][c]. Yakama Power, the tribal utility serving the Yakama Reservation, has reportedly had some success with this approach by offering customers high-speed internet service. Presentation by Raymond Wiseman, General Manager, Yakama Power, at the national workshop "Renewable Energy for Tribal Community Development," Denver, CO, June 28–30, 2011.

114 *See* Douglas C. MacCourt, Renewable Energy Development in Indian Country: A Handbook for Tribes 80–83 (2010) *available at* http://www.nrel.gov/docs/fy10osti/48078.pdf. *See also* Donald M. Clary, *Commercial-Scale Renewable Energy Projects on Tribal Lands*, 25:4 Nat. Res. & Env'. 19 (2011); Michael L. Connolly, *supra* note 109 (describing a farm developed through a lease of tribal land to a developer, in which the county derives as much revenue from taxes as the Tribe derives from the lease, even though the county provides no governmental services). It should be noted that, in meeting the requirement for federal agencies to purchase renewable electricity as provided in section 203 of the Energy Policy Act of 2005, tribal equity in a renewable energy facility is not required to qualify for the double credit a federal agency would receive for purchasing renewable energy that is produced on Indian lands. Pub. L. No. 109-58, § 203 (42 U.S.C. 15862). As of June 2010, however, this incentive had not been a factor in any renewable energy project on Indian lands. *See* Department of Energy, Energy Efficiency & Renewable Energy: Biennial Report to Congress on the Progress of the Federal Government in Meeting the Renewable Energy Goals of the Energy Policy Act of 2005 (June 2010), *available at* http://www1.eere.energy.gov/femp/pdfs/2008_epact_sec203_report.pdf.

utility should also develop expertise in the full range of financing options that could be used, including different kinds of bonds and related mechanisms.[115]

Of course, a tribe need not establish an electric utility to become engaged in providing various kinds of energy-related services, or in developing renewable energy projects to serve tribal needs or to sell power to others. Many of these kinds of services can be provided through existing government institutions or tribal enterprises, or through new entities created for specific purposes. Schools and tribal colleges should be prominently featured, since they can play key roles in community education about energy and climate issues and since they can help educate tribal citizens for green energy jobs.

Tribes could join together to address unmet needs. One kind of need that sometimes goes unmet is the incremental cost of incorporating energy efficiency, renewable energy, and green building features into major community-scale buildings. Such buildings are typically built with funds from a variety of sources, some federal, some tribal, some other. Sometimes there is just not enough to actually build the project with all the green features as designed. One approach to solving this problem would be to create a renewable energy development bank for Indian country. One model for such a development bank would be the Solar Energy and Energy Conservation Bank,[116] a federal agency that was authorized in 1980 and which went out of existence in 1988. A renewable energy development bank for Indian country could be chartered by federal legislation or it could be chartered by a collection of tribes. It could be capitalized, in part, with contributions from tribes with revenues from gaming or other sources. Tribes that contribute to such a development bank could reap substantial financial returns on their investments, as well as returns that cannot be quantified in monetary terms.

Conclusion

The climate crisis is real. The renewable energy revolution is just beginning. Whether it lives up to its potential to bring down CO_2 emissions on the order of magnitude we need is an open question. It surely will not happen without committed political leadership. Some of that leadership needs to come from American Indian and Alaska Native tribes and nations.

However, political leadership by itself will not be enough. That leadership must be able to produce programs and projects that actually deliver emissions reductions by eliminating reliance on energy technologies that burn fossil fuels. The building sector offers enormous opportunities. From a technological

115 *See* MacCourt, *supra* note 114, at 65–88. *See also* John C. Dernbach et al., *Energy Efficiency and Conservation: New Legal Tools and Opportunities*, 25:4 Nat. Res. & Env't 7 (2011).

116 Solar Energy and Energy Conservation Bank was authorized by Title V of the Energy Security Act of 1980, Pub. L. No. 96-294, 94 Stat. 719 (12 U.S.C. §§ 3601–3620).

perspective, buildings are the low-hanging fruit, which can be harvested with energy efficiency measures and passive solar design. This chapter has offered some ideas on how tribal governments could help lead in making net-zero energy the standard practice. Transportation and land use planning present challenges for tribes, especially for those in rural areas, but tribes do have some options, such as adopting land use policies that promote mixed-use walkable communities and that reduce reliance on motor vehicles. The electric power sector presents tribes with a wide range of challenges and opportunities. Tribal leaders should be proactive in bringing the smart grid to Indian country, which might entail creating tribal electric utilities. For tribes that have renewable resources with the potential to produce much more power than tribal communities need, utility-scale projects can deliver that power to off-reservation markets, if private investment capital can be tapped. Some changes in federal incentives would be helpful to promote tribal equity ownership of such projects.

Political leadership will also be needed to help articulate the reasons for pursuing the mix of programs and projects for moving toward a post-fossil fuels economy. Tribal leaders will surely want to draw attention to the short-term and local benefits of promoting energy efficiency and renewable energy, the lower operating costs, the jobs, and the quality of life benefits. We also need them to draw attention to the big picture. If ever there was an environmental crisis calling us to action with the welfare of the seventh generation in our minds and in our hearts, this is it.

Chapter 4

Application of Environmental Justice to Climate Change-Related Claims Brought by Native Nations

Elizabeth Ann Kronk[1]

Tribes in Alaska are facing nothing less than the loss of their entire culture.
National Tribal Air Association (2009)

Introduction

The Unique Impact of Climate Change on Native Nations

Native nations,[2] who often foretell the fate of the rest of the world, are disproportionately facing the profound impacts of climate change.[3] In the Inuit

1 J.D., University of Michigan School of Law; B.A. Cornell University. Assistant Professor of Law, Texas Tech University School of Law; Chief Judge, Sault Ste Marie Tribe of Chippewa Indians Court of Appeals. The author would like to thank her research assistant, Melissa Fales, for her helpful contributions to this article. The author would also like to thank the Woodrow Wilson International Center for Scholars and U.S.–China Partnership for Environmental Law at Vermont Law School for the opportunity to serve as an Environmental Justice Young Fellow this past summer. This piece is a direct result of the author's participation in the Environmental Justice Young Fellow's program. The author would also like to thank Professors Sarah Krakoff and Ezra Rosser for their helpful comments on earlier drafts of this chapter, but, of course, any mistakes contained herein are the author's alone. Finally, this chapter is dedicated to the Honorable Jenny Lee Kronk and Connor Warner for their unwavering support.

2 The author specifically chose the term "Native nations" for use throughout this article. This choice was made deliberately to be inclusive of Alaskan Natives and Native Hawaiians, who may not normally be included through word choices, such as "tribe" or "Indian country."

3 Most scholars agree that climate change is happening now. *See* National Congress of American Indians, Resolution #EWS-06-2004—Supporting a National Mandatory Program to Reduce Climate Change Pollution and Promote Renewable Energy (2006 Mid Year Session) ("the National Academy of Sciences (NAS) reviewed and declared global warming a real problem caused in part by human activities"). The vast majority of the climate change debate no longer centers on the reality of climate change, but rather on the extent of its impact on the environment. As a brief overview, it is believed that exacerbated climate change is related to the increased human production of greenhouse gases, such as

village of Shishmaref, Alaska, which has been inhabited for over 4000 years, homes are falling into the sea because melting permafrost has dramatically eroded the shoreline. Many Native nations across the Pacific Northwest face unprecedented insect infestations, which have attacked their woodlands, causing heavy forest mortalities. The Navajo Nation experienced an outbreak of the Hanta virus as a result of the substantial proliferation of mice scurrying onto the reservation in reaction to changing atmospheric conditions.[4] The impacts of climate change on Native nations are real, profound and immediate.

Because of the unique character of Native nations, these communities are more likely to be affected by climate change. First, because Native nations are often tied both legally and spiritually to specific areas of land, such as reservations, it is extremely difficult for them to leave these areas either to escape the effects of climate change themselves or perhaps to follow plant and animal species that are adapting to climate change. As species shift their ranges to follow their preferred climates, Native cultures may be threatened by the inability to access these species.[5] Alaskan Natives may be particularly hard hit by shifts in the ranges of species, such as caribou, because the Alaska Native Claims Settlement Act of 1971 extinguished Alaskan Natives' claims to aboriginal title and hunting and fishing rights.[6] Under the current ANCSA regime, Alaskan Natives will not be able to argue that they have a legal right, based on aboriginal title or use rights, to follow species that are the objects of traditional hunting and gathering because ANCSA extinguished their claim to aboriginal lands.

---

carbon dioxide. Greenhouse gases naturally heat the earth by trapping radiation within the earth's atmosphere. However, the increased amount of greenhouse gases has caused more radiation to be trapped in the atmosphere, thereby warming the earth's atmosphere and affecting the overall global climate. *See generally* Pew Center on Global Climate Change, *Climate Change 101*, *available at* http://www.pewclimate.org/global-warming-basics/climate_change_101/.

4 Terry Williams & Preston Hardison, *Impacts on Indigenous Peoples*, *in* CLIMATE CHANGE AND PACIFIC RIM INDIGENOUS NATIONS 19 (Alan Parker et al. eds. 2006), *available at* http://academic.evergreen.edu/g/grossmaz/IndigClimate2.pdf.

5 *Id.* at 23.

6 43 U.S.C. § 1603; Daniel Cordalis & Dean B. Suagee, *The Effects of Climate Change on American Indian and Alaska Native Tribes*, 22 NAT. RESOURCES & ENV'T 45, 47 (2008) ("Alaska may be experiencing the impacts of global warming more than any other place on Earth, and Alaska Native tribes are among the first American populations to feel the effects of global climate change. Erosion and flooding affect 86 percent of Alaska Native villages to some extent, with the greatest effects felt along the coast.") (citing U.S. GEN. ACCOUNTING OFFICE, GAO-04-142, ALASKA VILLAGES: MOST ARE AFFECTED BY FLOODING AND EROSION, BUT FEW QUALIFY FOR FEDERAL ASSISTANCE (2003)).

For these reasons, Native nations are among the first to feel the profound impacts of climate change.[7] Native communities are also among the most vulnerable in the United States,[8] given their unique relationship to the environment, as well as the extreme geographical locations of many of these communities.[9] These communities contribute little to the problem of climate change yet bear disproportionate impacts given their unique vulnerability.[10] Because Native nations are generally disproportionately impacted by climate change, legal claims brought by Native nations who are so impacted must be viewed through an environmental justice lens. As demonstrated by the case study presented below, however, it appears that such a lens is not being applied to these claims, which in turn results in the reality that Native nations may not be getting environmentally just outcomes.

---

7 Cordalis & Suagee, *supra* note 6, at 45 ("*The Fourth Assessment Report of the UN Intergovernmental Panel on Climate Change Working Group II* recognizes that American indigenous communities are among the most sensitive to climate change in North America and that 'indigenous communities in northern Canada and Alaska are already experiencing constraints on lifestyles and economic activity from less reliable sea and lake ice (for travelling, hunting, fishing and whaling), loss of forest resources from insect damage, stress on caribou, and more exposed coastal infrastructure from diminishing sea ice.'").

8 Beyond their vulnerability to the impacts of climate change, Native nations are generally one of the most vulnerable populations within the United States given their small population size, separateness, socio-political status and unique cultural attributes. Nell Jessup Newton, *Federal Power Over Indians: Its Sources, Scope, and Limitations*, 132 U. Pa. L. Rev. 195, 246 (1984) [hereinafter Newton, *Federal Power Over Indians*] ("Surely tribal Indians are among the most vulnerable of all racial and cultural groups to the majoritarian process. They comprise less than 1 percent of the nation's population. Tribal Indians live apart from other Americans on reservations; most tribes are poor; they often speak tribal languages and maintain aspects of their ancient cultures that differ substantially from dominant American cultural values.").

9 Peggy M. Shepard & Cecil Corbin-Mark, *Climate Justice*, 2 Envtl. Just. 163 (2009) ("Climate researchers report that vulnerable communities, even in the most prosperous nations, will be the first and worst hit [by climate change]. In this country, the most impacted areas will be communities-of-color, Indigenous Peoples, and low-income communities that are socio-economically disadvantaged, disproportionately burdened by poor environmental quality, and least able to adapt.").

10 Rebecca Tsosie, *Indigenous People and Environmental Justice: The Impact of Climate Change*, 78 U. Colo. L. Rev. 1625, 1628 (Fall 2007) [hereinafter Tsosie, *Indigenous People and Environmental Justice*]; National Tribal Air Association, Impacts of Climate Change on Tribes in the United States 12–13 (2009), *available at* http://epa.gov/air/tribal/pdfs/Impacts%20of%20Climate%20Change%20on%20Tribes%20in%20the%20United%20States.pdf ("Any impact to tribal resources due to climate change is largely the result of decades of emissions from sources outside of Indian Country (even the most developed and industrialized tribal carbon footprint is miniscule) … Although Tribal sources are not a significant cause of climate change, they are the ones most keenly feeling the effects.").

Case Study: Kivalina v. ExxonMobil

Given that Native communities bear disproportionate impacts from climate change, an environmental justice[11] perspective should be incorporated into the evaluation of claims raised by such communities. Simply put, failure to view these legal claims from an environmental justice perspective will be likely to end in a result that is not environmentally just. The Environmental Protection Agency (EPA) defines "environmental justice" as "the fair treatment and meaningful involvement of all people regardless of race, color, national origin, or income with respect to the development, implementation, and enforcement of environmental laws, regulations, and policies."[12] As demonstrated by the *Kivalina* case study described below, Native nations are being precluded from meaningful participation in the legal system, as courts, such as the U.S. District Court for the Northern District of California, are refusing to consider the merits of their legal claims related to climate change. In *Kivalina*, the court has denied Kivalina procedural justice. This is environmental injustice.

To understand how an environmental justice perspective should be applied to climate change-related claims brought by Native nations, this chapter examines the claims brought by the Native Village of Kivalina and City of Kivalina ("Kivalina"), against various corporate defendants involved in the oil and gas business.[13] The Native Village and City of Kivalina "are the governing bodies of an Inupiat village of approximately 400 people ... located on the tip of a six-mile barrier reef located ... some seventy miles north of the Arctic Circle."[14] Furthermore, the "Native Village of Kivalina is a self-governing, federally recognized Tribe established pursuant to the provisions of the Indian Reorganization Act of 1934 and amended in 1936."[15] According to the plaintiffs' complaint, historically, Kivalina was protected from strong winter storms by Arctic sea ice surrounding the barrier reef.[16] However, because of a warming environment related to climate change, the sea ice that traditionally protected the community is melting, and, as

11 EPA, *Environmental Justice, available at* http://www.epa.gov/environmentaljustice/ (last accessed October 1, 2010).

12 *Id.*

13 Kivalina filed its complaint against numerous private corporations who contributed substantial quantities of greenhouse gases to the environment, including: ExxonMobil Corporation, BP PLC, BP America, Inc., BP Products North America, Chevron Corp., Chevron U.S.A., Inc., ConocoPhillips Comp., Royal Dutch Shell PLC, Shell Oil Comp., Peabody Energy Corp., AES Corp., American Electric Power Comp., Inc., American Power Services Corp., DTE Energy Comp., Duke Energy Corp., Dynegy Holdings, Inc., Edison International, MidAmerican Energy Holdings Company, Mirant Corp., NRG Energy, Pinnacle West Capital Corp., Reliant Energy, Inc., The Southern Comp., and XCEL Energy, Inc. Complaint for Damages, Demand for Jury Trial (N.D. Cal. Feb. 26, 2008).

14 *Id.* at 1.

15 *Id.* at 4.

16 *Id.*

a result, Kivalina is experiencing a "massive erosion problem."[17] "Houses and buildings are in imminent danger of falling into the sea ... Critical infrastructure is imminently threatened with permanent destruction."[18] "The U.S. Army Corps of Engineers and the U.S. Government Accountability Office have both concluded that Kivalina must be relocated owing to global warming and have estimated the cost [of relocation] to be from $95 million to $400 million."[19]

In light of the massive injuries Kivalina is suffering and the impending loss of the land upon which the community is located, Kivalina filed a complaint in the U.S. District Court for the Northern District of California ("District Court") on February 26, 2008, against several private entities that allegedly contribute significantly to climate change through their emissions of greenhouse gases.[20] Kivalina included claims of federal public nuisance, state private and public nuisance, civil conspiracy, and concert of action.[21] Kivalina requested monetary damages for current injuries sustained, as well as a declaratory judgment "for such future monetary expenses and damages as may be incurred by Plaintiffs in connection with the nuisance of global warming."[22]

In response to Kivalina's complaint, Defendants filed motions to dismiss under Federal Rules of Civil Procedure 12(b)(1) and 12(b)(6), arguing that Kivalina's complaint failed to meet standing requirements and should be precluded under the political question doctrine. On September 30, 2009, United States District Judge Saundra Brown Armstrong dismissed Kivalina's claim, finding that the complaint was precluded under the political question doctrine and that Kivalina lacked standing.[23] In applying the six *Baker* factors,[24] which

17 *Id.* at 2.

18 *Id.*

19 *Id.* at 1.

20 Kivalina's complaint asserts that "Defendants in this action include many of the largest emitters of greenhouse gases in the United States." *Id.* at 1. The complaint then goes on to detail the actual greenhouse gas emissions for each defendant during certain years. *Id.* at 6–30; 39–44. For example, in 2006, BP emitted "65 million tons of carbon dioxide equivalent greenhouse gases," Chevron "emitted 68 million tons of carbon dioxide equivalent," and ConocoPhillips emitted "62.3 million tons." *Id.* at 6–8.

21 This article will focus on Kivalina's federal common law claim for public nuisance.

22 Complaint for Damages, Demand for Jury Trial, 67 (N.D. Cal. Feb. 26, 2008).

23 *Order Granting Defendants' Motions to Dismiss for Lack of Subject Matter Jurisdiction,* Case No. C 08-1138 SBA.

24 Baker v. Carr, 369 U.S. 186 (1962). In *Baker*, the Court explained that six factors may be used to determine whether or not a question is political in nature. If any of these factors applied to the question presented to a court, the court should decline to address the question presented given its political nature. These six factors included: (1) "Textually demonstrable constitutional commitment of the issue to a coordinate political department"; (2) "A lack of judicially discoverable and manageable standards for resolving it"; (3) "The impossibility of deciding without an initial policy determination of a kind clearly for nonjudicial discretion"; (4) "The impossibility of a court's undertaking independent

are applicable in determining when the political question doctrine attaches, the District Court held that the second[25] and third[26] *Baker* factors applied to Kivalina's complaint, and, as a result, its claims were barred under the political question doctrine. Furthermore, the District Court determined that Kivalina did not meet the requirements of Article III standing.[27] In determining that the questions presented by Kivalina were political in nature and that the Native nation lacked standing, the District Court effectively precluded Kivalina from meaningful participation in the legal system, as the case was dismissed for procedural rather than merit-based reasons. Moreover, as explained more fully below, the District Court's dismissal on these grounds demonstrated a failure to view the questions presented from an environmental justice perspective, which, in turn, led to an environmentally unjust result.

On March 10, 2010, Kivalina filed its opening brief in the U.S. Court of Appeals for the Ninth Circuit, appealing the District Court's decision.[28] In the time since the District Court's decision dismissing Kivalina's complaint, both the U.S. Court of Appeals for the Second Circuit[29] and Fifth

---

resolution without expressing lack of the respect due coordinate branches of government"; (5) "An unusual need for unquestioning adherence to a political decision already made"; and (6) "The potentiality of embarrassment from multifarious pronouncements by various departments on one question." *Id.*

25 *Order Granting Defendants' Motions to Dismiss for Lack of Subject Matter Jurisdiction*, Case No. C 08-1138 SBA at 13 ("Plaintiffs' global warming nuisance claim seeks to impose liability and damages on a scale unlike any prior environmental pollution case cited by Plaintiffs. Those cases do not provide guidance that would enable the Court to reach a resolution of this case in any 'reasoned' manner.").

26 *Id.* at 15 ("Plaintiffs ignore that the allocation of fault—and cost—of global warming is a matter appropriately left for determination by the executive or legislative branch in the first instance.").

27 *Id.* at 15–22.

28 *Appellants' Opening Brief*, No. 09-17490.

29 Connecticut v. AEP Comp. Inc., et al., 582 F.3d 309 (2d cir. September 21, 2009). On December 6, 2010, the U.S. Supreme Court granted the writ of certiorari and heard the appeal in this case. U.S. Supreme Court December 6, 2010 Order List, *available at* http://www.supremecourt.gov/orders/courtorders/120610zor.pdf. On June 20, 2011, the U.S. Supreme Court issued its decision in the case, *AEP v. Connecticut*, 564 U.S. _____ (2011). The Court was split, 4–4, on the issue of whether the claim amounted to a political question precluded from consideration by the courts. *Id.* Because the Court did not reach a majority opinion on this matter, the Second Circuit's decision finding that the claim was not a political question was upheld. This has important implications for the *Kivalina* matter. As previously explained, the District Court in *Kivalina* had declined to consider the merits of the claim, opting instead to dismiss the matter for procedural reasons, including a finding that the matter constituted a political question. After the Court's decision in *AEP v. Connecticut*, it should now be clear that the political question doctrine is not an impediment to a court considering the merits of Kivalina's claim. However, the Court's decision in *AEP v. Connecticut* will probably negatively impact Kivalina's claim, in that the Court

Circuit[30] have reached results contrary to the decision of the District Court on claims very similar to Kivalina's, based on the federal common law of public nuisance.

Given that Native nations suffer disproportionately from the impacts of climate change, this chapter examines the incorporation of an environmental justice perspective into claims brought by Native nations similarly situated to Kivalina. The first section briefly reviews the development of ideas and legal claims rooted in environmental justice. The section concludes that Native nations are environmental justice communities. Moreover, because Native nations contribute little by way of greenhouse gas emissions yet bear a substantial amount of the negative impacts of climate change, claims related to climate change raised by Native nations are environmental justice claims. Although Native nations are in fact environmental justice communities, the factors at issue in environmental justice claims brought by Native nations differ from the factors at play in claims raised by other environmental justice communities. Specifically, environmental justice claims arising in Indian country demand consideration of tribal sovereignty, the federal tribal trust responsibility, the ancient tribal trust doctrine, the unique connection between many Native nations and their land, and, finally, international considerations, such as the United Nations Declaration on the Rights of Indigenous Peoples. Ultimately, this chapter concludes that courts must incorporate an environmental justice perspective when evaluating climate change-related claims raised by Native nations to ensure that justice is served. Failure to do so results in

---

rejected similar claims brought by states in *AEP* that were based on the federal common law of public nuisance. *Id.* Here, the Court found that in cases such as *AEP*, and probably *Kivalina* as well, such claims are pre-empted by the fact that EPA has the authority under the Clean Air Act to regulate greenhouse gas emissions. *Id.* Federal common law actions are therefore pre-empted despite the fact the EPA has not yet implemented all of its proposed greenhouse gas regulations under the Clean Air Act. *Id.* Therefore, Kivalina's claim based on the federal common law of public nuisance will probably be dismissed as a result of the U.S. Supreme Court's decision in *AEP v. Connecticut*. However, its remaining claims, such as its claim based on the state law of public nuisance, will not be impacted by the Court's decision in *AEP*. This development may therefore increase the likelihood for a just environmental outcome, as the political question doctrine no longer appears to be a procedural impediment to Kivalina's claims and, therefore, the merits of its claims should be considered by the courts. Full discussion of the impacts of the Supreme Court's decision in *AEP v. Connecticut* on *Kivalina*, however, is outside the scope of this chapter.

30 Comer v. Murphy Oil U.S.A., 585 F.3d 855 (5th cir. Oct. 16, 2009). However, sitting *en banc*, the U.S. Court of Appeals for the Fifth Circuit dismissed the appeal when one of the nine judges recused herself, resulting in the court's determination that it lacked quorum to conduct judicial business. Comer v. Murphy Oil U.S.A., 607 F.3d 1049 (5th cir. May 28, 2010). Given the lack of a discussion of the merits of the climate-change related claim at issue in *Comer* by the court sitting *en banc*, this article will focus on the U.S. Court of Appeals for the Second Circuit's decision in *Connecticut v. AEP Comp. Inc.*

a situation similar to that facing Kivalina, where Native nations are deprived of meaningful participation in the legal system.

Application of Environmental Justice to Claims Arising within Indian Country[31]

"Modern" Environmental Justice Claims

Environmental justice is rooted in several social justice movements within the United States, including the Civil Rights Movement of the 1950s, 1960s, and 1970s, the Anti-Toxics Movement, Native American struggles,[32] the Labor Movement, and the traditional environmental movement.[33] Many scholars point to the 1982 protests in Warren County, North Carolina against a PCB dump and publication of the United Church of Christ Commission for Racial Justice's 1987 study, *Toxic Wastes and Race*, as catalytic events in the formation of the environmental justice movement.[34] Both of these events and subsequent efforts during the "first generation of environmental justice claims" focused on siting decisions and ensuring that people of color and lower socio-economic communities did not bear a disproportionate negative impact from environmental burdens and had equal access to decision-making.[35] Bunyan Bryant, a pioneer in the field of environmental justice, encapsulated this original understanding of environmental justice in his description of "environmental racism":

> It is an extension of racism. It refers to those institutional rules, regulations, and policies of government or corporate decisions that deliberately target certain communities for least desirable land uses, resulting in the disproportionate exposure of toxic and hazardous waste on communities based upon certain prescribed biological characteristics. Environmental racism is the unequal protection against toxic and hazardous waste exposure and the systematic exclusion of people of color from environmental decisions affecting their communities.[36]

---

31 Although the term "Indian Country" is a phrase of legal import, the author here is using the phrase broadly and intends to be inclusive of Native lands in Alaska.

32 Tsosie, *Indigenous People and Environmental Justice*, *supra* note 10, at 1629–30 ("Proponents of the environmental justice movement during the 1980s and 1990s generally considered Native Americans to be victims of 'environmental racism,' similar to other racial minorities, based on their similar history of exclusion, stereotyping, and economic and political disenfranchisement. Indeed, ample factual support exists for the perspective that Native peoples live in vulnerable communities, beset by a multitude of hazardous conditions.").

33 Luke W. Cole & Sheila R. Foster, From the Ground Up 19–30 (2001).

34 *Id.* at 20–21.

35 Tsosie, *Indigenous People and Environmental Justice*, *supra* note 10.

36 Environmental Justice: Issues, Policies, and Solutions 5 (Bunyan Bryant ed., 1995).

As the field of environmental justice has grown, it has included several different concepts of "justice." "Environmental justice, as a field, asks how environmental law fails to further values of distributive justice, procedural justice, corrective justice, and social justice."[37] The disproportionate impacts of environmental decision-making remain an important issue for many environmental justice advocates, but the umbrella of environmental justice has expanded throughout the ensuing decades. David Getches and David Pellow considered what constitutes an environmental justice issue in light of newly emerging considerations and challenges.[38] As they explain, "the ambit of environmental justice issues has stretched well beyond attacking the classically urban problem of undesirable facility siting and unequal pollution impacts."[39]

Given that "the ambit of environmental justice issues has stretched," the question of what now constitutes an environmental justice claim arises. Getches and Pellow conclude that environmental justice claims only extend to the claims of disadvantaged communities.[40] "The definition of the term *community* connotes some commonality in interests, backgrounds, occupations, or legal treatment among people, as well as the existence of ties to a particular place."[41] In addition to focusing on community concerns, modern environmental justice concerns are those where the inequality faced by the community intensifies the disadvantages facing the community.[42] Notably, just as Kivalina brought claims against private

---

37 Lesley K. McAllister, *On Environmental Enforcement and Compliance: A Reply to Professor Crawford's Review of Making Law Matter: Environmental Protection and Legal Institutions in Brazil*, 40 GEO. WASH. INT'L L. REV. 649, 673 (2009). Notably, Native nations are being denied procedural justice when courts refuse to consider the merits of their claims, instead opting to dismiss claims like the one brought by Kivalina on the basis of threshold legal questions such as standing. As previously explained, this leads to Native nations being excluded from meaningful participation and leads to unjust environmental results, both of which are demonstrated by the District Court's decision in *Kivalina*. Amy Hardberger, *Why We Do the Things We Do?: The Role of Ethics in Water Resource Planning*, 6 SANTA CLARA J. INT'L L. 129, 142–43 (2008) ("Procedural justice provides for equal treatment of citizens in many procedural aspects to ensure that everyone has a voice.") (citations omitted). Effective access to courts is an important consideration extending beyond environmental justice, as "it is nonetheless important to err on the side of ensuring that environmental standing continues to evolve in a way that affords meaningful access to the courts during this era of global environmental crisis in which we live." Randall S. Abate, Massachusetts v. EPA *and the Future of Environmental Standing in Climate Change Litigation and Beyond*, 33 WM. & MARY ENVTL. L. & POL'Y REV. 121, 176 (2008).

38 David H. Getches & David N. Pellow, *Beyond "Traditional" Environmental Justice*, *in* JUSTICE AND NATURAL RESOURCES: CONCEPTS, STRATEGIES, AND APPLICATIONS 3–30 (Kathryn M. Mutz et al. eds. 2002).

39 *Id.* at 5–6.

40 *Id.* at 25.

41 *Id.* at 24.

42 *Id.* at 26.

corporations, corporate deception can also lead to environmental justice claims.[43] Accordingly, modern environmental justice concerns are those facing communities of color and poor communities where the inequality faced by these communities intensifies environmental disadvantages.[44]

Environmental Justice Claims Arising in Indian Country

Native communities are environmental justice communities.[45] Although there are similarities,[46] environmental justice claims arising in Indian country differ from

---

43 Sarah Krakoff, *Tribal Sovereignty and Environmental Justice*, *in* JUSTICE AND NATURAL RESOURCES: CONCEPTS, STRATEGIES, AND APPLICATIONS 173 (Kathryn M. Mutz et al. eds. 2002).

44 As explained more fully in the section below, any "modern" definition of environmental justice must also include consideration of tribal sovereignty. *Id.* at 178 ("Because justice for tribal peoples requires support for tribes as distinct political entities, any definition of environmental justice must include the norm of tribal sovereignty. This is particularly important because of the paradoxical nature of tribal sovereignty: on the one hand, tribal sovereignty predates that of the federal or state governments and therefore requires no validation; on the other hand, as a practical matter the contours of tribal sovereignty are constantly being negotiated in this country's courts and legislatures. In other words, tribal sovereignty is sacrosanct yet entirely vulnerable. Its vulnerability calls for vigilant defense.").

45 *Id.* at 162 ("First, virtually all Indian tribes clearly fit into Getches and Pellow's definition of groups who come to the table with 'palpable and endemic disadvantage,' stemming from a long history of discrimination, exclusion, and deliberate attempts to destroy their cultural and political communities. Second, the obvious disproportionate environmental harms borne by Native peoples have meant that they are *already* a part of the discussion—to let them continue to be so without a conscious articulation of the role of tribal sovereignty would be counterproductive to determining appropriate remedial strategies."). For Native nations, meaningful participation therefore includes an acknowledgement of their sovereignty. Accordingly, courts considering claims brought by Native nations, like the one brought by Kivalina, must consider tribal sovereignty in order to effectively view the matter from an environmental justice lens. In *Kivalina*, the District Court, as previously discussed, failed to consider the Nation's sovereignty, especially in its discussion of the Nation's standing in the matter. As a result, Kivalina was deprived of an environmentally just outcome.

46 Like other environmental justice communities, Native nations faced historical discrimination. Of particular relevance is the fact that federal courts often discriminated against tribal and individual Indian claimants, especially before 1934. Newton, *Federal Power Over Indians*, *supra* note 8, at 216–18 (explaining in general reference to the nineteenth Century that "[u]ndoubtedly, racial and cultural prejudice played no small role in federal actions toward Indians during this period."). Given this history of discrimination that Native nations and individual Indians faced in federal courts, access to the courts is of increased importance today. In particular, federal courts should reject decisions such as the District Court's in the *Kivalina* matter that dispose of environmental justice claims for

environmental justice claims arising elsewhere by virtue of the fact that they involve Native nations.[47] These claims differ because they must be considered in light of tribal sovereignty, the federal trust responsibility between the federal government and Native nations, the ancient tribal trust, the unique connection between many tribal communities and their environment, and the United States' recent endorsement of the United Nations Declaration on the Rights of Indigenous Peoples. Each of these points will be discussed below.

Tribal sovereignty Native nations differ from other environmental justice communities because of their status as sovereign governments. While other environmental justice communities typically come together as informal groups whose legal rights flow from environmental laws, tribes' legal rights flow as an initial matter from their sovereignty and their related historical management of the land and resources. Native nations exist as entities separate from state and federal governments. Myriad historical legal developments led to this separateness. American Indian tribes are extra-constitutional, meaning that tribes exist apart from the American Constitution.[48] In the early nineteenth century, the U.S. Supreme Court affirmed the separateness of Native nations. In *Cherokee Nation v. Georgia*,[49] the U.S. Supreme Court held that American Indian tribes were "domestic dependent nations," highlighting their separateness from both state and federal governments. In *Worcester v. Georgia*,[50] the U.S. Supreme Court further clarified the separateness of American Indian tribes, finding that the laws of the states shall have "no force or effect" within the exterior boundaries of American Indian tribal territory.

---

procedural reasons without reaching the merits of such decisions. As a result of the District Court's decision, Kivalina was deprived of procedural justice, as previously explained.

47 "Indian country" is defined at 18 U.S.C. §1151, which states that "[e]xcept as otherwise provided in sections 1154 and 1156 of this title, the term 'Indian country', as used in this chapter, means (a) all land within the limits of any Indian reservation under the jurisdiction of the United States Government, notwithstanding the issuance of any patent, and, including rights-of-way running through the reservation, (b) all dependent Indian communities within the borders of the United States whether within the original or subsequently acquired territory thereof, and whether within or without the limits of a state, and (c) all Indian allotments, the Indian titles to which have not been extinguished, including rights-of-way running through the same."

48 Scholars have noted that "tribal sovereignty is both pre-constitutional and extra-constitutional." Ann Tweedy, *Connecting the Dots Between the Constitution, The Marshall Trilogy, and the* United States v. Lara*: Notes Toward a Blueprint for the Next Legislative Restoration of Tribal Sovereignty*, 42 U. Mich. J.L. Reform 651, 656 (Spring 2009) (citing Gloria Valencia-Weber, *The Supreme Court's Indian Law Decisions: Deviations from Constitutional Principles and the Crafting of Judicial Smallpox Blankets*, 5 U. Pa. J. Const. L. 405, 417 (2003)).

49 30 U.S. 1 (1831).

50 31 U.S. 515 (1832).

However, in the late nineteenth century, the relationship between tribal governments and the federal government changed. The absolute authority of Congress over Native nations was articulated by the U.S. Supreme Court in *United States v. Kagama*,[51] which held that Congress has plenary authority over Native nations. As an expression of its plenary authority over Indian country, on June 18, 1934, Congress passed the Indian Reorganization Act (IRA),[52] with the partial purpose of increasing local tribal self-government.[53] "In the modern era, as tribes have increasingly assumed governmental functions formerly performed by the Bureau of Indian Affairs and Indian Health Service, the relationship between the federal government and the tribes is often described as a government-to-government relationship."[54]

As American Indian tribal self-determination began to proliferate, fears within the dominant society arose regarding application and enforcement of tribal law.[55]

---

51 118 U.S. 375 (1886).

52 Pub. L. No. 73-383, 48 Stat. 984 (1934).

53 Mescalero Apache v. Jones, 411 U.S. 145, 152 (1973) ("The intent and purpose of the Reorganization Act was 'to rehabilitate the Indian's economic life and to give him a chance to develop the initiative destroyed by a century of oppression and paternalism.'") (quoting H.R. Rep. No. 73-1804, at 6 (1934)); Rose Cuison Villazor, *Blood Quantum Land Laws and the Race Versus Political Identity Dilemma*, 96 Cal. L. Rev. 801, fn. 40 (2008) ("Congress enacted the Indian Reorganization Act of 1934, 25 U.S.C. § 461 (2000), which had as its purpose the need to craft measures "whereby Indian tribes would be able to assume a greater degree of self-government.") (citing Morton v. Mancari, 417 U.S. 535, 542 (1974)); Honorable Sandra Day O'Connor, *Lessons from the Third Sovereign: Indian Tribal Courts* 1 (1998), *available at* http://www.icctc.org/CC%20manual/Lessons%20From%20the%20Third%20Sovereign.pdf ("Passage of the Indian Reorganization Act allowed the tribes to organize their governments, by drafting their own constitutions, adopting their own laws through tribal councils, and setting up their own court systems.").

54 Cordalis & Suagee, *supra* note 6, at 45 (citing Exec. Order No. 13,175, 2, 65 Fed. Reg. 67,249 (Nov. 6, 2000)). *See also* 25 U.S.C. § 3601 ("there is a government-to-government relationship between the United States and each Indian tribe …").

55 For example, in testimony related to what became known at the Indian Civil Rights Act, U.S. Senator Burdick stated, "In many cases the tribal courts are 'kangaroo courts.' One of the basic reasons for my statement is that the method of selecting tribal judges insures that an Indian appearing before tribal court, in too many cases, will not get fair treatment." Testimony of Senator Quentin Burdick, Hearings Before the Subcomm. on Constitutional Rights of the Senate Comm. on the Judiciary, 87th Cong. 88 (1962). More recently, in her comments on the then pending Tribal Law and Order Act of 2009, the Honorable Theresa Pouley indicated that concerns still seem to remain regarding the effectiveness of American Indian tribal courts. "At the hearing last month on the draft Tribal Law and Order Act, representatives from the Departments of Justice and Interior expressed concerns to this Committee regarding the extension of tribal court sentencing authority. DOJ and BIA expressed concerns as to whether tribal courts would adequately protect the rights of criminal defendants. DOI expressed similar concerns, and also raised issues regarding increased costs of longer detentions and possibly an increase in habeas petitions."

Perhaps in reaction to these fears, Congress and the U.S. Supreme Court took steps to limit the authority of Native nations.[56] As a result of these developments, Native nations have limited authority over non-Indians.[57] Today, the majority of matters handled by tribal courts include issues of property and family law.[58] This is consistent with the general policy of the American federal government to leave issues related to American Indian tribal members solely within the inherent tribal sovereignty of tribal governments.[59] Moreover, Congress has indicated its recognition of tribal sovereignty through passage of the Indian Self-Determination and Educational Assistance Act[60] and by subsequently amending various federal statutes to allow for increased tribal governance.[61]

Accordingly, environmental justice claims arising in Indian country differ from claims arising elsewhere given the inherent sovereignty still possessed by Native nations. As can be seen even from the brief description above, "[t]ribal sovereignty is thus a paradox. It transcends, and therefore requires no validation from, the U.S. government. At the same time, tribal sovereignty is vulnerable and requires vigilant and constant defense in our legal and political forums."[62] Moreover, unlike claims brought by other environmental justice communities, environmental

---

Prepared Statement of Hon. Theresa M. Pouley, Judge, Tulalip Tribal Court; President, Northwest Tribal Court Judges Association, 33–34 (July 24, 2009).

56 For example, see the Indian Civil Rights Act of 1968, which applied many of the protections of the U.S. Constitution to Indian country as well as limiting American Indian tribal court punishment authority to $5000 and/or one year in prison. 25 U.S.C. §§ 1301–1303. *See also* Oliphant v. Suquamish Indian Tribe, 435 U.S. 191 (1978) (holding that American Indian tribal courts do not have authority over non-Indians in criminal matters).

57 *See* Oliphant v. Suquamish Indian Tribe, 435 U.S. 191 (1978); Plains Commerce Bank v. Long Family Land & Cattle, 554 U.S. 316 (2008) (holding that although American Indian tribal courts have jurisdiction to regulate conduct on tribal lands, that power is lost once the land is transferred to non-Indians); *see also* Montana v. United States, 450 U.S. 544 (1981) (holding that American Indian tribal courts possess civil jurisdiction over non-Indians when the non-Indians either enter into a consensual relationship with the plaintiff allowing for tribal court jurisdiction or when the non-Indians' activities threaten the health, welfare, economic security or political integrity of the tribe).

58 Nell Jessup Newton, *Tribal Court Praxis: One Year in the Life of Twenty Indian Tribal Courts*, 22 Am. Indian L. Rev. 285, 308 (1998).

59 *See generally* Worcester v. Georgia, 31 U.S. 515 (1932) (holding that the laws of Georgia did not have any effect within the Cherokee Nation's territory); Santa Clara Pueblo v. Martinez, 436 U.S. 49 (1978) (holding that tribes have the power to determine tribal membership).

60 25 U.S.C. § 450 (2006).

61 Given the topic of this chapter, perhaps of special note are congressional amendments allowing tribal control over federal programs on reservations under the Clean Air Act, 42 U.S.C. § 7601(d)(1)(A), Clean Water Act, 33 U.S.C. § 1377(e), Safe Water Drinking Water Act, 42 U.S.C. § 300j-11, Federal Insecticide, Fungicide and Rodenticide Act, 7 U.S.C. § 136, and major portions of CERCLA, 42 U.S.C. §§ 9601–9657.

62 Krakoff, *supra* note 43, at 163.

justice claims raised by Native nations "must be consistent with the promotion of tribal self-governance."[63] This is because environmental justice claims arising from within Indian country include not only racial considerations but also political considerations, as Native nations have a special government-to-government relationship with the federal government.[64] The additional consideration of tribal sovereignty is crucial to any discussion of environmental justice claims arising in Indian country. Specifically, an environmental injustice occurs if courts, such as the District Court in *Kivalina*, fail to consider the sovereignty of Native nations, because Native nations cannot meaningfully participate in the legal process if courts fail to consider something so essential to Native nations as their sovereignty.[65] Moreover, because of the special government-to-government relationship that exists between American Indian tribal nations and the federal government, "the federal government must be prepared to defend vigorously the environmental self-determination that tribes already have."[66] Therefore, not only must courts consider Native nations' sovereignty when evaluating claims, such as *Kivalina*, in order to ensure an environmentally just result, but courts must also do so because of the federal trust relationship that exists between Native nations and the federal government.

Federal trust relationship with Native nations In addition to the consideration of tribal sovereignty, environmental justice claims arising from within Indian country require consideration of the unique trust relationship between the federal government and Native nations.[67] The trust responsibility incumbent

---

63 *Id.*

64 Additionally, individual American Indians have a political relationship with their tribal governments. Rebecca Tsosie, *Negotiating Economic Survival: The Consent Principle and Tribal–State Compacts Under the Indian Gaming Regulatory Act*, 29 Ariz. St. L. J. 25, 27 (1997).

65 Krakoff, *supra* note 43, at 163; Tsosie, *Indigenous People and Environmental Justice*, *supra* note 10, at 1652 ("Such a notion of justice must incorporate an indigenous right to environmental self-determination that allows indigenous peoples to protect their traditional, land-based cultural practices regardless of whether they also possess the sovereign right to govern those lands or, in the case of climate change, prevent the practices that are jeopardizing those environments.").

66 Krakoff, *supra* note 43, at 179.

67 Related to the federal trust responsibility doctrine is the concept that the federal government is morally obligated to act in the best interests of Native nations given the historical trauma heaped upon these governments by the federal government. For example, in the mid-twentieth century, the federal government set about "'terminating' the federal trust relationship with Native nations, abolishing reservations and subjecting Indians to the control of state laws. "Where it was implemented for particular tribes and reservations, this termination program created disastrous poverty and dislocation for Indian communities." Reid Peyton Chambers, *Compatibility of the Federal Trust Responsibility with Self-Determination of Indian Tribes: Reflections on Development of the Federal Trust*

upon the federal government arises from the unique history between the federal government and Native nations. As a result of this history, "the United States has a trust responsibility to each tribal government that includes the protection of the sovereignty of each tribal government."[68] This trust relationship emerged from the many cessions of both land and external sovereignty made by Native nations to the federal government.[69] The trust responsibility between Native nations and the United States imposes the most exacting duty on the federal government to protect the natural resources of Native nations.[70] "Scores of cases emphasize this duty of protection, and many hold that the duty imposes an affirmative obligation on government. Under well-established principles of private trust law, trustees may not sit idle and allow damage to occur to the trust."[71] In particular, the federal government owes federally recognized Native nations fiduciary obligations related to the management of tribal trust lands and resources.[72] Inclusive in this fiduciary obligation is the "affirmative duty to recoup monetary damages against third parties that destroy trust assets,"[73] such as the private entities targeted in the *Kivalina* litigation. "Failure to seek damages is, by all private trust standards, an abdication of trust responsibility."[74] The relationship between the federal government and federally recognized Native nations has evolved to the point where Native nations

---

Responsibility in the Twenty-First Century, 2005 Rocky Mtn. L. Inst. 13A-2 (citations omitted). However, a complete discussion of potential moral responsibility of the federal government to Native nations is beyond the scope of this chapter.

68 25 U.S.C. § 3601.

69 Mary Christina Wood & Zachary Welcker, *Tribes as Trustees Again (Part I): The Emerging Tribal Role in the Conservation Trust Movement*, 32 Harv. Envtl. L. Rev. 373, 387–88 (2008) ("A cornerstone of this relationship is the trust obligation, which arose from promises made by the federal government when it forced cessions of aboriginal land. The United States promised tribes that they would be secure on reservations and that the federal government would protect Native ways of life and autonomy.") (citations omitted); *See also* Newton, *Federal Power Over Indians*, *supra* note 8, at 207 ("The notion that the federal government had a property interest of some sort in Indian land provided the central analytical element for the guardianship power.").

70 Mary Christina Wood, *Advancing the Sovereign Trust of Government to Safeguard the Environment for Present and Future Generations (Part II): Instilling a Fiduciary Obligation in Governance*, 39 Envtl. L. 91, 93–94 (2009) [hereinafter Wood, *Instilling a Fiduciary Obligation in Governance*] ("Most importantly, a trust approach holds trustees to the 'most exacting fiduciary standards' … Trust law imposes a fundamental duty on the trustee to protect the assets of the trust from damage.") (citations omitted).

71 *Id.* at 94–95.

72 Cordalis & Suagee, *supra* note 6. "Recognizing that the United States has, under the Constitution, broad power over Indian affairs sufficiently extensive to make the tribes comparatively vulnerable to the exercise of that power, this guardian–ward construct also protects tribes from the peril to which that power potentially subjects them." Chambers, *supra* note 67, at 13A-9.

73 Wood, *Instilling a Fiduciary Obligation in Governance*, *supra* note 70, at 97.

74 *Id.* at 98.

may now regularly assume governmental functions that were previously held by the federal government.[75]

To better understand the trust responsibility that the federal government owes to Native nations, it is helpful to look to the history between the sovereigns. The federal trust responsibility doctrine has been the subject of many court decisions related to Indian country over the past two centuries. The doctrine has its origins in Chief Justice Marshall's opinion in *Cherokee Nation v. Georgia*, where the Chief Justice stated that Indians' "relation to the United States resembles that of a ward to his guardian."[76] As a result of the development of the federal trust responsibility doctrine, the federal government began to hold lands in trust for tribal governments. Several decades later, the Court reaffirmed its commitment to this doctrine in *United States v. Kagama*, where it held that "these Indian tribes *are* the wards of the nation. They are communities dependent on the United States … From their very weakness and helplessness … there arises the duty of protection and with it the power."[77]

In the ensuing twentieth century, the Court used the federal trust responsibility doctrine to define the scope of review of congressional legislation related to Indian country, and, as a result, whenever Congress takes action within Indian country it must do so as a trustee.[78] Furthermore, "because of the trust responsibility, it is well settled that statutes affecting Indians 'are to be construed liberally in favor of the Indians, with ambiguous provisions interpreted to their benefit.'"[79] In a more recent decision, the Court further defined the contours of the federal trust responsibility doctrine by following the common law trust principles as articulated in *Restatement (Second) of Trusts*, Sections 205–212.[80] In this regard, "[t]he courts

---

75 *Id.* ("In the modern era, as tribes have increasingly assumed governmental functions formerly performed by the Bureau of Indian Affairs and Indian Health Service, the relationship between the federal government and the tribes is often described as a government-to-government relationship.") (citations omitted).

76 30 U.S. (5 Pet.) 1, 17 (1831). "The concept of the trust responsibility under the Marshall Court decisions, then, was that tribes agreed to cede some of their lands in return for a federal obligation to protect the remaining lands and tribes rights to govern themselves free from interference by any other government." Chambers, *supra* note 67, at 13A-9.

77 118 U.S. 375, 383–84 (1886).

78 Chambers, *supra* note 67, at 13A-12 ("In *Delaware Tribal Business Committee v. Weeks*, the Supreme Court expressly rejected an argument that there could be no judicial review of statutes affecting Indians, and stated instead that federal legislation affecting Indians must be 'tied rationally to the fulfillment of Congress' unique obligation toward the Indians.' These cases thus teach that the trust responsibility provides a standard of review for legislation in the field of Indian affairs: whether the legislation is rationally related to the trust responsibility.") (citations omitted).

79 *Id.* at 13A-13 (citations omitted).

80 463 U.S. 206, 226 (1983). In developing the federal trust responsibility doctrine in this manner, the Court found that the doctrine applied whether there was a trustee (federal government), beneficiary (Indian nation) and trust corpus (tribal property, etc. to be managed

have also consistently rejected arguments that the government's conduct in its administration of the trust, can be tested simply by a standard of reasonableness, but have required that the government meet the higher standards applicable to private trustees."[81]

Recognition of the federal trust responsibility has not been limited to the courts. President Nixon recognized the federal trust responsibility in his 1968 Special Message to Congress on the Problems of the American Indian:

> The special relationship between Indians and the Federal government is the result of solemn obligations which have been entered into by the United States Government. Down through the years, through written treaties and through formal and informal agreements, our government has made specific commitments to the Indian people. For their part, the Indians have often surrendered claims to vast tracts of land and have accepted life on government reservations.[82]

Subsequent administrations have reaffirmed and even expanded upon Nixon's recognition of the federal trust responsibility doctrine.[83]

In addition to the specific trust responsibility between Native nations and the federal government, Professor Mary Christina Wood has argued that there is a general trust obligation on the part of governments to protect their citizens from the impacts of climate change.[84] A trust relationship includes a duty of loyalty from the trustee, in this case the federal government, to the beneficiary, Native nations.

---

by the federal government). *Id.* This understanding of the federal trust responsibility was re-affirmed recently in the Court's decision in *United States v. White Mountain Apache Tribe*, 537 U.S. 465 (2003).

81 Chambers, *supra* note 67, at 13A-17.

82 Special Message to Congress on the Problems of the American Indian: "The Forgotten American," 113 Pub. Papers (March 6, 1968).

83 "For example, President Reagan's Message to Congress on January 24, 1983 continued the commitment of the Nation to strong government to government relations with tribes and to support [sic] tribal self-government and economic self-sufficiency. President Clinton's Executive Order 13175 recognized 'the right of Indian tribes to self-government' and supported 'tribal sovereignty and self-determination.' President George W. Bush issued a Presidential Proclamation 7500 November 12, 2001 stating 'we will protect and honor tribal sovereignty and help to stimulate economic development in reservation communities.'" Chambers, *supra* note 67, at 13A-4 (citations omitted).

84 Wood, *Instilling a Fiduciary Obligation in Governance*, *supra* note 70, at 96 ("In the face of climate crisis, the most pressing matter is defining a fiduciary obligation for protecting the atmosphere, a trust asset that has never before been 'managed' … The scientifically established structure reflected in the Target, as adapted to comport with changed scientific understanding, can be invoked as a generic standard of fiduciary obligation applicable to each industrialized nation.").

> The duty of loyalty reaches its pinnacle with respect to natural assets necessary for public survival—like the atmosphere. Because such assets are crucial and irreplaceable, breaching the strict duty of loyalty may bring irreversible damage to society and future generations. Thus, the inquiry into fiduciary loyalty must be particularly demanding with respect to issues such as global warming. While it is true that government sometimes must balance competing public interests in managing the natural trust, that situation is much different than making a trade-off of public interests to benefit private singular interests.[85]

While this obligation is not yet settled as a matter of law, plaintiffs all over the country filed lawsuits against state and local governments based on a general atmospheric trust obligation.

In sum, the federal trust responsibility owed by the federal government to Native nations should inform consideration of any environmental justice claim arising in Indian country.[86] Failure to include consideration of this responsibility again results in Native nations being deprived of meaningful participation in the consideration of climate change-related claims, such as *Kivalina*, which are in fact environmental justice claims. Because of this responsibility, the federal government owes the most exacting obligation to Native nations to ensure that their natural resources are sustained. Moreover, the specific trust responsibility owed by the federal government to Native nations as a result of the unique history between the sovereigns is buttressed by the general trust responsibility owed by the federal government to all citizens, a duty of loyalty to protect American citizens from the negative impacts of climate change. As explained above, duties under the trust responsibility should extend to protecting Native nations from the harmful acts of private, third parties, such as the defendants in *Kivalina*. Trust responsibilities extend to the federal government as a whole. As a branch of the federal government, these obligations should be upheld by the federal judiciary.[87]

85 *Id.* at 100.

86 This argument, that the federal government owes certain duties and obligations to Native nations under the federal trust responsibility doctrine, may be seen as contrary to the previous assertion that decision-makers must also take into consideration tribal sovereignty when evaluating environmental justice claims arising in Indian country. However, both tribal sovereignty and the federal trust responsibility do exist within the current legal scheme applicable to modern day Indian country. Resolution of the apparent tension between these two legal concepts is beyond the scope of this chapter.

87 In fact, federal courts should apply a more "searching scrutiny" in evaluating these types of claims as they go to the very "personhood" of individual Natives. Territorial integrity is key to sovereignty. Without such integrity it is difficult to maintain the separateness that is fundamental to sovereignty. It is through their membership in such tribal nations that many Natives define themselves, their "personhood". Therefore, because climate change threatens the territorial integrity of many Native nations, it also threatens the very "personhood" of affected Natives. Such a threat certainly deserves a heightened level of review by federal courts. Newton, *Federal Power Over Indians*, *supra* note 8, at

In evaluating an environmental justice claim arising in Indian country, such as the *Kivalina* claim, it is critical that federal courts be mindful of, and uphold, the federal government's trust responsibility to Native nations. Failure to do so results in an environmental injustice, as seen in *Kivalina*.

Ancient tribal trust doctrine Federal courts considering environmental justice claims arising in Indian country, such as Kivalina's climate change-related claims, should also take into consideration the ancient public trust doctrine applicable to tribal management of lands.[88] Until relatively recently, Natives were responsible for the management of environmental resources found in what is today the United States of America, developing and applying an ancient tribal trust doctrine to the management of natural resources. This ancient tribal trust doctrine has been traditionally characterized by a restraint in the use of resources and a binding duty to preserve resources for future generations.[89] When tribal nations were conquered, "[a]uthority over Nature's Trust—the land and resources on this continent—accordingly became vested in a new set of trustees: federal and state governments."[90] The new trustees began to actively degrade the environment by opening "lands to consumption by private interests."[91] As articulated above, in addition to ensuring meaningful participation, claims based on environmental justice empower a community to assert itself so as to avoid further disproportionate negative impacts from environmental pollution. In this regard, environmental justice claims that allow Native nations to assert their control over sources of pollution and reassert management authority over natural resources both recognize the sovereignty of tribal nations and allow the same nations to "arrest

---

244 ("[T]ribal membership is at the core of Indian *personal* identity, reflecting much more than a shifting political value choice or voluntary association. The tribe is a projection of the autonomous Individual Indian. To some extent this unique interrelationship between tribe and individual identity is already recognized in the law: tribal membership as defined by the tribe is often the key element in determining whether a person is an Indian for some legal purposes.") (citations omitted). Moreover, Dean Nell Jessup Newton also has suggested that "Indian tribes meet other conditions the courts traditionally have found to justify heightened judicial scrutiny under the equal protection clause. The Court has observed that a suspect class is one subject to a 'history of purposeful unequal treatment.'" *Id.* at 246 (citations omitted).

88 Wood & Welcker, *supra* note 69, at 373 ("Until the most recent blink of human time, Indian tribes exercised territorial sovereignty over nearly all of the land on this continent—two billion acres. Nature was abundant and, for the most part, in a state of remarkable balance. Most tribes affirmatively managed resources to maintain a sustainable existence … Native peoples' understanding of their traditional role as stewards of the land—a gift from the Creator—was that the Earth should be protected in perpetuity for the sake of future generations.").

89 *Id.*

90 *Id.* at 374.

91 *Id.*

the hemorrhaging of natural systems brought about by federal and state trustee mismanagement of these assets."[92] In fact, tribal sovereignty, a key consideration related to environmental justice claims arising in Indian country, is inextricably bound to this ancient tribal trust possessed by Native nations.[93]

As with the federal trust responsibility discussed above, the responsibility to recognize and enforce the ancient tribal trust doctrine is not limited to the political branches of the federal government. The federal courts play a crucial role in this regard. In such cases where the trust responsibility between the federal government and Native nations applies, federal courts should take an active role in evaluating such matters to ensure that the resources at issue are sustained. To this end, courts should have both the inclination and tools to safeguard vital public trust assets as a last resort where the other branches have failed. Judges should be receptive to trust cases, understand the judiciary's role in the constitutional balance of power over ecological assets, be willing to enforce trust principles against the political branches, and be equipped to implement complex remedies where warranted.[94]

In the *Kivalina* matter, for example, such a searching inquiry would probably lead a federal court to conclude that there has been a violation of the ancient tribal trust and injury to the tribal trust corpus at issue. This is the case because the land is literally falling into the sea, prohibiting any chance that the Native community will be able to sustain itself for future generations under the present conditions.

Some may argue that application of the ancient tribal trust doctrine, which is protective of the tribal trust asset, must give way to private property interests, such as those of the defendants in the *Kivalina* litigation. However, such a conclusion would be in error. "Private property rights and licenses are subservient to antecedent public rights."[95] Furthermore, "[w]here a trust asset is at stake, the private property owner's ownership must recede to the superior property interest of the people as a whole."[96]

The ancient tribal trust doctrine links together the doctrines of tribal sovereignty and the federal trust responsibility. Before the formation of the United States, many Native nations generally managed their natural resources in a sustainable manner and for the use and benefit of future generations.[97] This strong commitment to sustainable natural resource management amongst many Native nations underlies any environmental justice claim arising in Indian country. In the case of Kivalina,

92 *Id.* at 375.

93 *Id.* at 385 ("Traditional Native sovereignty is inextricably connected to this spiritual conservation mandate. In effect, tribes use their sovereignty to exercise their spiritual duty to protect the interests of beneficiaries in distant generations … The duty to protect resources for coming generations is concurrently both a principle of religion and governance.").

94 Wood, *Instilling a Fiduciary Obligation in Governance*, *supra* note 70, at 136.

95 *Id.* at 106.

96 *Id.* at 117.

97 *See supra* n. 92.

the soil upon which the Nation sits is literally eroding away as a result of climatic changes. Kivalina is therefore being deprived of any opportunity to manage its natural resources. Such a complete deprivation of natural resources is antithetical to the ancient tribal trust doctrine and environmental justice. Moreover, the federal courts are capable of, and should act to, enforce this ancient tribal trust doctrine, and private property interests that may be at issue in claims involving climate change should yield to those related to the ancient tribal trust doctrine.

Unique tribal connection to the land and environment

> *We are the land.* (Paula Gunn Allen, Laguna Writer, *Iyani: It Goes This Way*)

Claims raised by tribal communities differ from many other environmental claims because most Native cultures and traditions are tied to the environment and land in a manner that traditionally differs from that of the dominant society.[98] "As Frank Pommersheim points out, land is important to Indian people in a multitude of ways—beyond a means of subsistence, land 'is the source or spiritual origin and sustaining myth which in turn provides a landscape of cultural and emotional means. The land often determines the values of the human landscape.'"[99] Similarity in connections to environment and the land among Natives result from the fact that most Native cultures are "land-based."[100] Moreover, many individual Natives and

98 The author recognizes that each Native nation has a different relationship with its environment and is hesitant to stereotype a common "Native experience," recognizing that there is a broad diversity of thought and experience related to one's relationship with land and the environment. In particular, the author would like to avoid traditional stereotypes of American Indians as "Noble Savages" or "Bloodthirsty Savages". *See* Rebecca Tsosie, *Tribal Environmental Policy in an Era of Self-Determination: The Role of Ethics, Economics, and Traditional Ecological Knowledge*, 21 Vt. L. Rev. 225, 271 (1996) [hereinafter Tsosie, *Tribal Environmental Policy in an Era of Self-Determination*] ("The problems of cross-cultural interpretation and the attempt to define 'traditional' indigenous beliefs raise a common issue: the tendency of non-Indians to glorify Native Americans as existing in 'perfect harmony' with nature (the 'Noble Save' resurrected) or, on the other hand, denounce them as being as rapacious to the environment as Europeans (the 'Bloodthirsty Savage' resurrected).").

99 Frank Pommersheim, *The Reservation as Place: A South Dakota Essay*, 34 S.D. L. Rev. 246, 250 (1989); *See also* National Congress of American Indians, Resolution #EWS-06-2004—Supporting a National Mandatory Program to Reduce Climate Change Pollution and Promote Renewable Energy (2006 Mid Year Session) ("climate-related changes to the weather, food sources, and local landscapes undermine the social identity and cultural survival of American Indians and Alaskan Natives.").

100 Tsosie, *Tribal Environmental Policy in an Era of Self-Determination*, *supra* note 98, at 274.

Native nations possess a spiritual connection with the land and the environment.[101] These communities "continue to have a deep relationship with ancestral homelands for sustenance, religious communion and comfort, and to maintain the strength of personal and interfamiliar identities. Through language, songs, and ceremonies, tribal people continue to honor sacred springs, ancestral burial places, and other places where ancestral communities remain alive."[102] The spiritual connection between many Native nations and their surrounding environment is crucial to the sovereignty of these Nations.[103]

Therefore, as the land changes owing to climate change, many communities may be faced with devastating impacts on their culture, spirituality and traditions. Such spiritual, cultural and historical connections to the land affected play an important role in any environmental justice claim arising in Indian country. This is because for many Native nations land, identity and sovereignty are uniquely connected. Failure to consider these interconnections by a court would negatively impact the quality of the Native nation's participation in the legal process. The District Court's decision in *Kivalina* exemplifies how Native nations may be negatively impacted, as the District Court failed to consider the importance of Kivalina's connection to the land and, as a result, rendered a decision that was environmentally unjust.

United Nations Declaration on the Rights of Indigenous Peoples Principles of international law may also be considered when evaluating environmental justice claims arising in Indian country. The potential applicability of international law to claims brought by Native nations has its roots in one of the foundational cases of federal Indian law, *Worcester v. Georgia*. In that case, "Chief Justice Marshall premised much of his eloquent defense of federal power on his view of the Indian tribes as sovereign nations whose rights of self-government predated the Constitution and whose dealings with the United States were governed by principles of international as well as constitutional law."[104] Moreover, some scholars have suggested that "tribal sovereignty" is a fundamental right.[105] Such fundamental rights transcend domestic law. Therefore, international law is an

101 *Id.* "American Indian tribal religions … are located spatially,' often around the natural features of a sacred universe. Thus, while indigenous people often do not care when the particular event of significance in their religious tradition occurred, they care very much about where it occurred." *Id.* at 282–83.

102 Wood & Welcker, *supra* note 69, at 381.

103 *Id.* at 424 ("Trust concepts therefore help to provide tribes with two essential tools of traditional Native self-determination: access to sacred lands and the ability to sustainably use the natural resources on those lands. These were, and remain today, vital tools of nation-building.").

104 Newton, *Federal Power Over Indians*, *supra* note 8, at 202.

105 *Id.* at 261 ("Nevertheless, it has been argued, chiefly by Barsh and Henderson, that tribal sovereignty should be protected as a fundamental political liberty. Their argument rests on sovereignty as a retained right of the people under the ninth amendment. The due

important piece to be considered in evaluating environmental justice claims arising in Indian country.

On December 16, 2010, President Barack Obama announced that the United States endorsed the United Nations Declaration on the Rights of Indigenous Peoples (UNDRIP). The UNDRIP is an international declaration, supported nearly unanimously by the countries of the United Nations, supporting and reaffirming the rights of indigenous peoples.[106] Although the Declaration is not binding international law, it is certainly persuasive given its broad support on the question of what rights indigenous peoples possess according to international law.

Of particular importance here is the UNDRIP's statements with regards to indigenous self-determination, property and redress. UNDRIP Article 3 states "[i]ndigenous peoples have the right to self-determination."[107] UNDRIP Article 8 states, "[i]ndigenous peoples and individuals have the right not to be subjected to forced assimilation or destruction of their culture."[108] UNDRIP Article 10 states "[i]ndigenous peoples shall not be forcibly removed from their lands or territories. No relocation shall take place without the free, prior and informed consent of the indigenous peoples concerned and after agreement on just and fair compensation and, where possible, the option to return."[109] UNDRIP Article 26 states "[i] ndigenous peoples have the right to the lands, territories and resources which they have traditionally owned, occupied or otherwise used or acquired … States shall give legal recognition and protection to these lands, territories and resources."[110] Finally, UNDRIP Article 28 states that "[i]ndigenous peoples have the right to redress, by means that can include restitution or, when this is not possible, just, fair and equitable compensation, for the lands, territories and resources which they have traditionally owned or otherwise occupied or used, and which have been confiscated, taken, occupied, used or damaged without their free, prior and informed consent."[111]

All of the UNDRIP rights mentioned above, as well as many other rights contained within the UNDRIP, are directly implicated by climate change-related litigation brought by Native nations, such as Kivalina's claim. As discussed in the Introduction, climate change is directly threatening the very land and natural resources upon which Native nations survive. Such a direct threat undermines the

---

process clause's protection of liberty, however, would be a more secure, even if less logical, repository for this right.") (citations omitted).

106 At the time of writing, 148 countries endorsed the UNDRIP, and apparently nine countries abstained from vote on the Declaration. Declaration on the Rights of Indigenous Peoples, G.A. Res. 61/295, Annex, U.N. Doc. A/Res/61/295 (Oct. 2, 2007), *available at* http://www.un.org/esa/socdev/unpfii/documents/DRIPS_en.pdf.

107 *Id.* at Art. 3.

108 *Id.* at Art. 8.

109 *Id.* at Art. 10.

110 *Id.* at Art. 26.

111 *Id.* at Art. 28.

very existence of Native nations, thereby threatening their inherent right to self-determination. As recognized by the UNDRIP Article 28, Native nations should have the opportunity to seek redress in domestic courts for the threat presented by climate change. Moreover, it is important to note that Article 26 affirmatively requires nation states, such as the United States, to protect the land and resources of Native nations. This affirmative responsibility under the UNDRIP mirrors the domestic federal trust responsibility discussed above. The fact that the United States has now endorsed the UNDRIP signals its recognition of the rights articulated therein. Accordingly, federal courts should keep this endorsement of the UNDRIP in mind when evaluating environmental justice claims arising in Indian country as the UNDRIP provides an important international legal component to buttress existing binding legal duties of the federal government under domestic law. Failure to consider these legal obligations owed by the federal government to Native nations results environmentally unjust outcomes, as demonstrated in *Kivalina*, where the District Court failed to acknowledge these legal obligations based on domestic legal principles let alone international principles.

Environmental justice claims of Native nations have traditionally fallen into two categories: those involving claims to regulate the tribal environment[112] and those involving claims requiring the inclusion of unique tribal interests in decision-making.[113] Environmental justice claims arising in Indian country differ from claims brought by other environmental justice communities, because these claims should include those considerations previously discussed. As explained at the beginning of this chapter, environmental justice requires that Native nations be given an opportunity for meaningful participation in the legal system when bringing forward claims of disparate environmental impact. The District Court's decision in *Kivalina* is an example where an environmentally unjust result occurred when the court failed to take these factors into consideration.

Conclusion: The Necessity of Environmental Justice Considerations in Climate Change-related Claims Brought by Native Nations

Environmental justice requires that courts consider the unique aspects of environmental justice communities in order to ensure adequate access to substantive or procedural justice. Climate change-related claims brought by Native nations are environmental justice claims. Although Native nations contribute little by way of greenhouse gas emissions, many Native nations are located in those

112 Tsosie, *Indigenous People and Environmental Justice*, *supra* note 10, at 1633 ("The lesson that emerged from the first generation of environmental justice claims for Native peoples was that equality of status of governments was the key to justice, rather than the 'equality of citizenship' that is the focus of civil rights-based environmental justice claims on behalf of poor and minority communities.").

113 *Id.* at 1627–28.

areas most vulnerable to the effects of climate change. A salient example of this is the devastating effects of climate change currently facing Kivalina. Despite emitting very few greenhouses to the environment, Kivalina is facing the complete loss of its land. In this way, Kivalina, like many other similarly situated Native communities, is an environmental justice community disproportionately facing the negative impacts of climate change.

Environmental justice issues arising in Indian country encapsulate considerations that differ from claims arising from other environmental justice communities. As discussed above, these considerations include tribal sovereignty, the federal trust responsibility toward Native nations, the ancient tribal trust doctrine, the recent endorsement of the United Nations Declaration on the Rights of Indigenous Peoples, and the unique cultural and spiritual connection many Natives have with their land. In sum, these additional legal and moral considerations combine to make environmental justice claims arising from Indian country particularly persuasive.

Moreover, meaningful access to the federal courts is critical for Native nations bringing claims related to climate change. By rejecting Kivalina's claims for procedural reasons, the District Court denied meaningful access to Kivalina and failed to take into consideration the environmental justice character of Kivalina's claim. As discussed above, meaningful access to the federal courts is crucial to remedy historical wrongs that have been wrought against Native nations.[114] Given the historical discrimination many Native nations faced in the federal courts, the need for access today is especially important. Such meaningful access is part of remedial diversity, as "remedial diversity addresses past structural wrongs without placing blame."[115] Moreover, meaningful access to the courts is important for the overall validity of the federal courts. Consideration of environmental justice claims brought by Native nations negatively impacted by the effects of climate change promotes viewpoint or substantive diversity and allows for the inclusion of the "voice of color," which in turn lends credibility to judicial decisions.[116] Finally, as part of the overall federal government, federal courts are equally responsible for upholding the federal trust responsibility owed by the federal government to Native nations.

Environmental justice considerations play an important role in any climate change-related claim brought by Native nations. The time has come for federal courts adjudicating these claims to seriously consider the disproportionate negative impacts Native nations bear as a direct result of climate change. Even if courts refuse to listen to these issues, as Nell Jessup Newton wisely said, "tribal advocates must keep them before the courts."[117] Throughout their history with the

---

114 *See supra* n. 45.

115 Sylvia R. Lazos Vargas, *Only Skin Deep?: The Cost of Partisan Politics on Minority Diversity of the Federal Bench*, 83 Ind. L.J. 1423, 1430 (2008).

116 *Id.* at 1429–37.

117 Newton, *Federal Power Over Indians*, *supra* note 8, at 287–88.

United States, Native nations have borne wars, plagues, starvation, assimilation efforts, and termination; they should not now be called on to bear the modern scourge that is climate change without legal remedy.

Tribal Lands

Chapter 5

The Promise and Perils of Renewable Energy on Tribal Lands

Sara C. Bronin[1]

In theory, the 95 million acres of tribal lands[2] in the United States are perfect sites for the renewable energy infrastructure that could help to meet the energy needs of not just tribes, but the rest of the nation. They often have plentiful sunlight, wind, and open space, resources that are important prerequisites for renewable energy production. They are not necessarily governed by the land use or environmental regulations that sometimes inhibit energy projects in more densely populated areas. At the same time, on-site renewable energy may provide direct economic benefits for tribes, including "green jobs," infrastructure improvements, and production revenues shared by the community. Moreover, on-site generation could significantly reduce energy expenses for tribal households, who pay more for energy than any other group in the country.

In keeping with this theory, the Indian Tribal Energy Development and Self-Determination Act (ITEDSA) was passed in 2005 to provide tribes with a

---

1 Associate Professor, University of Connecticut School of Law.

2 In this chapter, the term "tribal lands" is meant to be consistent with that definition in the Indian Tribal Energy Development and Self-Determination Act (ITEDSA) and includes "any land or interests in land owned by any Indian tribe, title to which is held in trust by the United States, or is subject to a restriction against alienation under laws of the United States." 25 U.S.C. § 3501(12). It is not intended to encompass all of those lands defined in ITEDSA as "Indian lands," which include:

(A) any land located within the boundaries of an Indian reservation, pueblo, or rancheria;
(B) any land not located within the boundaries of an Indian reservation, pueblo, or rancheria, the title to which is held—
(i) in trust by the United States for the benefit of an Indian tribe or an individual Indian;
(ii) by an Indian tribe or an individual Indian, subject to restriction against alienation under laws of the United States; or
(iii) by a dependent Indian community; and
(C) land that is owned by an Indian tribe and was conveyed by the United States to a Native Corporation pursuant to the Alaska Native Claims Settlement Act (43 U.S.C. 1601 et seq.), or that was conveyed by the United States to a Native Corporation in exchange for such land.

Id. at § 3501(2). The term "Indian lands" includes land that is owned by or in trust for individual Indians.

framework for developing renewable energy infrastructure. It aims to allow tribes to regulate the conveyance of their own energy resources, giving them, under certain circumstances, the ability to enter into leases and other agreements for the construction of renewable energy networks without federal supervision. Despite its expansive aims, ITEDSA is flawed in two significant ways. First, as written, ITEDSA fails to correct for misplaced financial incentives for renewable energy development by tribes. The law continues federal policies that ensure that non-Indians[3] and non-tribal business entities often reap far greater economic rewards than tribes or members of tribes.

Second, ITEDSA, if fully implemented, has the potential to increase the incidence of energy sprawl—that is, the occupation of vast, extra-urban or rural tracts of land by energy generation facilities. The negative effects of energy sprawl created by large-scale renewable facilities are well documented. To the extent that the renewable energy networks are used to serve tribal lands, it is important to encourage tribes to carefully assess environmental and ecological impacts. To the extent that transmission or distribution lines connected to facilities located on tribal lands extend beyond tribal lands, ITEDSA or some other statute must articulate how tribal members can or should influence such lines' siting.

This chapter analyzes the rationale for and substance of ITEDSA—the most significant federal law relating to renewable energy on tribal lands—and identifies ongoing challenges in the way the United States approaches renewable energy infrastructure siting on tribal lands. It does not offer a comprehensive set of solutions but rather identifies current issues in this area of law with a particular focus on the characteristics of tribal lands themselves.

Why Tribal Lands?

Tribal lands present a unique, and in many respects highly appealing, opportunity for the siting of renewable energy infrastructure. Renewable energy comes in many forms and includes any type of energy production that does not draw on finite resources. The National Renewable Energy Laboratory (NREL), a U.S. Department of Energy research and development facility that focuses exclusively on researching renewable energy, has identified seven basic sources of renewable energy: biomass, hydropower, wind, geothermal, solar, hydrogen, and ocean. Of these seven sources, biomass (derived from organic matter, such as food crops, plants, algae, and waste products and gasses) and hydropower (derived from the kinetic energy of flowing water) are the most common. Wind (derived from

3 As used in this chapter, the term "non-Indians" includes all those individuals who are not members of a Native American or Native Alaskan tribe, and non-tribal members, Indians who are not members of the relevant tribe. Non-tribal members include Native Americans living within the boundaries of a reservation who are not members of the tribe that regulates that reservation.

the kinetic energy of wind and processed primarily by turbines or windmills), geothermal (derived from the internal heat of the earth), and solar (derived from the conversion of sunlight, whether through photovoltaic or thermal means) are less common, but seem to have captured greater attention from policy-makers. Technical experts are still struggling to make hydrogen and ocean energy commercially feasible and they will not be considered further by this chapter. Currently in the United States, renewable energy comprises just 8 percent of energy consumed.[4]

Tribal lands, which are primarily located in the western United States, often have physical qualities highly conducive to the generation of renewable energy. The Department of Energy's Energy Information Administration (EIA) prepared a report in 2000 documenting these qualities.[5] It found that owing to latitude or topographical conditions, many tribal lands would serve as good to excellent sites for hosting renewable energy infrastructure such as solar photovoltaics, concentrated solar power, wind generation, biomass, and geothermal wells.[6] The EIA further identified tribal lands that would be best suited for central station development of electricity for renewable energy, and those that would be best suited for specific kinds of renewable energy.[7] For example, the EIA found that biomass potential, which roughly corresponds to arable land, was promising in 118 of 298 reservations, containing 56 percent of the tribal population studied by the EIA.[8] With respect to geothermal resources (which can be directed toward electricity production, direct heating, or geothermal heat pumps), the EIA cross-referenced maps produced by NREL and determined that 57 reservations may have potential for electricity production, with another 72 having potential for direct heat applications.[9] Four years later, NREL conducted a survey that found that tribal lands had the potential for solar power equal to 4.5 times the then-

---

4 U.S. Dep't of Energy Energy Information Administration, Renewable Energy Consumption and Electricity Preliminary Statistics 2009 (2010), *available at* http://www.eia.doe.gov/cneaf/alternate/page/renew_energy_consump/rea_prereport.html. Non-renewable resources including petroleum (37 percent), natural gas (25 percent), coal (21 percent), and nuclear power (9 percent) comprise the remaining 92 percent.

5 U.S. Dep't of Energy, Energy Information Administration, Energy Consumption and Renewable Energy Development Potential on Indian Lands, Apr. 2000, *available at* http://www.eia.doe.gov/Cneaf/Solar.Renewables/Ilands/toc.html [hereinafter Energy Consumption and Renewable Energy Development Potential on Indian Lands].

6 Assuming no significant topographical or boundary changes to the tribal lands analyzed by the EIA in 2000, these assessments hold true today.

7 Energy Consumption and Renewable Energy Development Potential on Indian Lands, *supra* note 5, at ch. 3.

8 *Id.* (citing potential greater than five megawatts per county for these reservations).

9 *Id.* (noting that generally geothermal production is very site-specific and that these projections are estimates only).

current national energy generation.[10] In addition, NREL found that the wind potential on tribal lands is 535 billion kilowatt-hours per year, an amount that equals as much as 14 percent of the U.S. electric generation.[11] All in all, the Bureau of Indian Affairs has estimated that tribal lands—which occupy just 5 percent of the land—have 10 percent of all energy resources (both renewable and non-renewable).[12] Harnessing the renewable component of these resources would help both tribes and the rest of the country reduce their dependence on fossil fuels.

Another characteristic that may make tribal lands more attractive for those building renewable energy projects is their relative absence of land use regulations, when compared with lands governed by non-tribal government. Many state, county, and local governments have enacted rigorous land use regulations, including zoning ordinances, growth controls, esthetic reviews, and environmental impact laws. The purpose of such regulations varies, but they primarily aim to control the way structures on real property look and are used. Public boards evaluate proposed projects for compliance with applicable regulations, and modifications may be required to accommodate certain requirements. On non-tribal lands, particularly in urban areas, renewable energy projects can become delayed, modified, or canceled as land use regulations require. For example, a jurisdiction's zoning ordinance may include a height restriction that prohibits the installation of tall windmills that harness wind energy. Preservation laws might prevent the erection of solar panels on roofs or in vacant lots in historic districts. Environmental regulations may thwart the drilling of geothermal wells.

Such restrictions may not apply to renewable energy development on tribal lands. Tribal governments have sovereign authority over tribal lands, and generally exercise jurisdiction with respect to these lands exclusive of state, county, or other local governments. Although some tribes have enacted zoning ordinances to regulate the way certain parcels are used, many tribes have not adopted land

---

10 U.S. Dep't of Energy, National Renewable Energy Laboratory, Potential Solar Generation from Tribal Lands (2004), *reproduced at* http://www.harvestcleanenergy.org/conference/HCE9/Post-conference/PPT/LizanaPierce.pdf (showing a map estimating generation "using an annual average solar resource from a tilt = latitude collector" and finding total tribal solar generation potential at 17,506 billion kilowatt-hours per year, with total U.S. electric generation at 3853 billion kilowatt-hours per year).

11 *Id.* (estimating generation "assuming 5 MW/km² of installed capacity, and capacity factors ranging from 25.1% (class 4) to 41.4% (class 7))." *See also* Office of Indian Energy and Economic Development, Native American Wind Resource Atlas (2010), *available at* http://www.bia.gov/idc/groups/xieed/documents/text/idc009842.pdf (cataloguing the potential for wind energy of 29 reservations across the continental United States).

12 Cited in U.S. Dep't of Energy, Office of Energy Efficiency and Renewable Energy, Lizana K. Pierce, DOE's Tribal Energy Program Power Point Presentation (2010), *available at* http://apps1.eere.energy.gov/tribalenergy/pdfs/2_doe_tep_overview_lkp.pdf [hereinafter DOE's Tribal Energy Program Power Point Presentation].

use regulations.[13] Even where such regulations have been adopted, they may not be as effective as the same regulations on non-tribal lands, owing to limitations on tribal authority imposed by court decisions and federal statutes.[14] In certain circumstances, land owned by a tribe may be subject to state, and not tribal land use regulations.[15]

Moreover, tribes that have enacted land use regulations may be hindered in fully enforcing those regulations within reservation boundaries on non-Indian land—that is, real property within reservation boundaries that is not owned by Native American individuals or tribes. The existence of non-Indian "islands" within reservation boundaries derives largely from the Dawes General Allotment Act of 1887[16] and companion laws and policies that carved up tribal lands into individual allotments, many of which become alienable to non-Indians, and also declared any remaining tribal lands to be "surplus," and also alienable to non-Indians. Scholars have estimated that, until that practice was reversed in 1934, almost 90 million acres of land was transferred to non-Indians.[17] Today, conflicts involving tribal management of non-Indian lands within reservation boundaries endure, and the Supreme Court has been reluctant to allow tribes to regulate non-Indian activities. In an important 1981 case, *U.S. v. Montana*, the Court held that tribes may regulate non-Indians on non-Indian lands only if they have a consensual relationship with the tribe or a tribal member, or their "conduct threatens, or has some direct effect on the political integrity, the economic security, or the health and welfare of the tribe."[18] Applying *Montana* to the land use context (and contrary to at least one circuit court interpretation of *Montana*),[19] a plurality of the Court wrote in *Brendale v. Confederated Tribes & Bands of Yakima Indian Nation* that tribes should be able to impose land use regulations on only those areas within the

13 Cohen's Handbook of Federal Indian Law § 4.01(2)(c) (Nell Jessup Newton et al. eds. 2005) [hereinafter "Cohen's Handbook"] ("Many tribes are now beginning to impose land use and zoning controls similar to those adopted by non-Indian communities as a means of preserving and protecting resources.") (citations omitted).

14 *Id.* at § 21.02(5)(b) (identifying both *Brendale* and the Indian Civil Rights Act as among the potential barriers to a fully effective and enforceable zoning regime).

15 Such is the situation in the State of New York, according to two recent cases, with respect to lands relatively recently acquired by tribes. *See* Seneca-Cayuga Tribe of Okla. v. Town of Aurelius, 233 F.R.D. 278 (N.D.N.Y. 2006); Cayuga Indian Nation of N.Y. v. Vill. of Union Springs, 390 F. Supp. 2d 203 (N.D.N.Y. 2005).

16 24 Stat. 388 (1887) (codified at 25 U.S.C. § 331 et seq.).

17 *See* Cohen's Handbook, *supra* note 13, at § 1.01 & § 1.04 ("In 1887, when the Dawes Act provided for allotting tribal lands to individual Indians, the American Indian's heritage in land totaled 138 million acres. Less than 50 years later, when the allotment policy was abandoned, only 48 million acres were left in Indian hands.").

18 U.S. v. Montana, 450 U.S. 544, 565 (1981).

19 *See, e.g.*, Knight v. Shoshone & Arapahoe Indian Tribes, 670 F.2d 900, 903 (10th cir. 1982) (finding that the tribes involved in the litigation had a significant tribal interest in enacting a comprehensive land use regulation scheme within a reservation).

reservation where tribal land predominated.[20] The absence of a majority opinion in *Brendale* has created difficulties for tribes and non-tribal governments attempting to reconcile conflicting land use regulations on the ground. With this unclear and unevenly enforced land use regulatory framework, owners of renewable energy projects may find flexibility that they would not find on non-tribal lands.[21]

Developers of renewable energy may be drawn to tribal lands for the foregoing reasons. Complementing this attractiveness to developers, Native American tribes have reason to want renewable energy production and distribution on tribal lands. Many tribes have cultures and religions rooted in concern for ecological balance,[22] and renewable energy that is sensitive to environmental concerns therefore might be a fitting choice. More practically, there is the potential for revenue generation. Energy facilities' output may be harnessed by tribal governments and, in the right economic conditions, reduce operating costs spent on more traditional forms of energy procurement. Arrangements between third parties, such as leasing land or equipment, may generate other income for the tribe as a whole, and jobs may be created for individual members of tribes, related to installing, constructing, and maintaining solar panels, wind turbines, and other renewable technologies.[23]

---

20 492 U.S. 408 (1989).

21 Much has been written about the issues surrounding *Montana* and *Brendale*. For broad context of tribal sovereignty over non-Indian land within Indian country, see Cohen's Handbook, *supra* note 13, at § 6.02(2)(b). *See also* Philip P. Frickey, *A Common Law for Our Age of Colonialism: The Judicial Divestiture of Indian Tribal Authority over Nonmembers*, 109 Yale L.J. 1 (1999) (characterizing *Montana* and *Brendale* as part of an incoherent, even "chaotic," *id.* at 44, line of cases); David H. Getches, *Conquering the Cultural Frontier: The New Subjectivism of the Supreme Court in Indian Law*, 84 Cal. L. Rev. 1573 (1996) (criticizing both *Montana* and *Brendale* as being part of a trend of overly subjective interpretations of tribal sovereignty by the Supreme Court); Judith V. Royster, *The Legacy of Allotment*, 27 Ariz. St. L.J. 1 (1995) (analyzing the cases in light of federal allotment law and policy and stating: "With each succeeding decision, the Court becomes more adamant about furthering the allotment policy and less amenable to protecting, or even perceiving, tribal interests.").

22 The contours of this assertion cannot be adequately explored by this chapter, but for a more nuanced analysis, see Rebecca Tsosie, *Tribal Environmental Policy in an Era of Self-Determination: The Role of Ethics, Economics, and Traditional Ecological Knowledge*, 21 Vt. L. Rev. 225, 272–87 (1996) (providing a thorough account of indigenous land ethics). Tsosie expands upon another scholar's assertion that tribes' traditional world views include, among other important aspects, "a concept of reciprocity and balance that extends to relationships among humans, including future generations, and between humans and the natural world." *Id.* at 276 (drawing from Ronald Trosper, *Traditional American Indian Economic Policy,* 19 Amer. Indian Culture and Res. J. 65 (1995)). She goes on to explain: "The interrelationship of people and land, combined with the deeply rooted ethics of reciprocity and balance, lead to a long-term view of ecological stability or, in contemporary terms, a concern with 'sustainability.'" *Id.* at 285.

23 *See* National Wildlife Federation, The New Energy Future in Indian Country: Confronting Climate Change, Creating Jobs, and Conserving Nature 15 (2010)

Renewable energy development could also help meet the needs of the many underserved households on reservations that lack access to reliable, affordable energy, and in doing so advance the cause of "energy justice," the movement that, according to one scholar, "seeks to apply basic principles of justice as fairness to the injustice evident among people devoid of life sustaining energy."[24] In 2000, the Census gathered information showing that over 5500 tribal housing units lack access to any fuel that would provide heat.[25] The Department of Energy reported that, in 1990, one in seven households (about 16,000 in total) on tribal lands lacked access to electricity or other arrangements that would provide electricity at no cost.[26] This rate is ten times the national average.[27] Recognizing this problem, the EIA report in 2000 identified 34 reservations, pueblos, and Tribal Jurisdiction Statistical Areas with high incidences of households without electricity and projected the availability of and the costs for solar, wind, biomass, and geothermal options.[28] Any of these options would have to take the form of distributed generation—that is, small-scale production facilities located very close to the households needing service—to reach the underserved communities on tribal lands. Large, concentrated energy-generating facilities on tribal lands would not necessarily meet their needs. Of the 16,000 households counted by the Census to be without electricity in 1990, over 75 percent were on the Navajo Reservation in Arizona and New Mexico, which actually has generation and transmission facilities within reservation boundaries.[29] On the Navajo Reservation and elsewhere, the presence of more generating facilities could help bring energy to underserved and remote areas and advance the agenda of the energy justice movement.

Native Americans on tribal lands also expend a larger portion of their financial resources on electricity than the national average. In 1990, the average tribal household paid twice as much for electricity when measured by a percentage

---

available at http://www.nwf.org/News-and-Magazines/Media-Center/News-by-Topic/Global-Warming/2010/~/media/PDFs/Global%20Warming/Reports/03-23-10_NWF_Tribal Lands_LoRes.ashx (listing such jobs).

24 Lakshman Guruswamy, *Energy Justice and Sustainable Development*, 21 Colo. J. Int'l Envtl. L. & Pol'y 231, 233 (2010). *See also* Lakshman Guruswamy, *Energy Justice*, in Climate Change: A Reader (William H. Rodgers, Jr, et al. eds. 2011); Hari M. Osofsky, *Energy Justice* (draft manuscript on file with author).

25 U.S. Census Bureau, Characteristics of American Indians and Alaska Natives by Tribe and Language 2000, 110 (table 16), *available at* http://www.census.gov/prod/cen2000/phc-5-pt1.pdf.

26 Energy Consumption and Renewable Energy Development Potential on Indian Lands, *supra* note 5, at ch. 2.

27 *Id.* at app. B table B.1.A. (showing a rate of 1.4 percent for all U.S. households and a rate of 14.2 percent for households on tribal lands).

28 *Id.* at ch. 3 (measuring costs for tribal lands ranging in size from the 239-person Iowa TJSA to the 123,944-person Navajo Reservation, in 1990 population figures).

29 *Id.* at ch. 2.

of income (4 vs 2 percent).[30] Across the country, the 10 percent of households spending the highest percentage of their incomes on electric costs spent an average of 9 percent of their income for such costs; the top decile of tribal households spent an average of 20 percent of their incomes.[31] With respect to natural gas costs as a percentage of income, the highest-paying decile of tribal households spent 15 percent of their incomes on natural gas, while the national average across all deciles was a mere 2 percent.[32] Renewable energy, if controlled directly by tribes and their members, could reduce costs for those Native Americans who live on reservations.

Recognizing the potential, and driven by the concerns described above, many tribes have begun to explore renewable energy development. Yet tribes have often been stalled in developing projects by cumbersome federal review requirements and limited financial resources, among other factors. With the recent passage of the Indian Tribal Energy Development and Self-Determination Act, Congress has attempted to help tribes more easily navigate this process, although as the next section will discuss, the Act has not yet met this goal.

The Unfulfilled Promise of ITEDSA

In 2005, Congress passed ITEDSA, which increases federal support of tribal energy projects and provides a mechanism within which tribes may regulate and develop their energy resources without constant consultation with the federal government.[33] Although the act itself does not define "energy resources," the regulations enacted in 2008 define the term to include a wide range of both renewable and non-renewable resources.[34] This chapter solely concerns itself with ITEDSA's applicability to renewable resources.

As written, the law affects tribes' ability to develop renewable energy in two primary ways. First, it provides for public support of certain development activities. Two offices created after ITEDSA handle its implementation and help to encourage tribal energy development: the Division of Indian Energy Policy Development within the Indian Energy and Economic Development Office of the Department of the Interior, and the Office of Indian Energy Policy and Programs in the Department of Energy. ITEDSA also requires or allows, as applicable, the Department of the Interior and the Department of Energy to offer grants, technical

30 *Id.* at app. B table B.2.A.

31 *Id.*

32 *Id.* (showing a rate of 1.4 percent for all U.S. households and a rate of 14.2 percent for households on tribal lands).

33 25 U.S.C. §§ 3501–3506.

34 "Energy resources" means "both renewable and nonrenewable energy sources, including, but not limited to, natural gas, oil, uranium, coal, nuclear, wind, solar, geothermal, biomass, and hydrologic resources." 25 C.F.R. § 224.30.

assistance, low-interest loans, and loan guarantees to tribes.[35] Federal grants may be used for technical assistance; energy conservation programs; studies relating to acquisition of energy supplies, services, and facilities; planning, construction, development, operation, maintenance, and improvement of tribal electrical generation, transmission, and distribution; the development of a tribal energy resource inventory; and other feasibility studies.[36] The statute does not specify the amount of funding required to be provided for any of these activities.

Second, and potentially more significantly, ITEDSA expressly authorizes tribes that meet certain criteria to enter into contracts and create rights of way for renewable energy projects.[37] More specifically, it allows tribes to enter into leases or business agreements for energy resource development on tribal land without approval by the Secretary of the Interior (the "Secretary") as long as the lease or business agreement is executed pursuant to a tribal energy resource agreement (TERA); the term does not exceed 30 years; and the tribe has entered into a TERA with the Secretary.[38] It also allows tribes to grant rights of way over tribal land for electric transmission or distribution lines without approval by the Secretary if: the right of way is executed in accordance with a TERA; the term does not exceed 30 years; and the line serves an electric generation, transmission, or distribution facility on tribal land or a facility on tribal land that possesses or refines energy resources developed on tribal land; and the tribe has entered into a TERA with the Secretary.[39] When a TERA exists, the federal government disclaims liability for any losses resulting from agreements entered into pursuant to the TERA, placing all responsibilities for such losses on the tribes.[40]

ITEDSA enhances tribes' ability to take actions without the approval of the Secretary, which reduces the time spent obtaining federal approvals and undergoing federal review. Under pre-ITEDSA protocols, tribes had to receive approval from the Secretary to engage in activities such as leasing land for renewable energy infrastructure development. Modifications and cancellations of such activities also required Secretarial approval. ITEDSA allows for tribes, in effect, to be "pre-approved" for activities covered by ITEDSA, which reduces the time spent petitioning and waiting for Secretarial approval.

---

35 25 U.S.C. § 3502.

36 25 U.S.C. §§ 3502–3503.

37 For a summary of the history of federal laws dealing with tribal self-determination including ITEDSA, see Judith V. Royster, *Practical Sovereignty, Political Sovereignty, and the Indian Tribal Energy Development and Self-Determination Act*, 12 Lewis & Clark L. Rev. 1065 (2008).

38 25 U.S.C. § 3504(a).

39 25 U.S.C. § 3504(b).

40 25 U.S.C. § 3504(e)(6)(D) ("the United States shall not be liable to any party (including any Indian tribe) for any negotiated term of, or any loss resulting from the negotiated terms of, a lease, business agreement, or right-of-way executed pursuant to and in accordance with a" TERA).

Tribes may also save time by using ITEDSA to avoid having to comply with the National Environmental Policy Act (NEPA).[41] NEPA requires that, for "major federal actions significantly affecting the quality of the human environment," a lengthy study called an environmental impact statement must document the environmental impact of the action, its adverse environmental effects, and any alternatives that could reduce any adverse effects.[42] For an energy infrastructure project overseen by a federal agency, an environmental impact statement might include information about the effects of the construction on flora and fauna, wind patterns, or historic artifacts. Environmental impact statements are notoriously time-consuming and expensive to assemble and do not necessarily result in any substantive changes to the action under review, since NEPA merely requires the preparation of the statement and does not mandate any substantive results. The Secretary's entering into the TERA is subject to NEPA, with the NEPA review period running concurrently with the public comment period for the TERA.[43] However, the NEPA process is avoided once a tribe enters into a TERA, because without the Secretary's involvement in the decisions covered by a TERA, the "federal action" trigger fails to be activated. The time and money saved results, in theory, in a greater likelihood that an energy project might be undertaken.

Finalizing a TERA with the Secretary, however, may be itself a time-consuming process for tribes. The Secretary has 270 days to review a proposed TERA and is only required to approve one if the tribe has demonstrated that it has the capacity to regulate the development of tribal energy resources and if the TERA includes certain provisions. For example, among other things, the TERA must: provide a process for identifying and evaluating significant environmental effects and for identifying mitigation measures if needed; incorporate a public input phase; and allow for the Secretary's periodic review, evaluation, and feedback. In addition, it must address how leases, business agreements, or rights of way with the tribes will meet environmental laws, provide for public notification, establish a consultation process with the states, allow for the Secretary's nullification of such agreements under certain circumstances, and become effective only when a copy is delivered to the Secretary, among other things. The statute gives the Secretary the power to suspend leases, business agreements, or rights of way or rescind approval of a TERA, if she determines that the tribe is not complying with the TERA.[44]

As several scholars have noted, ITEDSA is among a new wave of federal statutes that pushes tribes toward self-governance, treating the agreements between tribes and the federal government more like treaties between sovereign nations than like the top-down, paternalistic statutes of yesteryear.[45] Even with self-governance as

41 42 U.S.C. § 4321 et seq.

42 42 U.S.C. § 4332(C)–(E).

43 25 C.F.R. § 224.70.

44 25 U.S.C. § 3504(e); 25 C.F.R. §224.10-.185.

45 *See*, *e.g.*, Alex Tallchief Skibine, *Indian Gaming and Cooperative Federalism*, 42 Ariz. St. L.J. 253, 285–87 (2010); Royster, *supra* note 37, at 1080–82.

a goal, however, the number of requirements and the extent of the TERA process have proven to be so cumbersome, and the disclaimer of all federal liability so daunting, that as of mid-2011 no tribe had successfully negotiated a TERA with the Secretary. Thus while ITEDSA has an ambitious title and important aims, in practice it has changed little.

Remaining Challenges in Developing Renewable Energy on Tribal Lands

Unfortunately, ITEDSA has failed to spur tribe-controlled renewable energy development on tribal lands. Furthermore, additional challenges remain, even as the need to address tribes' unique obstacles during the renewable energy development process have become clear. These obstacles include: insufficient public support, inability to fully utilize the same financial incentives for renewable energy as private investors, and remote location far from existing regional transmission lines.[46] Each will be discussed in turn.

Tribes often lack enough readily available capital to study and plan multi-million dollar renewable energy projects, much less construct them.[47] Typically, development involves six phases: first, a market analysis; second, a scoping analysis to determine the viability of the project; third, load and transmission studies leading to a preliminary engineering design; fourth, legal and financial commitments are obtained; fifth, construction and commissioning of the project; and sixth, the project begins operating and ongoing maintenance also begins.[48] Each of these phases can be very expensive, especially for those communities without trained technical experts who could assist with the evaluation of alternatives.

Tribes' ability to even begin the process of developing renewable energy often depends on outside financial support. A range of federal agencies, from the Department of Energy to the U.S. Environmental Protection Agency, offer grants for strategic planning, analysis, business development, job training, and construction. Between 2002 and 2010, for example, the Department of Energy's Tribal Energy Program disbursed $30.4 million in support of feasibility studies

46 National Wildlife Federation, *supra* note 23, at 16 (summarizing these obstacles).

47 Because of their unique legal status, tribal members and tribal corporations face numerous challenges accessing capital and maximizing profitability beyond the renewable energy context. For recent scholarship describing these barriers, see two related articles by Professor Gavin Clarkson: *Accredited Indians: Increasing the Flow of Private Equity into Indian Country as a Domestic Emerging Market*, 80 U. Colo. L. Rev. 285 (2009); *Wall Street Indians: Information Asymmetry and Barriers to Tribal Capital Market Access*, 12 Lewis & Clark L. Rev. 943 (2008).

48 National Renewable Energy Laboratory & the Alliance for Sustainable Energy, LLC, Douglas C. MacCourt, Renewable Energy Development in Indian Country: A Handbook for Tribes 10–11 (2010), *available at* http://www.nrel.gov/docs/fy10osti/48078.pdf.

or construction of 129 tribal projects.[49] In addition, the U.S. Department of Agriculture, the Bureau of Indian Affairs, and the U.S. Department of Housing and Urban Development offer a variety of low-interest loans and loan guarantee programs, and the American Recovery and Reinvestment Act pumped millions more into renewable energy programs, with tribal set-asides. Still, with a single solar installation alone costing several million dollars, these federal programs cannot possibly offset all costs. It is not clear how many of the 565 federally recognized tribes are currently interested in pursuing renewable energy projects, but significantly more money must be set aside for tribal development projects across the country to ensure that the tribes who do want help can get enough.

Public financial support is more important for tribes than for other groups, as tribes cannot take advantage of the same financial incentives for renewable energy as taxable private entities. Private investment in renewable energy has been spurred, in large part, by incentives such as tax credits that offset the costs of projects. The federal production tax credit, for example, gives a tax credit of 1.5 cents per each kilowatt-hour to the producer of electricity produced from wind, biomass, geothermal, solar, and other sources.[50] The federal energy investment tax credit provides a tax credit of up to 30 percent of certain costs for qualifying wind, solar, fuel cell, and other projects.[51] Tribes, however, do not pay federal taxes to which such credits would apply, and the credits are not transferable from tribes to taxable entities.

The inability to take advantage of tax credits and other incentives forces tribes eager to build renewable energy projects to make hard choices. Instead of entering into joint venture relationships, in which a tribe and non-tribal entity co-own infrastructure, tribes and tribal entities more commonly enter into leasing arrangements, in which tribes lease their land and the non-tribal entities build and own the infrastructure. As landlords, tribes must often pay state taxes on leasing income, which reduces the value of the lease. Moreover, lease terms may be longer than would otherwise be preferable so that the non-tribal entity can take advantage of tax credits or other incentives. Leases may also hinder tribes' efforts to negotiate the transmission of energy to their own people, if the non-tribal entity owning the infrastructure anticipates higher profits from non-tribal end users. Making renewable energy-related tax credits transferable, as some have suggested, would help to make partnering with non-Indian taxable entities more lucrative for tribes.

Finally, neither ITEDSA nor any other law clearly addresses the effects of energy sprawl on or beyond tribal lands. Energy sprawl, a term coined by the Nature Conservancy in 2009, refers to the amount of land occupied by energy production and the related impacts on ecosystems, habitat, and wildlife activity.[52]

49 DOE's Tribal Energy Program Power Point Presentation, *supra* note 12.

50 26 U.S.C. § 45.

51 26 U.S.C. § 48.

52 Robert I. McDonald et al., *Energy Sprawl or Energy Efficiency: Climate Policy Impacts on Natural Habitat for the United States of America*, 4 PLoS ONE 1, 1 (2009).

The Nature Conservancy measured the land-intensivity of different methods of energy production and found that even the "greenest" of technologies disturbs land, both directly and indirectly. For example, solar photovoltaic energy is estimated to disturb 37 square kilometers per terawatt-hour produced annually, while wind development is estimated to disturb 72 square kilometers per terawatt-hour.[53] Biomass, meanwhile, is estimated to disturb a startling 550 kilometers per terawatt-hour, owing to the large quantities of plant or crop material needed to produce each unit of energy.[54]

The potential for energy sprawl may actually be more significant on and near tribal lands than elsewhere. Many tribal lands are vast territories with populations living far less densely than in urban areas, so unless distributed generation is used to deploy small-scale renewable energy to smaller groups of end users, infrastructure within tribal lands must be built across long distances. For those end users off tribal lands, to whom sales may be part of the economic calculus of the project, transmission of energy from a tribal generating facility may also be space-consuming. Even if an energy project is situated at or near a border, getting energy from a tribal energy project to non-Indian end users could require extensive (not to mention expensive, at perhaps $10,000 a linear mile) transmission and distribution infrastructure.

Further compounding the energy sprawl problem, as noted above, environmental and land use controls on tribal lands may be less rigorous than in other areas. As a result, the impact of the construction of renewable energy infrastructure may go understudied, and less care may be taken in its siting. Even ITEDSA, which attempts to facilitate renewable energy projects on tribal lands, could have the unintended consequence of allowing for siting to occur in a detrimental fashion, by advancing a mechanism for tribes to avoid complying with NEPA. Although NEPA does not require the least environmentally disruptive alternative, it at least requires the documentation and consideration of environmental impacts. ITEDSA requires tribes seeking to enter into a TERA to propose a process for environmental review, but it is not clear whether this review would have to include impacts of infrastructure development on the land and ecosystems.[55]

Moving the engines of production closer to their end users is one way to reduce energy sprawl,[56] but for tribes with limited resources to invest in renewable energy, small-scale production serving small groups seems unlikely to occur. So

53 *Id.* at 4.

54 *Id.*

55 Judith Royster has identified other concerns with ITEDSA's approach to environmental review, including its public review requirements, which she feels "conflict [...] sharply with tribal self-governance." Royster, *supra* note 37, at 1086, 1090–95.

56 *See, e.g.*, Sara C. Bronin, *Curbing Energy Sprawl with Microgrids*, 43 Conn. L. Rev. 547 (2010) (recommending small-scale microgrids that produce energy to help reduce energy sprawl).

for the large-scale projects anticipated by ITEDSA, siting guidelines are needed to minimize environmental impacts.

Conclusion

As the United States pushes for more renewable energy infrastructure, tribal lands rich in opportunities for siting renewable projects must be seen as part of the solution. The current legal framework for using tribal land for renewable energy projects fails, however, to adequately address the needs of tribes and the environment. As a result, some of the land most suitable for renewable energy projects continues to lie dormant, while some land being developed for energy projects may be in jeopardy of long-term damage.

Where do we go from here? As a starting point, policy-makers should fully fund or expand existing programs giving public support to tribes for renewable energy projects and make it easier for tribes and their members to obtain grants, technical assistance, low-interest loans, and loan guarantees. The expansion of these financial incentives depends on political will and budget priorities, but a factor cutting in favor of expansion is that even moderate public subsidies of renewable energy generate significant tribal and non-tribal private investment.[57] Along the same lines, Congress and state legislatures should make renewable energy tax credits fully transferrable by tribes to taxable entities willing to pay for them.[58]

As a second step, the portions of ITEDSA that relate to tribal energy resource agreements should be reconsidered and revised. The revision process must fully involve diverse tribes, and tribal sovereignty must underlie all decisions.[59] Several key areas call for revisions. The time limit on the terms of lease and business agreements—currently 30 years—might be lengthened or abandoned. The number of days the Secretary may take to review a proposed TERA may be shortened from the current figure, 270. Perhaps most significantly, tribes and policy-makers could consider how better to allocate liability for losses related to agreements the tribes make under a TERA. A careful review of ITEDSA's TERA provisions, and

---

57 *See* Elizabeth Ann Kronk, *Alternative Energy Development in Indian Country: Lighting the Way for the Seventh Generation*, 46 Idaho L. Rev. 449 (2010) (describing barriers to renewable energy projects on tribal land and focusing on projects in the Navajo Nation, Kumeyaay Tribe, and Blackfeet Nation).

58 *See* Mark Shahinian, Note, *The Tax Man Cometh Not: How the Non-Transferability of Tax Credits Harms Indian Tribes*, 32 Am. Indian L. Rev. 267 (2007–2008) (providing a detailed argument in favor of fully transferable tax credits).

59 James M. Grijalva's chapter in this book proposes the same framework for the environmental review context. He analyzes recent attempts to adapt federal public participation regulations to the tribal context and argues that true environmental justice is possible only when tribal sovereignty underlies the adapted environmental review processes.

reforms approved by both policy-makers and tribes, would encourage tribes to take advantage of the self-determination powers granted by ITEDSA.

Finally, tribes' obligations with regard to their impact on the natural environment should be clarified in ITEDSA and other statutes. As noted above, although ITEDSA mandates an environmental review for projects subject to a TERA, the statute fails to delineate tribes' specific obligations. It also omits any siting guidelines that might reduce the negative effects of energy sprawl. Even if, in consultation with tribes, Congress changed ITEDSA to include more specific environmental review and siting procedures, such procedures would probably only apply to projects built pursuant to a TERA. Accordingly, other legislation must be drafted to account for these important priorities outside the TERA context.

This chapter, which has focused on identifying current issues regarding siting renewable energy on tribal land, concludes with these broad suggestions, while leaving the articulation of specific solutions to others. A comprehensive solution to overhaul the tax, jurisdictional, and land use laws to facilitate tribes' use of renewable energy cannot come too soon for these important projects.

Chapter 6
At the Margins: Border Tribes' Struggles to Protect Reservation Lands, Waters, and Communities

Allison M. Dussias[1]

Our people wonder what has brought you so far from your homes. ... Your people trespass upon our hunting grounds. You flock to our shores. Our waters grow warm; our lands melt like a cake of ice ... The warm wave of the white man rolls in upon us and melts us away.[2]

We have a constitutional responsibility to our tribal members, to keep them safe and to allow them to live in harmony.[3]

The lands of a number of tribes lie along, or near, the borders that divide the United States from Canada and from Mexico. The borders, and related international agreements and policies, can have profound impacts on tribal nations. The borders divided some tribes and their lands, without their consent. International agreements and national policies related to the borders may fail to take into account tribal rights and responsibilities, and impede tribes' efforts to manage and protect their lands, waters, and communities. At the same time, the U.S. government may rely on tribes for assistance in pursuing national goals. Tribal rights and responsibilities run the risk of being marginalized as the government focuses on its own agenda and on its international agreements and relationships, indifferent to their impact on tribes.

Among the tribes located near international borders that are impacted by border-related policies and agreements are the Chippewa tribes of the Great Lakes Basin and the Tohono O'odham Nation of Arizona. This chapter focuses on these tribes to explore some of the ways in which border-related agreements and issues can impact tribes' rights and responsibilities with respect to the natural resources of their homelands.

---

1 Professor of Law, New England Law, Boston.

2 Chief O-Ge-maw-ke-to, *quoted in* United States v. Michigan, 471 F. Supp. 192, 214 n.3 (1979).

3 Isidro Lopez, Vice Chairman, Tohono O'odham Nation, *quoted in* Lucinda Hughes-Juan, *Establishing Boundaries, Protecting Citizens*, Indian Country Today, Sept. 15, 2009.

The first part of the chapter analyzes Chippewa tribes' experiences with the implementation of a 1909 U.S.–Canadian agreement, the Boundary Waters Treaty, and an agreement that sprang from it, the Great Lakes Water Quality Agreement. The Chippewa tribes signed treaties reserving some lands while ceding others, subject to retained rights to hunt, fish, and harvest other resources. Despite treaty rights and the active role that the tribes accordingly play in Great Lakes Basin fisheries management, these bi-national agreements have failed to guarantee tribes a role in implementing their provisions. The second part examines the experiences of the Tohono O'odham Nation, whose Reservation is bounded on the south by the U.S.–Mexican border. While the border divides O'odham lands and communities, it also functions as a conduit for human and drug trafficking. These illegal activities, and U.S. officials' actions in response, damage reservation lands, threatening sacred and culturally significant sites and burial places and undermining tribal efforts to return to the consumption of traditional desert foods. The third part offers some concluding observations and argues that it is imperative for these tribes to have the opportunity to participate, as sovereigns and true partners, in making decisions and implementing policies that affect the resources and communities that their reservations and treaties were meant to protect.

Bordering the Grandmother's Land: Chippewa Experiences with the Boundary Waters Treaty and Great Lakes Water Quality Agreement

As governments, we expect a separate mechanism. We do not sit with organizations and businesses, but as government to government. Since you are established by your respective governments and we are governments, then we look for equal seating at whatever processes there are.[4]

The Boundary Waters Treaty and the International Joint Commission

The Boundary Waters Treaty of 1909 ("BWT") provides for joint U.S.–Canadian management of the waters along the 5000-mile border, which crosses about 150 lakes and rivers.[5] The BWT was intended to prevent disputes and settle questions regarding the use of boundary waters, defined as:

4 Public Hearing, Int'l Joint Comm'n, Int'l Lake of the Woods and Rainy River Watershed Task Force (Sept. 1, 2010) (remarks of Mike Myers, President, Network for Native Futures), http://www.ijc.org/conseil_board/rainy_river_watershed/sites/default/files/Kenora.pdf.

5 Noah D. Hall, *The Centennial of the Boundary Waters Treaty: A Century of United States–Canadian Transboundary Water Management*, 54 Wayne L. Rev. 1417, 1419–20 (2008).

> The waters ... of the lakes and rivers and connecting waterways, or the portions thereof, along which the international boundary ... passes, including all bays, arms, and inlets thereof, but not including tributary waters which in their natural channels would flow into such lakes, rivers, and waterways, or waters flowing from such lakes, rivers, and waterways, or the waters of rivers flowing across the boundary.[6]

The Parties' principal concerns were navigation and access to boundary waters. Accordingly, Article I provided that navigation of all boundary waters would remain free and open for commerce to both countries equally. Other provisions relate to the use and diversion of waters, such as Article II, which reserved to each Party control over the use and diversion of waters on its side of the border that flow across the border or into boundary waters, but ensured relief for injuries caused to the other Party. Under Article III, neither Party can use, obstruct, or divert boundary waters (other than for ordinary use for domestic and sanitary purposes) so as to affect "the natural level or flow of boundary waters on the other side of the line," without the approval of a new bi-national body, the International Joint Commission ("IJC"). Article IX empowered the IJC to investigate and report on questions and disagreements referred to it by the Parties.

Dealing with another potential source of conflict, Article VI addressed the waters of the St Mary and Milk Rivers (in Montana, Alberta, and Saskatchewan), which were to be measured and apportioned equally between the Parties, under the IJC's direction. Although water quality was not a focus of the BWT, Article IV stated that "boundary waters and waters flowing across the boundary shall not be polluted on either side to the injury of health or property on the other."

The IJC has proven to be a significant mechanism for transnational co-management and cooperation. The IJC's reports and recommendations have been used repeatedly as the basis for resolving water disputes and for new water protection policies.[7] Consequently, having a role in the IJC's work provides the opportunity to shape important decisions.

Tribes located in border states, such as the Chippewa tribes of Michigan, Minnesota, and Wisconsin, signed treaties in the nineteenth century guaranteeing their rights to continue subsistence practices, including fishing, in some cases even on lands ceded by treaty. Although the exercise of these rights can be affected by decisions as to boundary waters, tribes were ignored when the BWT was drafted and signed. Given that the BWT's key concern was navigation, it is perhaps unsurprising that tribes were not consulted, as the Parties would not have seen them as having a substantial interest in boundary waters navigation. Poverty and federal dominance in many aspects of reservation governance also stood in the way of tribes partnering with other governments in the early twentieth century. In

---

6 Boundary Waters Treaty, U.S.–Gr. Brit. (for Can.), Jan. 11, 1909, prelim. art., 36 Stat. 2448 [hereinafter BWT].

7 Hall, *supra* note 5, at 1422.

addition, although *United States v. Winans*[8] upheld tribal treaty fishing rights in 1905, other decisions upholding treaty fishing rights, including rights in the Great Lakes Basin, lay in the future. While these considerations may explain the failure, in 1909, to treat tribes as governments whose sovereignty and treaty rights are implicated by actions and decisions that affect boundary and connected waters, they cannot explain the exclusion of tribes from formal participation in the BWT regime today. As Little Traverse Bay Bands Tribal Chairman Frank Ettawageshik put it, "It's not 1909 anymore."[9]

The Continuing Exclusion of Tribes

The reach of the BWT's water management regime was expanded by later bi-national agreements, such as the Columbia River Treaty,[10] the Great Lakes Charter,[11] and (the focus here) the Great Lakes Water Quality Agreement, which also failed to include tribes as Parties. The first Great Lakes Water Quality Agreement was signed in 1972 ("1972 GLWQA"),[12] following several years of IJC-fostered study of Great Lakes water pollution.[13] The 1972 GLWQA declared the Parties' intent to prevent further pollution of the Great Lakes System, as required by Article IV of the BWT.[14] The 1972 GLWQA set objectives for Great Lakes System boundary waters' quality[15]—a matter that impacted tribes' treaty fishing rights. The IJC was given an important role in implementation, along with two new bodies, the

8 United States v. Winans, 198 U.S. 371 (1905).

9 Frank Ettawageshik, *Remarks of Tribal Chairman Frank Ettawageshik*, 54 Wayne L. Rev. 1477, 1479 (2008).

10 Treaty Relating to Cooperative Development of the Water Resources of the Columbia River Basin, Can.–U.S., Jan. 17, 1961, 15 U.S.T. 1555.

11 Council of Great Lakes Governors, Great Lakes Charter, Principles for the Management of Great Lakes Water Resources 1 (Feb. 11, 1985), *available at* http://www.cglg.org/projects/water/docs/GreatLakesCharter.pdf. The Charter was signed by the governors of Illinois, Indiana, Michigan, Minnesota, New York, Ohio, Pennsylvania, and Wisconsin and by the premiers of Ontario and Quebec. *See also* Jacqueline Phelan Hand, *Protecting the World's Largest Body of Fresh Water: The Often Overlooked Role of Indian Tribes' Co-management of the Great Lakes*, 47 Nat. Resources J. 815, 823 (2007).

12 Great Lakes Water Quality Agreement, U.S.–Can., Apr. 15, 1972, 23 U.S.T. 301 [hereinafter 1972 GLWQA].

13 Hall, *supra* note 5, at 1431.

14 1972 GLWQA, *supra* note 12, at pmbl.

15 The "Great Lakes System" is "all of the streams, rivers, lakes and other bodies of water that are within the drainage basin of the St. Lawrence River at or upstream from the point at which this river becomes the international boundary between Canada and the United States." *Id.* art. I(d). "Boundary waters of the Great Lakes System" means the boundary waters (as defined in the BWT) that are within the Great Lakes System. *Id.* art. I(a), 23 U.S.T. at 1.

Great Lakes Water Quality Board and the Research Advisory Board, which did not include tribal members.

In 1978, a new Great Lakes Water Quality Agreement ("GLWQA") was adopted to address water quality impairment caused by persistent organic chemicals and other persistent toxic substances,[16] such as mercury—a toxin that poses a grave threat to tribal fishing rights.[17] Adopting an ecosystem approach,[18] the GLWQA highlighted the goal of restoring and maintaining the integrity of the waters of the Great Lakes Basin Ecosystem: "the interacting components of air, land, water and living organisms, including man," within the drainage basin.[19] Despite embracing the holistic approach that characterizes traditional tribal relationships with the environment, the GLWQA failed to ensure a role for tribes in its implementation. None of the bodies designated to play a central role in implementation (the IJC, the Great Lakes Water Quality Board, and the new Science Advisory Board and Great Lakes Regional Office) included tribal representatives as members. The 1987 amendments to the GLWQA also failed to prescribe a formal role for Great Lakes Basin tribes. The Parties agreed to develop Remedial Action Plans ("RAPs") for designated "areas of concern" and Lakewide Management Plans for open water lakes.[20] Although the RAPs' goal of restoring "impaired beneficial uses—both ecological and cultural"[21] recognizes that environmental degradation can have cultural impacts, the entities most at risk for suffering impaired cultural (and ecological) uses were still left out as GLWQA Parties.

Tribal Water Protection and Fisheries Management Endeavors

Although they were omitted as Parties to the BWT and GLWQA and as members of bodies established under these agreements, Chippewa tribes, and other tribes whose rights are affected by decisions made under the auspices of the BWT or GLWQA, have come to play an important role in the protection and restoration of water bodies and fisheries. Tribes and intertribal organizations have launched water and fisheries protection initiatives as part of exercising treaty fishing rights. They have also participated in some aspects of the implementation of the

---

16 Great Lakes Water Quality Agreement, U.S.–Can., Nov. 22, 1978, art. II, 30 U.S.T. 1383 [hereinafter GLWQA].

17 *See* Allison M. Dussias, *Spirit Food and Sovereignty: Pathways for Protecting Indigenous Peoples' Subsistence Rights*, 59 Clev. St. L. Rev. 273, 286–87 (2010).

18 Mimi Larsen Becker, *The International Joint Commission and Public Participation: Past Experiences, Present Challenges, Future Tasks*, 33 Nat. Resources J. 235, 252 (1993).

19 GLWQA, *supra* note 16, art. I(g).

20 Protocol on Great Lakes Water Quality, Amending the 1978 Agreement Between the United States of America and Canada, U.C.–Can., Nov. 18, 1987, annex 2, T.I.A.S. No. 11551.

21 Lake Superior Binational Program, Lake Superior Lakewide Management Plan (LaMP) 2000 Summary Edition 5 (2000) [hereinafter LSBP, LaMP 2000 Summary].

BWT and GLWQA themselves, despite not being treated as full partners under these agreements.

Protecting and exercising treaty rights Under treaties signed in 1836, 1837, 1842, and 1854, covering western Lake Superior, the St Croix River, and the upper Mississippi River,[22] tribes ceded land but retained off-reservation hunting, fishing, and gathering rights. The 1836 treaty, addressing the rights of the eastern Chippewa and Ottawa bands, provided for the cession of Chippewa and Ottawa lands in the northwest quarter of Michigan's Lower Peninsula.[23] Western Chippewas (denominated the Lake Superior and Mississippi bands) ceded lands in eastern Minnesota and north-central Wisconsin (1837) and as far east as Marquette, Michigan (1842).[24] The 1854 treaty recognized reservations in Michigan's Upper Peninsula, northeastern Minnesota, and northern Wisconsin.[25] The treaties guaranteed rights to resources in the ceded territories: "[t]he privilege of hunting, fishing, and gathering the wild rice, upon the lands, the rivers, and the lakes" (1837); "the right of hunting …, with the other usual privileges of occupancy" (1842); and "the right to hunt and fish" (1854).

It took litigation to convince non-Indians that the tribes' off-reservation rights were still viable. In 1979, *United States v. Michigan* upheld the right of 1836 Treaty tribes to fish in the Great Lakes, free of state regulation of the manner or exercise of the right.[26] This litigation led to the establishment of a tribal–state cooperative management system for Great Lakes fisheries in Michigan, pursuant to a 2000 Consent Decree.[27] A 2007 Consent Decree records the current agreement

22 Jennifer G. Read, Great Lakes Fisheries Leadership Inst., Institutional Arrangements for Great Lakes Fisheries Management 33 (2003), *available at* http://www.miseagrant.umich.edu/downloads/fisheries/read_prensentation.pdf.

23 Treaty with the Ottawa, Etc., at Washington, 7 Stat. 491 (1836).

24 Treaty with the Chippewa at St. Peters, 7 Stat. 536 (1837); Treaty with the Chippewa at LaPointe, 7 Stat. 591 (1842).

25 Treaty with the Chippewa at LaPointe, 10 Stat. 1109 (1854).

26 United States v. Michigan, 471 F. Supp. 192, 281–82 (W.D. Mich. 1979) (involving the Bay Mills Indian Community, Grand Traverse Band of Ottawa and Chippewa Indians, Little River Band of Ottawa Indians, Little Traverse Bay Bands of Odawa Indians, and the Sault Ste Marie Tribe of Chippewa Indians). *See generally* Karen Ferguson, Comment, *Indian Fishing Rights: Aftermath of the* Fox *Decision and the Year 2000*, 23 Am. Indian L. Rev. 97 (1998–1999).

27 Consent Decree, United States v. Michigan, No. 2:73 CV 26 (W.D. Mich. Aug. 8, 2000), *available at* http://1836cora/pdf/2000consentdecree.pdf (governing the allocation, management, and regulation of state and tribal fisheries in the waters of Lake Huron, Lake Michigan, Lake Superior, and connecting waters that are within the areas ceded in the 1836 Treaty).

with respect to Chippewa and Ottawa treaty rights on lands and inland waters within the 1836 Treaty ceded areas.[28]

In a Wisconsin case, *Lac Courte Oreilles Band of Chippewa Indians v. Voigt* (1983), the Seventh Circuit Court of Appeals concluded that off-reservation fishing, hunting, and gathering rights included in the 1837 and 1842 treaties continued to be valid tribal property rights.[29] The scope of these rights was laid out in a series of judicial decisions,[30] which established that the Chippewa tribes could hunt, fish, and gather all natural resources using any method they wished in the ceded territory at a level that would provide a moderate living[31] and that generally tribes alone can regulate members' off-reservation hunting, fishing, and gathering rights.[32]

In Minnesota, a suit by the Grand Portage, Fond du Lac, and Bois Forte Bands of Chippewa, arguing that the tribes retained the right to hunt and fish free of state regulation in a northeastern Minnesota area ceded under the 1854 Treaty, resulted in a 1988 settlement agreement providing that tribes would regulate members' harvest activities in the ceded area.[33] The Supreme Court ultimately addressed Minnesota off-reservation treaty rights in *Mille Lacs Band of Chippewa Indians v. Minnesota* (1999),[34] in which the Court upheld tribal harvest rights (to be exercised largely free of state regulation) in the area ceded by the 1837 Treaty, a conclusion that also affected other 1837 Treaty tribes.[35]

Tribes in Michigan, Minnesota, and Wisconsin play an important role in water and fisheries protection through activities related to management of resources covered by treaty rights upheld in the litigation described above. The exercise of the off-reservation treaty rights in Great Lakes Basin fisheries is facilitated

---

28 Consent Decree, United States v. Michigan, No. 2:73 CV 26 (W.D. Mich 2007), *available at* http://www.1836cora.org/documents/2007InlandConsentDecree.pdf.

29 Lac Courte Oreilles Band of Lake Superior Chippewa Indians v. Voigt, 700 F.2d 341 (7th cir. 1983), *cert. denied*, 464 U.S. 805 (1983).

30 Charles F. Wilkinson, *To Feel the Summer in the Spring: The Treaty Fishing Rights of the Wisconsin Chippewa*, 1991 Wis. L. Rev. 375, 399–402 (1991). *See also* Kenneth D. Nelson, Comment, *Wisconsin, Walleye, and the Supreme Law of the Land: An Overview of the Chippewa Indian Treaty Rights Dispute in Northern Wisconsin*, 11 Hamline J. Pub. L. & Pol'y 381, 386–403 (1990).

31 Lac Courte Oreilles Band of Lake Superior Chippewa Indians v. Wisconsin, 653 F. Supp. 1420, 1426–28, 1434, 1435 (W.D. Wis. 1987).

32 Lac Courte Oreilles Band of Lake Superior Chippewa Indians v. Wisconsin, 668 F. Supp. 1233, 1240, 1241 (W.D. Wis. 1987).

33 Minnesota Dep't of Natural Resources, Laws and Treaties, 1854 Treaty, Legal History, http://www.dnr.state.mn.us/aboutdnr/laws_treaties/1854/litigation.html.

34 Minnesota v. Mille Lacs Band of Chippewa Indians, 526 U.S. 172 (1999).

35 The other tribes (which had joined the lawsuit) were the Fond du Lac Band (Minnesota) and the Bad River, Lac du Flambeau, Lac Courte Oreilles, Red Cliff, and St. Croix Bands and the Sokaogon Chippewa Community (Wisconsin). *Mille Lacs*, 526 U.S. at 186 n. 2.

by intertribal organizations such as the Chippewa Ottawa Resource Authority ("CORA"), the Great Lakes Indian Fish and Wildlife Commission ("GLIFWC"), and the 1854 Treaty Authority. CORA regulates the exercise of the treaty fishing rights of five Michigan tribes. Separate committees oversee Great Lakes and inland matters, with the Great Lakes Resource Committee managing the 1836 Treaty fishery and the Inland Lands and Waters Resources Committee overseeing inland resource matters.[36] GLIFWC represents eleven Michigan, Minnesota, and Wisconsin signatories of the 1836, 1837, 1842, and 1854 Treaties. It provides members with services related to natural resource management and conservation; legal and policy analysis; public education; and intergovernmental relations.[37] The 1854 Treaty Authority implements the 1854 Treaty rights settlement agreement with Minnesota for the Grand Portage and Bois Forte Bands and has established regulations for the commercial harvest of resources, spearing, and netting. The Treaty Authority also plays an important role in monitoring and habitat protection.[38]

In summary, tribes and intertribal organizations diligently work to protect the lands and waters of their reservations and other lands in which they hold treaty rights. These efforts can be undermined by decisions made under the BWT and GLWQA without tribal input and consent.

Participating in BWT and GLWQA activities and programs: IJC public comment submissions Article XII of the BWT directs the IJC to give all interested parties a "convenient opportunity to be heard" on all matters under consideration. Tribes, as parties with rights at stake when the IJC and other entities created under the BWT make decisions, have accordingly submitted comments on pending matters of interest to them. In 2006, for example, the St Regis Mohawk Tribe, whose lands along the St Lawrence River are divided by the U.S.–Canadian border, commented on the final report of the Lake Ontario and St Lawrence River Study Board, formed by the IJC to evaluate the environmental impacts of water level changes. The report presented three options for managing water levels and flows. The Tribe wrote in support of Plan B+, the "Balanced Environmental Plan," which would promote improvement in wetland meadow marsh communities, thus enhancing fish and wildlife habitats and making planned restoration projects more

---

36 Chippewa Ottawa Resource Authority, http://www.1836cora.org/index.php. The member tribes are the Bay Mills Indian Community, Grand Traverse Band of Ottawa and Chippewa Indians, Little River Band of Ottawa Indians, Little Traverse Bay Bands of Odawa Indians, and Sault Ste Marie Tribe of Chippewa Indians.

37 Read, *supra* note 22, at 33. The member tribes are the Bay Mills Indian Community, Keweenaw Bay Indian Community, and Lac Vieux Desert Band (Michigan); the Fond du Lac and Mille Lacs Bands (Minnesota); and the Bad River, Lac Courte Oreilles, Lac du Flambeau, Red Cliff, and St Croix Bands and Sokaogon Chippewa Community (Wisconsin). *Id.* n. 2.

38 1854 Treaty Authority, General Information, Organizational Information, http://www.1854treatyauthority.org/about/history.htm.

feasible.[39] The Tribe knew that the IJC's decision on water levels and flows would have a major impact on tribal projects to address damage from industrial release of hazardous substances. The U.S. Fish and Wildlife Service ("USFWS") agreed that Plan B+ was the best option.[40]

The IJC nevertheless ultimately backed "Plan 2007," a variant of a plan that the Tribe had concluded offered the least environmental benefits. The IJC stated that it was "impossible" to adopt Plan B+ "without unduly reducing the benefits and protections currently accorded to other interests."[41] Opposition to Plan 2007 ultimately led the IJC to conclude that a new proposal, based on restoring more natural water flows, was needed.[42] A working group (devoid of tribal representation) continues to work on developing a new proposal.[43]

The St Regis Mohawk Tribe's experience shows that, while tribes are willing to take part in the IJC's public review process, there is no guarantee that their views will be respected. Moreover, there is a profound difference between contributing to policy development as a member of the public and participating as an interested government, with a right and duty to participate as such. Because tribes are political entities whose peers are other governments, limiting them to public participation mechanisms fails to respect their governmental status and treaty rights.

Tribes' meaningful participation, as tribes, is critical not only because of their status and treaty rights, but also because of the very nature of the BWT and GLWQA regime, which seeks to bring together interested governments to protect boundary and related waters, recognizing their right, and power, to participate in making decisions that could affect their territory. Great Lakes Basin tribes clearly are interested governments. Some tribes have reservations bordering the Great Lakes or have Great Lakes fishing rights, while others have reservations elsewhere within the Basin that touch waters that are part of the watershed. Tribal governments have power to regulate tribal members' on-reservation and off-reservation conduct related to water, including fishing. Some tribes carry out federal Clean Water Act programs on their reservations.[44] Tribal governments' authority over water use and other conduct that affects water establishes that they should be included among

---

39 Letter from James W. Ransom, Chief, and Lorraine M. White, Chief, Saint Regis Mohawk Tribe, to Secretary, U.S. Section, Int'l Joint Comm'n (Sept. 15, 2006), *available at* www.ijc.org/en/activities/losl/documents/2006_09_15_Ransom_White.pdf.

40 *Id.*

41 Int'l Joint Comm'n, Your Guide to the IJC's Proposed New Order of Approval and Plan 2007 at 4, *available at* http://www.ijc.org/LOSLdocuments/pdf/LOSL_guide_e.pdf.

42 Letter from Irene Brooks, Chair, U.S. Section, Int'l Joint Comm'n, to Condoleezza Rice, U.S. Sec'y of State (Sept. 4, 2008), *available at* http://www.ijc.org/en/activities/losl/documents/ 2008_09_04_Rice_Emerson.pdf.

43 *See, e.g.*, Int'l Joint Comm'n, Lake Ontario–St. Lawrence River Working Group Holds Sixth Meeting (Feb. 17, 2011), http://www.ijc.org/rel/news/2011/110221_e.htm.

44 *See generally* Dussias, *supra* note 17, at 313–32 (discussing tribal water regulation under the auspices of the Clean Water Act).

the governments that develop water policy under the BWT and its progeny, rather than be regarded simply as members of the public. Moreover, ensuring tribes' participation as such recognizes the importance of input from all entities that may be looked to as partners in water protection, which will be more invested in working to implement policies that they have helped to develop.

Participating in BWT and GLWQA activities and programs: GLWQA program implementation Some Great Lakes Basin tribes and intertribal organizations have carved out a role in GLWQA implementation, especially as to fisheries protection, that is more in keeping with tribal rights and status. A number of tribes have become member agencies of the GLWQA's Binational Program to Restore and Protect Lake Superior.[45] The Lake Superior Lakewide Management Plan ("L.S. LaMP") assesses the state of the Lake Superior ecosystem and identifies actions required to achieve goals and targets set by the L.S. LaMP, which the Program's member agencies implement. Management decisions are made by the Lake Superior Task Force, composed of U.S. and Canadian federal, provincial, state, and tribal representatives. The Program's publications have acknowledged that culture affects what is at stake for tribes in protecting the Lake Superior ecosystem: "Native Americans/First nations are one cultural group at increased risk of exposure to environmental contaminants. Because this group has a strong relationship with its physical environment through spiritual, medicinal, hunting, gathering and fishing traditions, its population has a higher potential for exposure."[46] Tribes also participate in the volunteer Lake Superior Binational Forum[47] and have been leaders in initiatives under the L.S. LaMP. Tribes and tribal organizations have been involved in the development and implementation of Lake Superior Remedial Action Plans, designed to restore specific impaired beneficial uses (ecological and cultural) in degraded areas (called "Areas of Concern") within the Great Lakes Basin.[48]

The GLIFWC has taken the lead in a fish consumption study and in projects to control invasive plants[49] and to identify lake sturgeon spawning habitat and juvenile lake sturgeon habitat requirements.[50] The Chippewa/Ottawa Treaty Fishery Management Authority (CORA's predecessor) acted as a lead agency on lake trout rehabilitation projects. The Red Cliff Fisheries Department has also

45 The tribes are the Keweenaw Bay Indian Community (Michigan); the Fond du Lac Band and Grand Portage Band of Lake Superior Chippewa (Minnesota); and the Bad River Band and Red Cliff Band of Lake Superior Chippewa (Wisconsin). LSBP, LAMP 2000 SUMMARY, *supra* note 21, at i.

46 *Id.* at 19.

47 *Id.* at 7.

48 LAKE SUPERIOR BINATIONAL PROGRAM, LAKE SUPERIOR LAKEWIDE MANAGEMENT PLAN (LAMP) 1–9 (2008) [hereinafter LSBP, LAMP 2008].

49 LSBP, LAMP 2000 SUMMARY, *supra* note 21, at 22 & 28.

50 *Id.* at 38.

worked on projects focused on lake trout and lake sturgeon rehabilitation.[51] The Bad River Band partnered with the USFWS on a project studying obstacles to lake sturgeons' trip up the White River to spawn.[52]

The Grand Portage Band and the Red Cliff Band have participated, along with federal agencies, in efforts aimed at rehabilitation and stocking of coaster brook trout, including conducting a survey of trout in Lake Superior waters along their reservations.[53] The GLIFWC and the Keweenaw Bay Indian Community, along with the USFWS and the Michigan Department of Natural Resources, conducted a project to assess stocking efforts and the status of Lake Superior sturgeon.[54] The Fond du Lac Band's Resource Management Division launched a hydrologic study and restoration activities and has developed a management plan for habitat restoration.[55]

> Tribes and tribal organizations have also been involved in management activities related to Lake Michigan, such as the implementation of the Lake Michigan Lakewide Management Plan ("L.M. LaMP").[56] Tribal activities aimed at supporting the L.M. LaMP's goals, such as the recovery of the lake sturgeon population, include a sturgeon rearing program operated by the Little River Band of Ottawa Indians.[57] Tribes serve as members of the Lake Michigan Management Committee, which oversees development and implementation of the L.M. LaMP.[58]
>
> The work of the Lake Huron Binational Partnership has also benefited from tribal participation. While tribes and First Nations are not viewed as part of the "core" of the Lake Huron Binational Partnership, they are included on an issue-by-issue basis under the Partnership's "flexible membership" concept.[59] CORA has participated in activities of the Partnership, such as projects to assess and rehabilitate lake trout and cisco and to survey the fish community of the St. Mary's River.[60]

Tribes and tribal organizations have proven, particularly through work on fisheries management, that they can make invaluable contributions to efforts to preserve and restore the Great Lakes Basin environment. It seems absurd that

---

51 *Id.*

52 LSBP, LaMP 2008, *supra* note 48, at 6–22.

53 *Id.* at 6–20.

54 *Id.* at 6–23.

55 *Id.* at 6–10.

56 Lake Michigan Lakewide Management Plan (LaMP) 2008 9–3 & 10–1.

57 *Id.* at 4–12.

58 *Id.* at G-3.

59 Lake Huron Binational Partnership 2008–2010 Action Plan 1 (2008).

60 *Id.* at 66 & 74.

tribes are active in management of the waters and fisheries of the Great Lakes Basin, through their own efforts related to exercising treaty rights and through participation in some GLWQA programs, yet are not recognized as entities that should be parties to the agreements aimed at managing waters in which they have a strong interest and have treaty rights. Moreover, there is no assurance that tribes will continue to be included in GLWQA implementation endeavors, given that they are not GLWQA Parties. This is the nonsensical situation facing Great Lakes Basin Chippewa tribes today.

Down Mexico Way: The Experiences of the Tohono O'odham Nation

> *We are older than the international boundary with Mexico and had no role in creating it. But our land is now cut in half, with O'odham communities, sacred sites, salt pilgrimage routes, and families divided. We did not cross the 75 miles of border within our reservation lands. The border crossed us. And the border comes at a price.*[61]

The reservation of the 28,000-member Tohono O'odham Nation (historically referred to by outsiders as the Papago Tribe) contains 75 miles of the U.S.–Mexican border in southwestern Arizona. The Tribe is concerned about the border's impact on the Tribe's members, who need to cross the border to visit family and friends residing on the other side, as well as to visit sacred sites and participate in cultural activities. Since September 11, 2001, a passage that was once hassle-free is so no longer, and a border fence has created a physical barrier between the Tribe's U.S. and Mexican members.

At the same time, the Tribe is concerned about threats posed by outsiders, who engage in human and drug trafficking on Reservation lands, taking advantage of the main Reservation's border location, size, and remoteness to carry out their illegal activities. The United States shares this concern and has turned to the Tribe for assistance with border security. U.S. officials have noted that the "Tohono O'odham Nation is committed to doing its part by working with federal authorities to protect the U.S. homeland," described the United States and the Tribe as partners in security endeavors, and touted "the mutual commitment of the DHS and the Tohono O'odham Nation to enhance border security and

61 *Walls and Waivers: Expedited Construction of the Southern Border Wall and Collateral Impacts to Communities and the Environment: Joint Oversight Field Hrg. Before the Subcomm. on Nat'l Parks, Forests & Public Lands and the Subcomm. on Fisheries, Wildlife and Oceans of the H.R. Comm. on Natural Resources*, 110th Cong. 31 (2008) (testimony of Ned Norris, Jr., Chairman, Tohono O'odham Nation) [hereinafter Norris 2008 Testimony].

combat threats of terrorism and transnational crime."[62] The Tribe participates in the Homeland Security Advisory Council Southwest Border Task Force[63] and members serve in the Shadow Wolves, an elite unit of patrol officers who have worked since the 1970s with U.S. Immigration and Customs Enforcement and U.S. Customs and Border Protection ("CBP") to help identify and track traffickers on the Tribe's lands.[64] Both the illegal activities and the efforts to combat them have raised another pressing issue for the Tribe: how to deal with the consequent environmental and cultural damage.

The Tohono O'odham Nation and Reservation

The Tohono O'odham Reservation today comprises four non-contiguous parcels embracing over 2.8 million acres in Arizona's Sonoran Desert. The main, 2.7 million acre parcel, located along the border, was established as a reservation by executive orders in 1916 and 1917.[65] Most of the Reservation land consists of natural desert and open range, with small villages and family compounds.[66] The Tribe's name, meaning "Desert People," reflects the landscape.[67]

O'odham aboriginal lands extended north to the Gila River, south to the Gulf of California, east to the San Pedro River, and west to the Colorado River. In this arid territory, productive resources were spread thinly and migration over a large area was a necessary part of life.[68] Tribal members were accustomed to travelling freely on paths that cross what is today considered an international border, to harvest resources and participate in the annual round of traditional ceremonies.[69]

62 Dep't of Homeland Security, Department of Homeland Security and Tohono O'odham Nation Announce Agreement to Develop Enhanced Tribal Card (Nov. 3, 2009), http://www.dhs.gov/ynews/releases/pr_1257272243349.shtm.

63 Dep't of Homeland Security, Secretary Napolitano Announces Southwest Border Task Force (June 4, 2009), http://www.dhs.gov/ynews/releases/pr_1244145382319.shtm.

64 George A. Van Otten & Juana C. Jose, *Social, Cultural, and Economic Manifestations of Illegal Immigration and Smuggling on the Tohono O'odham Reservation*, J. Homeland Sec. 8 (Feb. 2009), http://www.homelandsecurity.org/journal/BrowseArticles.aspx?catid=1.

65 Exec. Order No. 2524 (Feb. 1, 1917) & Exec. Order No. 2300 (Jan. 14, 1916). Land had previously been reserved for the Tribe at San Xavier (1874) and Gila Bend (1882). Papago Tribe v. United States, 19 Ind. Cl. Comm. 394 (1968).

66 Van Otten & Jose, *supra* note 64, at 3.

67 Tohono O'odham Nation, http://www.tonation-nsn.gov/.

68 Sara Singleton, Not Our Borders: Indigenous People and the Struggle to Maintain Shared Lives and Cultures in Post-9/11 North America 4 (Border Policy Research Institute Working Paper No. 4, Jan. 2009), *available at* http://www.wwu.edu/bpri/files/2009_Jan_WP_No_4.pdf.

69 *Id.* at 5.

The Gadsden Purchase of 1854, creating the present U.S.–Mexican boundary, ignored tribal sovereignty by dividing O'odham territory without consent.[70]

The length of the Reservation's southern border, coupled with the remote character of the Reservation, renders the Reservation vulnerable to illegal cross-border activities. This vulnerability has been exacerbated by unilateral U.S. government decisions. Officials decided to focus on closing down what they viewed as key points of entry and on bolstering manpower and resources at places like San Diego, Yuma, and El Paso, which had the effect of displacing human and drug trafficking to other, more sparsely populated areas, with inhospitable conditions for these activities,[71] such as the Tohono O'odham Reservation.[72] Expansion of illegal activities has led to a corresponding increase in security and environmental problems on the Reservation. Consequently, while the United States focuses on the Reservation's southern border as a U.S. security risk, the Tribe also sees the border as not only a barrier to tribal unity, but also as a funnel for environmentally and culturally harmful activities.

The costs of decisions by U.S. government officials that turn the Reservation into a conduit for human and drug trafficking are borne by the Tribe, while the United States itself reaps the benefits of (allegedly) enhanced border security. As one commentator has explained, whatever *benefits* accrue from tightened border security take the form of a public good—the benefits are available to all and are roughly equal in value for everyone. The *costs* of increased border security, however, are distributed asymmetrically, raising questions of fundamental fairness.[73]

The Impact of the Reservation's Border Location

The environmental impact of illegal activities The funneling of illegal drug trafficking to the Tohono O'odham Reservation led to the Reservation becoming second only to Nogales, Arizona in terms of the quantities of drugs smuggled across the border.[74] In 2009, for example, a record 319,000 pounds of marijuana were seized on the Reservation from drug traffickers. Drug smuggling scouts hide out on the Reservation to monitor the movement of U.S. Border Patrol ("USBP")

---

70 *Border Infrastructure and Technology Integration Act: Hearing on S.2295 Before the Senate Comm. on Commerce*, (June 17, 2004) (testimony of Ned Norris, Jr., Vice-Chairman, Tohono O'odham Nation), *available at* http://www.usborderpatrol.com/Border-Patrol704_X.htm [hereinafter Norris 2004 Testimony]. *See also* Gloria Valencia-Weber & Antoinette Sedillo Lopez, *Stories in Mexico and the United States About the Border: The Rhetoric and the Realities*, 5 INTERCULTURAL HUM. RTS. L. REV. 241, 262–66, 291–304 (2010) (discussing the formation of the border and issues related to the division of the Tohono O'odham Nation).

71 Singleton, *supra* note 68, at 5.

72 Norris 2004 Testimony, *supra* note 70.

73 Singleton, *supra* note 68, at 2–3.

74 *Id.* at 6.

agents, causing tribal members to long for a return to the days when they could walk on the Reservation without fear and without the disruptions caused by drug smugglers (and USBP agents).[75] The statistics on the extent of illegal migration and human trafficking through Reservation lands are also staggering. In some years, about 1500 undocumented migrants have crossed the Reservation every day.[76] Tribal members' homes are broken into by migrants searching for food, water, and money.[77]

Migrants and human traffickers leave behind bottles, clothing, backpacks, food containers, and other items on the Reservation. Struggling to survive while crossing a harsh landscape in searing heat, migrants leave behind anything that they no longer need, or can no longer carry, along their route, then often abandon anything that they are still carrying once they reach a planned pick-up point.[78] In 2004, for example, six tons of trash was left each day by undocumented migrants, which contributed to the 113 open pit dumps on the Reservation.[79] Five years later, estimates placed the daily trash accumulation at one ton per day, left by several hundred migrants.[80] Human waste is also left behind by migrants and traffickers.[81]

Traffickers even abandon automobiles. In one eighteen-month period, 2675 abandoned vehicles were found, of which 303 had been stolen.[82] The result of all of this activity is a reservation landscape that is littered with trash, vehicles, and human waste, creating hazards (including infectious disease risks) to wildlife, domestic animals, and tribal members.[83] Environmental damage to sacred sites, burial grounds, and sensitive vegetation also results from the creation of roads for trafficking activities and from off-road driving.[84]

Most disturbing of all, dozens of corpses are found on the Reservation each year. In July 2010 alone, 44 people died while trying to cross the Reservation. The Tribe is left to pay for burial and autopsy costs resulting from these tragedies.[85]

---

75 Eric Eckholm, *In Drug War, Tribe Feels Invaded by Both Sides*, N.Y. Times, Jan. 24, 2010, at A1. The USBP is the law enforcement component of the CBP.

76 Singleton, *supra* note 68, at 6.

77 *Id.*

78 Good Neighbor Environmental Board, A Blueprint for Action on the U.S.–Mexico Border 40 (2010) [hereinafter GNEB 2010 Report].

79 Norris 2004 Testimony, *supra* note 70.

80 GNEB 2010 Report, *supra* note 78, at 40.

81 Van Otten & Jose, *supra* note 64.

82 *Id.* (Jan. 2003–June 2004).

83 GNEB 2010 Report, *supra* note 78, at 40.

84 Good Neighbor Environmental Board, Air Quality and Transportation & Cultural and Natural Resources 39 (2009).

85 Amanda Lee Myers & Julie Watson, *Migrants: Crossing is Worth the Risk*, Chi. Daily Herald, Sept. 5, 2010, at 25; Norris 2004 Testimony, *supra* note 70 (noting that an autopsy costs $1400).

Tribal authorities and residents of Reservation villages and ranches each year incur significant costs, in both time and money, in dealing with waste left on the Reservation. Tribal agencies also must cope with needs for services that arise from illegal activities. Each year, the Tribe spends $3 million of its limited law enforcement funds on efforts to secure the border—a matter that is a *federal* obligation.[86] Health care costs for undocumented migrants (about $2 million annually) have been paid for out of Indian Health Care funding intended for tribal members, putting a strain on tribal health care.[87]

Environmental damage caused by U.S. government activities The wellbeing of Reservation communities is also threatened by the actions of U.S. government employees and contractors, whose presence has changed the character of parts of the Reservation, transforming them into areas "bristling with weapons, new roads, spotlights and military surveillance vehicles."[88] A concrete fence to block cars and a barbed wire fence to block foot traffic now cut across Reservation land. CBP agents search the Reservation, man roadside checkpoints, and patrol by air and all-terrain vehicles.[89] Agents have camped on sacred sites, such as the Baboquivari Peaks, which the O'odham regard as the home of the I'itoi, the creator, and left trash behind.[90]

The U.S. government's determination to subordinate everything to the objective of improved border security is made clear by the statutory grant of authority to the Secretary of the Department of Homeland Security ("DHS") to waive all legal requirements, including provisions of environmental and cultural resource protection statutes, to expedite construction of border security infrastructure.[91] In 2008, DHS Secretary Michael Chertoff waived requirements under 36 statutes with respect to 470 miles of the border, on which border barriers were to be installed.[92] Although this stretch of the border included 55 miles on the Reservation, the Tribe was not consulted.[93] Among the statutes waived were the Archaeological Resources Protection Act, the Native American Graves Protection

---

86 Norris 2008 Testimony, *supra* note 61, at 30; Dep't of Homeland Security, Dep't of Homeland Security Missions and Responsibilities, http://www.dhs.gov/xabout/responsibilities.shtm#two (responsibility of the DHS to "secure and manage" U.S. borders).

87 Norris 2004 Testimony, *supra* note 70.

88 Singleton, *supra* note 68, at 5.

89 Lee Rood, *Arizona's Border Tighter, Arrests Down, But at a Cost*, Des Moines Register, Sept. 12, 2010, at A1.

90 Brenda Norrell, *Indigenous Border Summit Opposes Border Wall and Militarization* 5, *in* Citizen Action in the Americas 5 (Oct. 2006).

91 REAL ID Act, Pub. L. No. 109-13, sec. 102, 119 Stat. 302, 306 (May 11, 2005) (amending the Illegal Immigration Reform and Immigrant Responsibility Act of 1996 (8 U.S.C. sec. 1103 note) and granting the DHS Secretary authority to waive "all legal requirements").

92 73 Fed. Reg. 18,293 (Apr. 3, 2008).

93 Norris 2008 Testimony, *supra* note 61, at 31.

and Repatriation Act, and the American Indian Religious Freedom Act. The waiver covered the construction of roads and barriers and of various kinds of detection equipment, as well as their upkeep once constructed.

Secretary Chertoff claimed that it was the DHS's goal to "implement measures to minimize the effects of construction on cultural, biological and natural resources wherever possible."[94] The DHS has a poor track record of keeping such commitments, however, as exemplified by a 2007 incident. The Tribe objected to construction methods being used within a jaguar habitat near the Reservation's eastern border. The CBP said that the project would be postponed for two weeks for additional review yet nonetheless proceeded with construction a few days later. Bird kills, in violation of the Migratory Bird Treaty Act, have occurred at border construction sites when contractors failed to cap bollards. The Tribe had approved the construction of barriers that would block illegal vehicle traffic but not harm animal migration.[95]

Border construction projects have even damaged burial sites. After environmental assessments on O'odham ancestral lands identified the location of archaeological sites, barriers and the border road nonetheless were built over an area in which fragments of human remains were found in tire tracks left by heavy equipment.[96] Fence construction activities in the San Pedro River valley, which lies within the Tribe's ancestral territory, have uncovered human remains and artifacts of the Hohokam. Tribal Chairman Ned Norris has explained the impact of burial site destruction of in appropriately stark terms: "Imagine a bulldozer parking in your family graveyard, turning up bones. This is our reality."[97]

Even if the DHS were willing to follow cultural resource protection laws, the agency may well have a different sense of what mitigation-focused activity is appropriate. In the case of the border barrier, Secretary Chertoff boasted of the funding of some excavations along the construction route "to allow archaeologists to gather information about pre-historic and Native American culture"[98] without acknowledging that this would provide little satisfaction to those who view any grave disturbance as desecration.

While damage caused by migrants and by human and drug traffickers can be understood as the actions of individuals with no relationship with, and owing no responsibilities to, the Tribe, the situation is different where government conduct is concerned. The United States has a government-to-government relationship with,

---

94 Dep't of Homeland Security, *Statement of Secretary Michael Chertoff Regarding Exercise of Waiver Authority* (Apr. 1, 2008), http://www.dhs.gov/xnews/releases/pr_1207083685391.shtm [hereinafter Chertoff Statement].

95 Norris 2008 Testimony, *supra* note 61, at 32.

96 *Id.* at 30.

97 *Id.* at 32.

98 Chertoff Statement, *supra* note 94.

and a trust obligation toward, the Tribe and its land.[99] Tribal officials have long complained of the DHS's failure to appropriately consult the Tribe and reimburse it for expenditures made to deal with border security-related problems. Federal officials have, the Tribe contends, failed to respond properly to the Tribe's funding needs and its responsibility and right to act as a partner (rather than a subordinate) in planning and implementing border security programs.[100]

In commenting on plans to construct the border barrier, Secretary Chertoff noted that the DHS held meetings with Native American tribes as part of its efforts to provide "all interested stakeholders the opportunity to provide input and comments regarding proposed projects."[101] Tribes, however, should be treated *as governments*, with the right to be consulted as such, rather than simply being treated as "stakeholders" on a par with local landowners and other community members. This failure to afford tribes treatment commensurate with their status is a mistake repeated by other federal agencies, such as the Department of the Interior ("DOI"). Tribal Chairman Ned Norris has noted that the DOI also has jurisdiction over the border and is mandated by Executive Order 13,175 to recognize tribes' "inherent powers over their members and territory." Although the DOI initially admitted that it could not endorse the DHS's border infrastructure proposal because of obligations under the Wilderness Act and other statutes, the DOI ultimately supported Chertoff's use of his waiver power. The DOI never consulted tribal officials before, as Chairman Norris put it, "turning its back on the Nation [and] the land it is sworn to protect."[102] Moreover, when the DHS wanted to increase its presence on the Tribe's lands, the BIA, without consulting the Tribe, gave the DHS permission to do so.[103]

Land use and traditional foods The threats to tribal lands and communities caused by illegal activities and by the efforts to combat them are occurring at a time when the Tribe is trying to address another serious threat to the Tribe's wellbeing: the high incidence of non-insulin-dependent diabetes mellitus (commonly referred to as type II diabetes) among tribal members. The key to solving this problem may lie in a return to the consumption of desert plants, both cultivated and wild, that sustained the Tribe for many generations.

The Tribe's roots in the Sonoran Desert homeland run deep. Thousands of years ago, the Hohokam people settled along the Salt, Gila, and Santa Cruz Rivers and grew cotton, tobacco, corn, beans, and squash, irrigated by sophisticated canal systems. Following in Hohokam footsteps, the Tohono O'odham established

99 The Tribe's ongoing breach of trust case against the United States indicates that this is not the only context in which the United States has failed to live up to its trust responsibilities. United States v. Tohono O'odham Nation, 131 S. Ct. 1723 (2011).

100 Singleton, *supra* note 68, at 6.

101 Chertoff Statement, *supra* note 94.

102 Norris 2008 Testimony, *supra* note 61, at 32.

103 *Id.* at 44.

planting, harvesting, and ceremonial cycles, along with complex systems for storing and delivering water. They developed a seasonal settlement pattern adapted to the environment, migrating during warm weather to cooler homes in the mountains from homes in the valleys, where crops were raised near washes.[104] Their diet historically included cultivated crops such as brown and white tepary beans; varieties of cantaloupes, squash, and watermelon that were adapted to the arid environment; and white-kernel corn (nutritionally superior to yellow sweet corn). They also harvested plant foods from the desert, such as cholla buds, prickly pear fruit, saguaro fruit, and mesquite bean pods.[105] The metabolism of the O'odham was well adapted to these crops and desert foods, which helped to control blood sugar levels and to increase insulin sensitivity.[106]

Over the course of the twentieth century, nutritionally inferior processed foods and other Western dietary staples, some supplied by the government as surplus commodities, replaced traditional foods in the O'odham diet.[107] The Bureau of Indian Affairs encouraged tribal members to take jobs as laborers in off-reservation cotton fields rather than growing food crops on the Reservation.[108] Extensive groundwater pumping after World War II, to satisfy Tucson's growing water demands, reduced the river flooding and runoff that were needed for crop irrigation.[109] As the highly processed, low-fiber grains and fat-laden meats of the Western diet replaced traditional foods, which are high in fiber and complex carbohydrates, the incidence of type II diabetes soared, leading to the Tribe having the highest rate of diabetes in the United States. Today, more than half of tribal members develop the disease.[110]

---

104 Tohono O'odham Nation, History & Culture, Tohono O'odham History, http://www.tonation-nsn.gov/ton_history.aspx.

105 David Rich Lewis, Neither Wolf Nor Dog: American Indians, Environment, & Agrarian Change 125 (1997).

106 Daniel Lopez et al., Tohono O'odham Cmty. Action & Tohono O'odham Cmty. Coll., Community Attitudes Toward Traditional Tohono O'odham Foods 10 (2002), *available at* http://www.safs.msu.edu/culturaldiv/Tohono%20%27odham%20Foods.pdf.

107 *Id.* at 9; David V. Fazzino II, *Whose Food Security? Confronting Expanding Commodity Production and the Obesity and Diabetes Epidemics*, 15 Drake J. Agric. L. 409–10 (2010). *See also generally* Michael P. Milburn, *Indigenous Nutrition: Using Traditional Food Knowledge to Solve Contemporary Health Problems*, 28 Am. Indian Q. 411 (2004) (discussing Western and traditional indigenous dietary patterns and their health implications).

108 Charles Wilkinson, *Filling in the Blank Spots on Powell's and Stegner's Maps: The Role of Modern Indian Tribes in Western Watersheds*, 23 J. Land Resources & Envtl. L. 41, 54 (2003).

109 *Id.*

110 Lopez et al. , *supra* note 106, at 10; Fazzino, *supra* note 107, at 411–12. *See also* Dale A. Coddington & John J. Hisnanick, *Clinical Characteristics of Non-insulin-dependent Diabetes Mellitus among Southwestern American Indian Youths*, 19 J. Health Popul. Nutr. 12 (Mar. 2001) (study of diabetes among O'odham youths).

Tribal members are working on restoring the growing, harvesting, and consumption of traditional foods, such as tepary beans. The significance of beans in the traditional O'odham diet is made clear by the name that other tribes (and the United States) gave to the Tribe: Papago, meaning "bean eaters." In the 1930s, tribal members grew over one and a half million pounds of tepary beans each year; in 2001, less than 100 pounds were grown. Tepary beans are now grown on a 125-acre farm established by an organization founded by tribal members, Tohono O'odham Community Action ("TOCA"). Tepary beans and other traditional foods have additional cultural significance, appearing in stories and ceremonies. Tepary beans, scattered across the sky by Coyote, make up the Milky Way. Embracing traditional foods and their cultivation thus also recaptures ties to ancestors and their lifeways. As tribal member Terrol Johnson explains, "With all the foods we're growing, … there's a connection with the language, and the stories, and the songs."[111]

Tepary beans are beneficial in combatting diabetes because the soluble fiber and insulin that they contain help to reduce blood sugar levels and improve insulin production and sensitivity.[112] In addition to increasing cultivation of tepary beans, tribal members are being encouraged to harvest traditional desert foods, such as cholla buds (gathered from varieties of the cholla cactus) and prickly pears. These plants contain mucilage, which slows the digestion and absorption of starches and consequently lowers the insulin response.[113] Thus these foods, like tepary beans, may help to reduce the incidence of diabetes and its severity.[114]

Elders' recollections of crops that were grown in their youth but for which seeds are now difficult to find led to efforts to locate seeds in other communities on the Reservation and in O'odham communities in Mexico. Seed exchanges were launched to supply seeds to communities that needed them.[115] A cooperative called Native Seeds/SEARCH works on collecting and distributing native plant seeds to consumers both on and off the Reservation.[116] To encourage young people to

---

111 Anne Minard, *O'odham Encouraged to Grow Crops Rooted in Their Tradition*, ARIZ. DAILY STAR, July 5, 2005, at B1 (quoting Terrol Johnson). *See also Arizona Café Makes Healthy Fare for Native Americans*, NPR: ALL THINGS CONSIDERED (June 19, 2009); Daisy Hernandez, *Got Tradition? American Indians Use Native Foods to Fight Diabetes and Revive Indian Culture*, 8 COLORLINES MAG. 24 (June 22, 2005).

112 LOPEZ ET AL, *supra* note 106, at 11.

113 *Id.* at 11; Fazzino, *supra* note 107, at 411.

114 LOPEZ ET AL., *supra* note 106, at 11; Fazzino, *supra* note 106, at 411. *See also* Desmond E. Williams et al., *The Effect of Indian or Anglo Dietary Preference on the Incidence of Diabetes in Pima Indians*, 24 DIABETES CARE 811 (2001) (study suggesting that following an Indian diet, rather than a Western diet, reduces diabetes risk among Pimas, who are closely related to the Tohono O'odham).

115 *Traditional Native American Crops Face Extinction: Native Seeds/SEARCH Group Works to Preserve Culture and History Through Seed Gathering and Preservation*, 1 NATIVE VOICE (iss. 8), July 5, 2002, at 3.

116 Wilkinson, *supra* note 108, at 55.

consume traditional foods, a Food and Fitness Initiative was launched to introduce traditional foods into Reservation school lunch programs. Such projects are imperative, it seems, given the fact that 76 percent of Reservation sixth to eighth graders are overweight or obese,[117] which increases the likelihood that they will develop diabetes.

Tribal members have also begun growing traditional crops with low water demands using the ak-chin method, which utilizes water from summer rains. Relying on elders' knowledge of where ak-chin fields used to be cultivated, they have reclaimed traditional farmland. By 2005, one reclaimed family farmland was growing 14,000 pounds of tepary beans.[118] Indeed, tepary beans grow best with limited water—well-irrigated plants produce a lot of foliage, but plants given limited water have a greater harvestable yield.[119] This project, and others aimed at reviving dry based farming, can also improve Reservation food security.[120]

As tepary beans, cholla buds, and prickly pear and saguaro cactus fruits are re-introduced into the tribal diet, there are some initial reports that diabetes rates may be starting to fall.[121] Tribal members have reaped benefits beyond improved health from the resurgence in the growing and harvesting of traditional foods, as O'odham young people participating in community garden projects learn from elders about the plants and about traditions related to the land.[122]

The continued success of these efforts depends, however, on the ability of tribal members to freely cultivate and harvest traditional plants on Reservation lands that are already negatively impacted by human and drug trafficking and law enforcement efforts. Security concerns have already led some tribal elders and others to no longer gather desert plants.[123] Moreover, tribal resources that could be

117 Tristan Reader, Tohono O'odham Cmty. Action, The Health Effects Caused by the Loss of the Traditional Food System (2010), http://www.tocaonline.org/www.tocaonline.org/Oodham_Foods/Entries/2010/3/30_The_Health_Effects_Caused_by_the_loss_of_the_Traditional_Food_System.html. *See also* Paul W. Franks et al., *Childhood Obesity, Other Cardiovascular Risk Factors, and Premature Death*, 362 New Eng. J. Med. 485, 488 (2010) (28.7 percent of Pima and Tohono O'odham children in a study on risk factors for premature death were obese).

118 Minard, *supra* note 111, at B1; Kim Severson, *Native Foods Nourish Again*, N.Y. Times, Nov. 23, 2005, at F1.

119 Albert H. Markhart, III, *Comparative Water Relations of* Phaseolus vulgaris *L. and* Phaseolus acutifolius *Gray*, 77 Plant Physiol. 113, 116 (1985) (tepary bean (*Phaseolus acutifolius* Gray) plants produce extensive vegetative growth if well irrigated but produce maximum harvestable yield with limited water supply).

120 Christina Fox, Comment, *Teach a Man: Proactively Battling Food Insecurity by Increasing Access to Local Foods*, 4 J. Food L. & Pol'y 243, 253–54 (2008).

121 Patricia West-Barker, *Author to Host Native Foods Talk*, Santa Fe New Mex., Aug. 20, 2008, at D1.

122 Lourdes Medrano, *O'odham Youths Learn Traditions of Farming*, Ariz. Daily Star, Oct. 31, 2006, at B1.

123 Norris 2004 Testimony, *supra* note 70.

used to expand support for growing traditional crops instead must be used to deal with border-related problems. The U.S. policies that funnel illegal activities to the Reservation thus go beyond causing environmental and health problems to also threaten cultural preservation and revitalization.

Toward True Partnership with Tribes "at the Margins"

> *We've become an afterthought all over again ... Here we are, right on the frontlines, yet nobody asks us what we think.*[124]

As tribal nations subsumed within the borders of the United States, without their consent and despite the resulting division of their lands and peoples, the Tohono O'odham Nation and the Chippewa tribes confront many of the same challenges with which tribes located far from international borders must also grapple. At the same time, as the first two parts of this chapter have shown, they are faced with some issues that arise from, or are further complicated by, their proximity to an international border. For the Tohono O'odham, this has meant that they are subjected to serious security threats from human and drug trafficking funneled onto their Reservation by the location of the border and by U.S. border security policies. The Chippewa tribes, for their part, encounter a Great Lakes water management regime developed at a nation-state-to-nation-state level, without ensuring a place for them and for their treaty rights. As the Tohono O'odham and the Chippewa tribes then deal with the U.S. government on crucial issues, such as the protection of reservation environments and communities and the exercise of treaty rights, the government's response can be shaped not only by domestic policies and concerns, but also by international security and international relations policies and agreements. A potential path forward for the tribes, in the midst of this complicated picture, is explored below.

Common Struggles

Although the ecosystems in which the Chippewa tribes and the Tohono O'odham Nation make their homes seemingly have little in common, this is not the case with respect to the struggles that they face. Lands were reserved for these tribes in recognition of their desire, and their right, to continue to enjoy the natural resources of their homelands, in some cases even as to ceded lands. Their lands are located near international borders with respect to which the United States has developed policies that, like the borders themselves, were established without tribal consent. On the Canadian border, this has meant signing bi-national agreements and establishing a water protection regime, while on the Mexican

124 Robert Holden, *quoted in* Hernan Rozemberg, *Tribes on the Border*, San Antonio Express-News, Nov. 1, 2006, at 1A.

border security decisions have been made that funnel illegal activities (and environmentally destructive conduct) to Reservation land. Water protection and reservation security and pollution issues can have a profound impact on tribes' rights to enjoy reservation lands and exercise off-reservation treaty rights. The failure to treat tribes as necessary participants when decisions on these issues are being made, by leaving them out of agreements like the BWT and GLWQA and excluding them from the development of border security policies, undermines the ability of tribal governments to carry out their responsibility to protect significant resources, whether they be fish or desert plants.

Where tribal and U.S. interests overlap, U.S. officials have relied on tribes for their assistance, recognizing that tribes possess knowledge and skills that are valuable in the implementation of federal policies and programs. Chippewa tribes participate, albeit not as fully fledged partners, in efforts to preserve Great Lakes Basin resources under the GLWQA, while also being active in fisheries management pursuant to treaty rights. The Tohono O'odham Nation has shouldered a burden in the area of U.S. national security that is far out of proportion to the size of its resources.

Respect for tribes' contributions has not, however, translated into respect for the tribes as necessary and permanent partners. In a sense, the tribes' participation is at sufferance. Not guaranteed a right to participate in the development of policies and programs that affect them, tribes could find themselves shut out entirely of future involvement. In addition, tribal and federal priorities may not match up, even where common goals are concerned, leading to tribal priorities being marginalized. The DHS and CBP, for example, are unlikely to view the Tohono O'odham Nation's interest in restoring consumption of traditional foods as equal in importance to U.S. security.

The Case for Partnership

A new approach to the participation of tribes like the Chippewa tribes and the Tohono O'odham Nation in the development and implementation of policies that affect them is long overdue. In view of the tribal rights and interests that are at stake, in view of tribal sovereignty, and in view of federal policies recognizing tribes as fellow governments, it is time for tribes to be treated as true partners, with a right to be heard and heeded. Where border-related issues are at stake, there is a need for a tri-national, or multinational, approach to replace the current bi-national approach, in order to recognize that border area tribes are nations that, along with the United States, Canada, and Mexico, have rights and responsibilities tied to these issues. If the United States looks to tribes to cooperate in policies and programs that pursue common goals and confront common threats, whether related to environmental protection or border security, then tribes should be involved, as partners, in the development of such policies. Just as their expertise and their collaboration with federal and state agencies have fostered better implementation of existing policies, tribes' involvement as partners in developing environmental and border policy can lead to more effective policy development.

Respect for treaty rights and sovereignty The marginalization of the Chippewa tribes and the Tohono O'odham Nation by U.S. officials explored above is inconsistent with the fact of tribal sovereignty and treaty rights. The importance of tribal political status and of treaty rights has been affirmed by the courts and Congress, and recognized in Executive Order 13175, "Consultation and Coordination with Indian Tribal Governments," which noted that the United States has a "unique legal relationship with Indian tribal governments" and "supports tribal sovereignty and self-determination." Agencies were directed to respect tribal sovereignty and honor treaty rights when formulating and implementing policies that have tribal implications and to follow prescribed consultation guidelines.[125] In a 2009 memorandum, President Obama stated his Administration's commitment "to regular and meaningful consultation and collaboration with tribal officials in policy decisions that have tribal implications" and said that the starting point for fulfilling this commitment was "complete and consistent implementation of Executive Order 13175."[126] The continued failure to include interested tribes as parties to the BWT and the GLWQA, and to include border tribes as full partners in the formulation of border policies, clashes with the respect for treaty rights and sovereignty and the consultation directive of Executive Order 13175 and the 2009 memorandum.

A better approach to tribal involvement than the ones described in this chapter—one that shows respect for tribes' treaty rights and their governmental status—was followed in the creation of the Great Lakes Regional Collaboration ("GLRC"), formed pursuant to a 2004 Executive Order. The GLRC has recognized tribes as "valuable partners"; acknowledged "the United States' unique treaty obligations and trust responsibilities toward Tribal nations and their communities," and admitted that "most environmental problems, and particularly habitat degradation, disproportionately impact the culture, religious practices and other life ways of Tribal communities." Consequently, the GLRC "supports particular priorities that Collaboration member Tribal Nations have identified" and is committed to addressing "these priorities to help sustain the overall health and well-being of Tribal communities and of the natural resources on which they rely."[127] Tribal representatives are members of the Steering Committee that guides the implementation of the GLRC's Wetlands and Habitat Initiative,[128] launched in

125 Exec. Order No. 13175, 65 Fed. Reg. 67,249 (2000).

126 Tribal Consultation: Memorandum for the Heads of Executive Departments and Agencies, 74 Fed. Reg. 57,881 (2009).

127 GLRC, Great Lakes Regional Collaboration Strategy to Restore and Protect the Great Lakes 12–13 (2005), *available at* http://www.glrc.us/documents/strategy/GLRC_Strategy.pdf.

128 Great Lakes Habitat Initiative, Final Report and Implementation Plan 7 (2008).

response to the determination that habitat and wetlands degradation is a key threat to the protection of the Great Lakes. While it remains to be seen what impact tribal involvement will have on the work of the GLRC, guaranteeing tribes a role at the outset is an important step forward.

Recognition of the value of tribal input: tribes, like ecosystems, transcend boundaries Lands, waters, and communities of tribes located near international borders often transcend them. Chippewa tribes exist not only in the United States but also in "the Grandmother's Land," as Sitting Bull referred to Canada.[129] O'odham communities exist on both sides of the U.S.–Mexican border. Their lands are divided by the borders on paper, but not in the lives of tribal members. Water bodies and waterways along the borders may be divided by boundary lines on maps, but not in tribal members' memories and experiences.

Ecosystems, too, transcend boundaries, as victims of cross-border pollution know all too well. By failing to include tribes as signatories to the BWT and GLWQA, Canada and the United States miss the opportunity for regular input from tribal nations that can work with their counterparts in the same ecosystem on the other side of the border. These nations can approach cross-border environmental issues with a greater sense of unity than can U.S. and Canadian representatives, who may be burdened by national disagreements on other fronts. Moreover, the right of indigenous peoples, particularly those who are divided by international borders, to "maintain and develop contacts, relations and cooperation, including activities for spiritual, cultural, political, economic and social purposes, with their own members as well as other peoples across borders" is recognized by the United Nations Declaration on the Rights of Indigenous Peoples.[130]

Illustrating this cross-border unity, tribal leaders from both sides of the border, representing over 120 tribal nations, responded to their exclusion from the Great Lakes Charter by signing the Tribal and First Nations Great Lakes Water Accord. The Accord noted that "Tribes and First Nations continue to exercise cultural and spiritual rights of self-determination and property rights within traditional territories" and that their governments have, as do all governments, "the duty to protect the interests and future rights of our peoples." The failure to include the direct participation of tribal governments, "because of the interconnectedness of the worldwide ecosystem, endangers the interests of the earth." The Accord demanded equal, highest-level tribal participation in efforts to protect Great Lakes

129 Dee Brown, Bury My Heart at Wounded Knee: An Indian History of the American West 419 (1970).

130 United Nations Declaration on the Rights of Indigenous Peoples art. 36, G.A. Res. 61/295, U.N. GAOR, 61st Sess., 107th plen. Mtg., U.N. Doc. A/RES/61/295 (Sept. 13, 2007).

Basin waters and committed the signatories to work with each other, as well as with other Basin governments, "to secure a healthy future for the Great Lakes."[131]

Along the Mexican border, the United States has recognized the importance of Tohono O'odham tribal members' knowledge of their Reservation's landscape in border protection efforts by its reliance on the Shadow Wolves and through the participation of tribal members in other law enforcement endeavors. In 2010, the Tribe approved a Memorandum of Understanding with the U.S. Marshals Service, under which the tribal police department will participate in a Fugitive Apprehension Task Force with federal, state, and local law enforcement authorities.[132] Because their knowledge of O'odham territory transcends the U.S.–Mexican border, tribal members are in a position to support U.S.–Mexican cooperative efforts to track human and drug traffickers not only on the Tribe's U.S. lands but also in Mexico's Sonoran Desert.

Recognition of the value of tribal input: tribes bring a new, old perspective to resource management At the celebrations commemorating the BWT's 100th anniversary, a Tuscarora Nation member read from the Haudenosaunee Thanksgiving Address: "We give thanks to all the Waters of the world for quenching our thirst and providing us with strength. Water is life. We know its power in many forms—waterfalls and rain, mists and streams, rivers and oceans. With one mind, we send greetings and thanks to the spirit of water."[133] Tribes seek to protect water and other natural resources, not just because they are good in and of themselves, but because of their role in sustaining the lives of communities. This is an ethic of use, but not of abuse.

The traditional environmental ethic of many tribes is imbued with a holistic, ecosystem-based approach to natural resources stewardship. Different beings are understood as related and interconnected in the web of life, such that threats to one species can pose threats to others as well. The water protection regime stemming from the BWT and its progeny, which has only recently recognized the necessity of an ecosystem-based approach, can learn from those who have long espoused an "all my relations" vision of the natural world and the role and responsibility of humans in it.

Also relatively new to non-native governments is the ethic of environmental sustainability, which encompasses a sense of the responsibility of those who today make decisions that impact the environment to ensure that future generations will be able to survive on the land and waters that they inherit. This ethic has, however, long been a part of tribes' view of the environment. Non-native government

131 Tribal and First Nations Great Lakes Water Accord, *quoted in* Ettawageshik, *supra* note 9, at 1480. About 30 more tribal nations subsequently signed. *Id.* at 1481.

132 Resolution No. 10-052 of the Tohono O'odham Legislative Council, Feb. 18, 2010, *available at* http://tolc-nsn.org/docs/actions10/10052.pdf.

133 U.S. Dep't of State, DipNote, U.S., Canada Celebrate Boundary Waters Treaty Centennial, http://blogs.state.gov/index.php/entires/boundary_waters_treaty_centennial/.

officials have much to learn from peoples, like the Great Lakes Basin tribes, whose relationship with the natural world has been shaped by a "Seven Generations" philosophy of stewardship. To quote Chairman Ettawageshik, "[W]e are to think of the consequences of our actions through a time period long enough to encompass seven generations," a forward-looking perspective that makes "decisions that seem difficult in the short term … easier to make; things that seem important now fade in long-term importance."[134]

The Tohono O'odham Nation's commitment to environmental protection, and to sustainability and cross-generational stewardship, is set out in the tribal constitution:

> It shall be the policy of the Tohono O'odham Nation to encourage productive and enjoyable harmony between members of the nation and their environment; to promote efforts which will preserve and protect the natural and cultural environment of the Tohono O'odham Nation, including its lands, air, water, flora and fauna, its ecological systems, and natural resources, and its historic and cultural artifacts and archeological sites; and to create and maintain conditions under which members of the nation and nature can exist in productive harmony and fulfill the social, economic, and other requirements of present and future generations of members of the Tohono O'odham Nation.[135]

The Tribe is concerned that environmental protection is being ignored in favor of the actions that the federal government claims are necessary for border security. U.S. officials need to remember that Executive Orders and Memoranda direct them to act in ways that respect tribal sovereignty, which is embodied in tribal constitutions like that of the Tohono O'odham Nation. They are also directed to consult with tribes about prospective decisions that would affect them, and such consultations provide an opportunity for tribes to express views that are based on traditional environmental ethics. Finally, officials would do well to remember that short-sighted decisions that ignore long-term environmental impacts can come back to haunt us. Ignoring the potential environmental consequences of security measures, such as by waiving compliance with environmental statutes, and subordinating all interests to security concerns, is a perilous path to follow.

Professor Charles Wilkinson has commented eloquently on the contributions that tribes can make toward environmental preservation:

> With no sense of romanticism—and looking only to the force of the words, the intellectual and cultural tie to the natural world, the integrity of knowing intimately a particular landscape for more generations than can be counted, and a world view at once ecological and spiritual—I believe that, of all the

---

134 Ettawageshik, *supra* note 9, at 1482.

135 Const. of the Tohono O'Odham Nation, art. XVIII, sec. 1, *available at* http://tolc-nsn.org/docs/Constitution.pdf.

> societies in the West, none can put forth a voice for the land in more articulate, knowledgeable, and authentic terms than the American Indian tribes.[136]

Paying attention to what tribes have to say about the environment is not a matter of indulging a wistful, romantic attachment to the 1970s television depiction of a tearful Indian, weeping at the sight of pollution.[137] Rather, it is a matter of recognizing that tribes have developed a sense of the environment and of the practical need to protect it from which all peoples can learn and benefit.

Prospects for Partnership

This chapter has argued for the need for a true partnership between the tribes discussed above and the United States in addressing border-related issues of common interest, which recognizes that tribes' sovereignty and treaty rights entitle them to meaningful participation in decision-making that affects them and that their fuller involvement can improve policy development and implementation. The details of such a partnership are left for another day, and will be best addressed by tribes and intertribal organizations. Yet what are the prospects for any movement in the direction of fuller partnership?

As to the GLWQA, perhaps the time is ripe for some meaningful change. A 2007 report, the product of a review of the GLWQA through bi-national working groups,[138] concluded that the GLWQA "should recognize the critical role and essential participation of other orders of government, including … Tribes and First Nations … [which] should be included in the revision and implementation of the Agreement." This recommendation recognized that the success of the GLWQA to date stemmed from the Parties' working together with tribes.[139] As Chairman Ettawageshik put it, "The Great Lakes Water Quality Agreement is only words on paper; it takes people to get things done."[140] Tribes must be counted among the key implementers of the GLWQA, with whom effective coordination and collaboration are needed to achieve the GLWQA's goals.[141]

Commenting on the draft review report, the GLIFWC observed that, because the successful exercise of ceded territory treaty rights depends "on clean and

---

136 Wilkinson, *supra* note 108, at 55.

137 Amy Waldman, *Iron Eyes Cody, an Actor, and Tearful Anti-Littering Icon*, N.Y. Times, Jan. 5, 1999, at A15 (obituary of Iron Eyes Cody, who portrayed an Indian weeping over pollution in a 1970s "Keep America Beautiful" public service message).

138 Agreement Review Comm., 1 Report to the Great Lakes Binational Executive Committee 1 (2007), *available at* http://binational.net/glwqa/v1_glwqareview_en.pdf.

139 *Id.* at 21.

140 *Id.* at 51.

141 *Great Lakes Water Quality Agreement Governance and Institutions: Workshop Review Report to the ARC by the Canadian and U.S. Convenors*, *in* Agreement Review Comm., 2 Report to the Great Lakes Binational Executive Committee 318, 327 (2007), *available at* http://binational.net/glwqa/v2_glwqareview_en.pdf.

abundant natural resources, tribes have a meaningful stake in the management of the Great Lakes basin." Moreover, because of the commitment of the tribes—just like the GLWQA Parties—to protecting and effectively managing the Great Lakes, "tribal treaty rights present significant opportunities to advance the effective implementation of the Agreement." The GLIFWC noted the need for governance and institutional frameworks to provide for effective coordination and praised the report's "recognition of the tribes' role as governments whose actions can help accomplish the purpose of the Agreement." Once at last identified "as key players" needed to implement the GLWQA, tribes should be included "in all aspects of the Agreement."[142]

The Sault Ste Marie Tribe of Chippewa Indians has also submitted comments on the revision of the GLWQA. The Tribe stressed the need for multi-national collaboration, involving individual tribes, to manage and protect the Great Lakes, in place of the bi-national regime, which "limits the resilience and the full potential" of the GLWQA. A multi-national approach would provide the GLWQA with "greater stability and accountability in the face of socio-political change, a more thorough and inclusive understanding of Great Lakes waters and management, and the necessary components for effective implementation by all nations." The Tribe noted that the success of the 2000 Consent Decree relating to treaty-based fishing rights "depends on maintaining a healthy environment for fish populations, which obviously includes water quality related concerns." As a signatory to the Consent Decree, the United States has a responsibility to protect the treaty fishing rights, which "can only be accomplished by involving the affected tribes as a partner in all planning and regulatory activities."[143] While it remains to be seen whether the GLWQA will be amended[144] to ensure a stronger role for tribes—one that respects their treaty rights and governmental status and recognizes their contributions to protection of the Great Lakes Basin—at least the possibility is on the table for discussion.

Recent work by the DHS on developing a tribal policy provides a basis for cautious optimism that the Tohono O'odham Nation will have the opportunity to assume a role with respect to border-related policies that is commensurate with it governmental status and recognizes its value as a partner. In 2010, DHS Secretary Janet Napolitano released the DHS's Plan of Action to develop a tribal consultation

142 Letter from James E. Zion, Executive Administrator, Great Lakes Indian Fish and Wildlife Commission, to Mark Elster, U.S. EPA (July 13, 2007), *in* AGREEMENT REVIEW COMM., 3 REPORT TO THE GREAT LAKES BINATIONAL EXECUTIVE COMMITTEE 62, 63–65 (2007), *available at* http://binational.net/glwqa/v3_glwqareview_en.pdf.

143 Letter from Darwin McCoy, Tribal Chairman, Sault Ste Marie Tribe of Chippewa Indians, to James Schardt, Great Lakes National Program Office, EPA (Feb. 15, 2010), *in* GREAT LAKES WATER QUALITY AGREEMENT 2010 RENEGOTIATIONS, COMPILATION OF BINATIONAL.NET COMMENTS (2010), *available at* http://binational.net/glwqa/glwqa_comments_e.pdf.

144 *See* Amending the Great Lakes Water Quality Agreement, http://binational.net/glwqa_2010_e.html (summarizing work in the GLWQA review process).

and coordination policy to comply with the 2009 Obama Memorandum. Drafted by the DHS Office of Intergovernmental Affairs' Tribal Desk in consultation with tribal governments, the Plan acknowledged that the DHS has a responsibility to help meet the "significant Federal obligations" to tribes and that working in partnership with tribes "will lead to better policy outcomes and will ultimately help the DHS achieve its mission." The Plan identified three main themes that emerged from extensive tribal input: consultation must be rooted in recognition of sovereignty; Executive Order 13175's "*substantive* goals of tribal self-government and fulfillment of the Federal trust responsibility" must not continue to be overshadowed by a focus on its *procedural* requirements; and post-consultation agency accountability mechanisms are needed. The Plan outlined steps to be taken to (a) create a consultation policy and internal procedures to institutionalize tribal consultation and (b) improve communication and collaboration with tribes.[145] Although the consultation policy has not yet been finalized, progress has been made on fulfilling several aspects of the Plan and work on others, carried out with tribal input through a number of mechanisms, is ongoing.[146] Perhaps the newfound appreciation of the contributions by tribes like the Tohono O'odham Nation to achieving common goals and the commitment to tribal sovereignty and self-determination voiced in the 2009 Obama Memorandum will at last lead to true partnership between the Nation and the United States.

* * *

Accepting tribes as full, rather than junior, partners, by respecting tribal sovereignty and treaty rights and avoiding marginalization of tribal rights and priorities, can provide a new path forward toward the accomplishment of common goals. As tribal nations and nation-states alike confront environmental and border security problems affecting their lands, resources, and communities, it is time, to paraphrase Sitting Bull, for us to "put our minds together, as partners, and see what kind of life we can make for our children."[147]

---

145 Dep't of Homeland Security, Plan to Develop a Tribal Consultation and Coordination Policy Implementing Executive Order 13175, http://www.dhs.gov/xlibrary/assets/dhs_tribal_consultation_coordination_policy_plan_implementing_eo_13175.pdf (emphasis added).

146 Dep't of Homeland Security, Progress Report on the Plan of Action to Develop a Tribal Consultation and Coordination Policy Implementing Executive Order 13175 (Aug. 2010), http://www.dhs.gov/xlibrary/assets/tribal-plan-of-action-progress-report-082010.pdf.

147 *See* Christine Whiteswan Sterne, *Sitting Bull*, http://www.manataka.org/page57.html. The original quote reads: "Let us put our minds together and see what kind of life we can make for our children."

Tribal Environmental Protection

Chapter 7

Co-operating to Protect the Shining Big Sea Water and its Siblings: Consultation with Native Peoples in Protecting the Great Lakes

Jacqueline Phelan Hand[1]

> *Our ancestors have inhabited the Great Lakes Basin since time immemorial, long before the current political boundaries were drawn. Our spiritual and cultural connections to our Mother earth are Manifest by our willingness to embrace the responsibility of protecting and preserving the land and waters.*
>
> Statement of Mother Earth Water Walkers

The women who form the Water Walkers held their first walk around Lake Superior in April 2003. "Several women from different clans came together to walk around the Great Lakes … to raise awareness that our clean air and clear water is being constantly polluted."[2] The women have since walked around Lake Michigan in 2004, Lake Huron in 2005, and Lake Ontario in 2006, carrying a bucket of water to symbolize water's importance to life. Despite their demonstrated commitment to the Great Lakes, the Water Walkers, as members of American Indian Tribes, have been denied effective participation in their management.

Until the Environmental Decade of the 1970s, natural resource management fell primarily within the jurisdiction of the states, with a few obvious exceptions, mostly relating to shared resources or federal land. As a strong constituency for environmental protection developed, a variety of federal statutes were passed, many involving forms of "co-operative federalism," under which the federal government sets minimum standards, which are then implemented by the states. This comfortable symmetry is compromised by the fact that the federal government and the states are not the only sovereigns with rights and responsibilities for protection of the land and its resources. The third type of sovereign is the American

---

1 Professor of Law, University of Detroit Mercy. J.D., Wayne State University, 1978. The author is Director of the University of Detroit Mercy Indian Law Center. This chapter draws extensively from an article I published in the Natural Resources Journal prior to the entry into effect of the Great Lakes Compact and Agreement in 2008. *See* Jacqueline Phelan Hand, *Protecting the World's Largest Body of Fresh Water: The Often Overlooked Role of Indian Tribes' Co-Management of the Great Lakes*, 47 Nat. Resources J. 815 (2007).

2 Mother Earth Water Walk, http://www.motherearthwaterwalk.com (select "About Us" tab).

Indian nations, whose governments also have inherent rights and duties to protect and manage natural resources. Each of these sovereigns, thus, has interests in management of the Great Lakes. Recent agreements between the Great Lakes states and Canadian provinces do not reflect this trifurcated allocation of interests. This chapter tells the story of how the agreements developed without the Tribes' genuine participation, and describes why it is important to include Tribes going forward. It further suggests that the best way to do so is to strengthen the duty to consult the Tribes, which was required by the agreements.

Sovereignty and the Management of Natural Resources

The legal histories with respect to indigenous rights to self-government and resource management in the U.S. and Canada are distinct. In the United States, treaties forged in the eighteenth and nineteenth centuries form the basis both for the Tribes' retention of inherent sovereignty and for their consequent right to protect and manage their resources. After repeated policy shifts, U.S. current laws and policies at least theoretically reflect a commitment to tribal self-government.

By contrast, the relation between the Canadian government and its First Nations has developed somewhat differently. Many aboriginal land claims, rather than being settled by nineteenth-century treaties, are still being resolved in a process that began in earnest in the early 1980s, triggered by the then new Canadian constitution.[3] As a result, the Canadian Supreme Court has, through a series of cases, developed an approach for integrating the rights of First Nations into the broader fabric of the legal system.[4] This line of cases offers a template for procedural and substantive integration of indigenous peoples into decision-making about shared resources, which should be followed in implementing the Great Lakes Compact and Agreement.

U.S. Tribal Off-reservation Hunting and Fishing Rights

The property claims of American Tribes are often not limited to reservation land. Many of the treaties under which Indian Tribes ceded land to the federal government include a reservation of hunting and fishing rights on non-reservation

3 Constitution Act, 1982, s.35, being Schedule B to the Canada Act 1982 (UK), 1982, c 11.

4 Many of these cases involve determining First Nation rights to impact decisions about resources before their underlying land claims have been resolved. In this situation deference to First Nations interests is partially a function of the court's judgment on the strength of the underlying claim. *Haida Nation v British Columbia* (Minister of Forests), [2004] 3 S.C.R. 511, 2004. SCC 73.

lands.[5] For example, while the exact nature of the reserved right is dependent on the precise language of the treaty, generally tribal members exercising such rights to hunt or fish are not required to pay a state license fee.[6] The treaties in the Pacific Northwest, principally concerned with salmon, generally involve the reservation of the right to fish at "all usual and accustomed places."[7] This language, combined with treaty language recognizing that the Indians' right to fish is secured "in common with all citizens of the territory," led to many years of bitter litigation over exactly what portion (if any) of the yearly salmon run was to be allocated to the tribes.[8] The matter was finally resolve by the U.S. Supreme Court, which held that Indian fishermen should have a right to up to 50 percent of the available fish, limited by the state's right to determine how many fish could safely be harvested without endangering the resource.[9]

A comparable struggle, which occurred in Michigan, the only state completely within the Great Lakes Basin, resulted in the clear judicial recognition of the rights of Michigan Tribes to fish in the Great Lakes. The process began when a Chippewa tribal member, William Le Blanc, was charged by the state with failing to secure a commercial fishing license and for using a gill net. The Michigan Supreme Court upheld Le Blanc's right to fish without a license but also upheld the State of Michigan's right to subject him to its gill net regulations because it believed preservation of the fishery required that the regulation be applied to Indians as well as non-Indians.[10] (The practical political issue involved the competition between tribal commercial fishermen and non-Indian sport fishermen.) The state decision was trumped in relatively short order by the federal district court decision in *U.S. v. Michigan*, which held that the tribes have a sovereign right to fish in the Great Lakes and therefore the state has no power to regulate the manner or exercise of Indian fishing rights in the Great Lakes.[11] Similarly, other Great Lakes tribes hold treaty rights according to a series of cession treaties under which the bulk of Michigan, Wisconsin, and Minnesota were conveyed to the federal government in the first half of the nineteenth century.[12] These off-reservation treaty rights of the tribes were also affirmed by a series of state and federal court decisions

5 *See* Minn. v. Mille Lacs Band of Chippewa Indians, 536 U.S. 172 (1999).

6 Tulee v. Wash., 315 U.S. 681 (1942).

7 *See* United States v. Winans, 198 U.S. 371 (1905).

8 *See* Judith Royster & Michael C. Blumm, Native American Natural Resources Law: Cases and Materials 508–37 (2nd ed. 2008) (2007).

9 Wash. v. Wash. State Commercial Passenger Fishing Vessel Ass'n, 443 U.S. 658 (1979).

10 People v. Leblanc, 399 Mich. 31, 248 N.W.2d 199 (1976).

11 U.S. v. Mich., 471 F. Supp 192 (W.D. Mich, 1979). Fishing rights of the Milles Lacs Band under the 1837 treaty were affirmed by the U.S. Supreme Court in *Minn. v. Mille Lacs Band of Chippewa Indians*, 536 U.S. 172 (1999).

12 1837 Treaty with Chippewa, July 29, 1837, 7 Stat. 536, *available at* http://digital.library.okstate.edu/kappler/vol2/treaties/chi0491.htm.

recognizing rights to fish in various areas of the Great Lakes. In effect, the various Great Lakes Tribes are co-tenants with the states and provinces bordering the lakes and in matters of fishing often take priority over them. These tribes have not acted as passive rights holders but have been very active in managing the lakes and their piscine inhabitants.

Cooperative Tribal Institutes

The effective transfer of control of much of the fishery to the tribes has not led to its degradation, as many critics suggested in the period prior to the *U.S. v. Michigan* decision. In fact, the Great Lakes Tribes have developed institutions that have effectively protected the fisheries and the waters on which they depend as well as protecting off-reservation hunting and fishing rights. The two most prominent of these are the Great Lakes Fish and Wildlife Commission (GLIFWC)[13] and the Chippewa Ottawa Resource Authority (CORA).[14]

The Great Lakes Tribes' sovereign claim to the lakes, which arises out of the treaties and rights reserved (i.e. not transferred) under them, does not rest on proof of governmental effectiveness. Nevertheless the existence and competency of CORA and GLIFWC do suggest a practical as well as spiritual concern for protecting the ecosystem and a willingness to expend energy and resources for its protection. Tribes' successful participation in the cooperative management of the Lakes' fisheries and waters forms part of the backdrop for the recent international negotiations and agreements. As discussed below, unfortunately this demonstrated competence has not translated into genuine participation.

The Great Lakes Agreements

The five Great Lakes (Erie, Huron, Michigan, Ontario, and Superior) form a considerable part of the boundary between the eastern United States and Canada.

13 This conservation and management institution was formed by ten individual bands of Ojibwa in three states. It has a permanent staff of approximately 60 full-time employees who work to manage fisheries in the Great Lakes. *See* Sue Erikson, A Guide to Understanding Ojibwe Treaty Rights 22–25 (2005), *available at* http://www.glifwc.org/publications/pdf/TreatyRights06.pdf. Member tribes are: Bay Mills Indian Community, Grand Traverse Band of Ottawa and Chippewa Indians, Little River Band of Ottawa Indians, Little Traverse Bay Band of Odawa Indians and the Sault Ste Marie Tribe of Chippewa Indians. (Notice that Bay Mills is a member of both organizations.) About Us, Chippewa Ottawa Resource Authority, http://www.1836cora.org/About-us.php.

14 CORA was formed by the six Michigan tribes with off-reservation treaty fishing rights. It operates a comprehensive program of fishery management including enforcement in treaty waters.

The Great Lakes Basin is the largest freshwater system in the world, constituting nearly 20 percent of the world's supply of fresh water. The Great Lakes, along with the St Lawrence River and all connecting channels, make up the basin. The basin provides a home for a wide range of flora and fauna and provides drinking water for more than 30 million people.[15] The importance of this resource to both the United States and Canada is such that efforts at cooperation began a century ago. The first of these efforts was the Boundary Waters Treaty of 1909.[16] The treaty established the still operating International Joint Commission, consisting of an equal number of Canadian and American representatives to adjudicate matters between the parties.[17] It also recognizes one of the primary concerns relating to the Lakes, that no individual party should be allowed to unilaterally remove large quantities of water from the basin without the approval of the other parties who have rights in the resource.

For many years following the Boundary Waters Treaty, water use issues in the area remained relatively static. The perceived abundance of water meant that usage, including usage detrimental to the ecosystem, remained substantially unregulated.[18] Beginning in the 1950s, proposals began to surface for large-scale diversions of water from the basin; however, these repeatedly fell by the wayside as economically infeasible. By the 1980s, proposals to divert water from the basin to the increasingly populated but arid western states appeared more imminent and viable.[19] In the same decade, the U.S. Supreme Court ruled that ground water is an article of interstate commerce and as such its transfer cannot be prohibited by the states.[20] The Supreme Court ruling raised the specter of unlimited exploitation of the region's key resource by outside interests, such as states located in more arid regions.

---

15 Great Lakes Commission for the Great Lakes States and Provinces, Toward a Water Resources Management Decision Support System for The Great Lakes–St. Lawrence River Basin 9 (2003), *available at* http://www.glc.org/wateruse/wrmdss/finalreport.html (select Executive Summary). *See, e.g.*, U.S. Policy Committee for the Great Lakes, Great Lakes Strategy 2002: A Plan for the New Millennium, *available at* http://www.epa.gov/grtlakes/gls/gls2002.pdf.

16 Boundary Waters Treaty, U.S.–U.K. (for Canada) at Jan.11, 1909, 36 Stat. 2448, U.K.T.S. 1910 No. 25. Since Lake Michigan is located completely within the United States, it is generally not covered by the treaty.

17 *Id.* at Art.VII, 36 Stat. at 2451.

18 For example, until late 2006, with the passage of the Water Legacy Act, Michigan had no system limiting removal of ground water. For a thoughtful description of the role that the Great Lakes play in the culture and identity of the people of the Great Lakes, see Marcia Valiante, *Harmonization of Great Lakes Water Management in the Shadow of NAFTA*, 81 U. Det. Mercy L. Rev. 525, 527 (2004).

19 *See, e.g.*, Michael J. Donahue, Alicia A. Bixby & David Siebers, *Great Lakes Diversions and Consumptive Use: The Issue in Perspective,* 18 Case W. Res. J. Int'l L. 19 (1986) (describes several proposals).

20 Sporhase v. Nebraska, 458 U.S. 941 (1982).

Great Lakes Charter

Recognition of the lack of regulatory protections, combined with increased concern that large quantities of water could be removed from the basin, initially led the Great Lakes States and Canadian Provinces[21] to adopt the Great Lakes Charter.[22] The Charter, created under the auspices of the Council of Great Lakes Governors, is a non-binding good faith agreement, intended to provide the basis for the development of a coordinated regime aimed at protecting the region as a whole. Charter signatories agreed to three key principles:

1. The states and provinces agree to regulate new or increased removals from the Great Lakes, whether consumptive or diversions, which are more than 2 million gallons per day.[23]
2. The parties agree to notify and consult with all other parties for all new or increased diversions or consumptive uses of water greater than 5,000,000 gallons per day.[24]
3. The parties commit to gather and report information on all new or increased withdrawals of more than 100,000 gallons per day.

Although the Charter on its face provides that diversions will be limited to those consistent with the long-term preservation of the resource, it reflects a strong preference for no diversions at all.[25] The Charter embodied and reaffirmed the commitment of the states and provinces to develop a joint strategy to manage and protect the waters of the basin.[26]

---

21 The Great Lakes States are Illinois, Indiana Michigan, Minnesota, New York, Ohio, Pennsylvania and Wisconsin. The Canadian Provinces are Ontario and Quebec.

22 Council of Great Lakes Governors, Great Lakes Charter: Principles for the Management of Great Lakes Water Resources (1985), *available at* http://www.cglg.org/projects/water/docs/GreatLakesCharter.pdf

23 A "consumptive use" is defined as "that portion of water withdrawn or withheld from the Great Lakes Basin and assumed to be lost or otherwise not returned to the Great Lakes Basin due to evaporation, incorporation into products, or other processes." *Id.* at 6. A "diversion" is defined as a "transfer of water from the Great Lakes Basin into another watershed, or from the watershed of one of the Great Lakes into that of another." *Id.*

24 *See, e.g.*, Noah D. Hall, *Toward a New Horizontal Federalism: Interstate Water Management in the Great Lakes Region.* 77 U. Colo. L. Rev. 405, 424–26 (2006) (noting that the other parties' rights are limited to consultation; if the state or province chooses to go ahead, there is no practical remedy).

25 Valiante, *supra* note 18, at 528.

26 *See* Peter V. McAvoy, *The Great Lakes Charter: Toward a Basin wide Strategy for Managing the Great Lakes,* 18 Case W. Res. J. Int'l L. 49 (1986).

Water Resources Development Act and Similar Measures

The approach of the Great Lakes Charter was approved of and reinforced by the U.S. Congress in 1986 with the passage of section 1109 of the Water Resources Development Act ("WRDA").[27] The WRDA provides that any governor can veto any diversion from the United States side of the border:

> No water shall be diverted or exported from any portion of the Great Lakes, within the United States, or from any tributary within the United States of any of the Great Lakes, for use outside of the Great Lakes basin unless such diversion or export is approved by the Governor of each of the Great Lake [sic] States.[28]

A key impetus behind the passage of this section of WRDA was to insulate the governors' decisions from attack under the commerce clause of the Constitution.[29]

In the years immediately following the passage of WRDA, proposals for large-scale diversions essentially dried up, although a number of proposals were put forward that contemplated the use of Great Lakes water outside the watershed but within one of the Great Lakes states. A typical example was the proposal for a small "temporary" diversion from Lake Michigan to Pleasant Prairie, Wisconsin, located immediately outside the basin; the town's drinking water had been contaminated by radium.[30] As time went on, awareness of the weaknesses and shortcomings of the regime created by the WRDA and the Great Lakes Charter grew. It did not cover consumptive uses or groundwater removal. Lacking enforcement provisions, The Great Lakes Charter provided no limitations on the vetoes by individual states of other states' projects and no remedy for failure to follow the Charter's consultation provisions. In addition, it did not cover the Canadian provinces even in a non-binding way. Finally, it did not indicate any awareness of the status of indigenous nations as sovereign co-owners of the Lakes.

Immediate Response to Great Lakes Water Removal Schemes

In the 1990s, several events occurred which brought to the fore concerns about large exports of water from the Great Lakes Basin to other regions. First, the North American Free Trade Agreement ("NAFTA") between the United States, Canada, and Mexico was signed in 1992. Although it was soon supplemented by the North American Agreement on Environmental Cooperation in 1993, fears remained that trade policy would trump the ability of the states and provinces to prohibit such

27 42 U.S.C. § 1962d-20(d) (2000).

28 *Id.* Diversions approved prior to passage of WRDA are not covered. *See* 42 U.S.C. § 1962d-20(f).

29 Valiante, *supra* note 18, at 529.

30 *Id.* at 530.

exports.[31] These fears were further exacerbated in 1998 when the Nova Group applied for and initially received a permit from the Province of Ontario to export water from Lake Superior to Japan. The permit was rescinded after a vociferous and near universal outcry, but the reality check created by the incident led to broad recognition that more explicit protections were needed. Several immediate responses materialized. The U.S. Congress passed an amendment to WRDA that extended its coverage to the "export" of water from the Great Lakes, as well as explicitly encouraging the states to cooperate with the Canadian provinces to create "common conservation standards" to control withdrawals of Great Lakes waters.[32] The Canadian government passed comparable legislation, encouraging the Canadian provinces to prohibit export of water from, *inter alia*, the Great Lakes Basin.[33] Most importantly, for purposes of this discussion, the Great Lakes Governors and Premiers began negotiations, which resulted in the agreement known as Annex 2001.[34] Throughout this preliminary period, the indigenous peoples on both sides of the border were completely ignored.

Annex 2001: The Negotiation Process

Annex 2001, a subsidiary to the Great Lakes Charter, reflected a commitment to work toward developing a binding agreement that would be acceptable to all ten jurisdictions by 2004. The focus of the negotiations was the development of a common standard for all withdrawals within the basin, i.e. one not limited solely to diversions. The withdrawal standard was meant to incorporate principles of conservation, ecosystem protection, and improvement, not merely maintenance of the resource. This standard was expected to be applied to all withdrawals from the basin, with larger withdrawals to be regulated by decisions of a regional decision-maker.

The Annex 2001 signatories used the existing institution of the Council of Great Lakes Governors to implement its directives. A Water Management Working Group was established, consisting of state, local, and federal officials, which was

31 In an effort to quash such fears the governments of the three countries issued a joint statement asserting that "water in its natural state in lakes, rivers, reservoirs, aquifers and the like is not a good or product" and therefore is not covered by trade agreements. Statement by the Governments of Canada, Mexico and the United States, THE FREE TRADE OBSERVER, No. 51, Dec. 2, 1993, at 855.

32 42 U.S.C. § 1962d-20 (2000) (*as amended*).

33 *See* Water Resources Preservation Act, S.Q., ch. 63 (1999), amended by ch. 48, 2001 S.Q. (Can.), *Water Taking and Transfer* 285/99 R.O. § 3. *See, e.g.*, Valiante, *supra* note 18, at 532.

34 COUNCIL OF GREAT LAKES GOVERNORS, THE GREAT LAKES CHARTER ANNEX: A SUPPLEMENTARY AGREEMENT TO THE GREAT LAKES CHARTER (2001), *available at* http://www.cglg.org/projects/water/docs/greatlakescharterannex.pdf.

supplemented by an Advisory Group made up of representatives of various water user sectors and conservation organizations. American Indian Tribes and First Nations were the only claimants to the water in the Great Lakes who were not allocated a "place at the table." This exclusion continued the approach that has characterized the process from the beginning of the twentieth century. After the Working Group produced its first draft of the proposed agreement on July 19, 2004, over 30 public hearings were held on both sides of the border in an effort to make the process transparent to the public. The Tribes and First Nations could attend and make comments, but only as members of the public, not as sovereigns with inherent claims to the water in question.

Two separate but coordinated Agreements resulted from this process. The first, the Great Lakes–St Lawrence River Basin Resource Compact,[35] went into effect in 2008 after being ratified by the legislatures of each participating state, followed by the consent of the U.S. Congress and a presidential signature.[36] The initial intent of the Annex 2001 signatories was to create one document, which would bind both states and provincial governments. Concerns about the constitutionality of such a pact led instead to the development of a separate non-binding companion agreement, the Great Lakes–St Lawrence River Basin Sustainable Water Resources Agreement.[37] It is clear that the system set up by the two agreements, while far from perfect, is substantively a great improvement on previous efforts to protect the Great Lakes. However, the processes by which it was reached, as well as the process under which it is currently being implemented, are defective in that they did not, and do not, recognize the role of the relevant Native American Tribes and First Nations in managing the resource.

The Indian Tribes, as sovereigns, are effectively co-tenants with the states in claims to Great Lakes waters.[38] Nevertheless, when the Annex 2001 process began, the relevant Tribes were effectively ignored, shutting them off from the practical

35 Great Lakes–St Lawrence River Basin Resource Compact (2005), *available at* http://www.cglg.org/projects/water/docs/12-13-05/Great_Lakes-St_Lawrence_River_Basin_Water_Resources_Compact.pdf. The Great Lakes–St Lawrence River Basin Resource Compact will remain a proposed compact until approved by the legislatures of all eight states and the U.S. Congress.

36 *Id.* at 26–27 § 9.4. The Compact will remain in force unless five of the eight states vote to terminate. *Id.* at 26 § 8.7.

37 For an excellent discussion of the history and content of both agreements, see Hall, *supra* note 24.

38 At the initial meeting of the Working Group on March 15, 2002, when asked "How will Tribes be addressed?" The response was "Each State and Province will work individually with Tribes." Meeting Summary Memorandum, Joint Water Management Working Group/Advisory Committee Meeting (Mar. 15, 2002), at 6, *available at* http://www.cglg.org/projects/water/docs/MeetingSummaries/3-15-02MeetingSummary.doc. Both the states and the tribes are subject to the superior power of the federal government under the Commerce Clause and the Indian Commerce clause of the U.S. Constitution, and tribes are not subject to state jurisdiction.

development of the Compact and Agreement. The reasons for this exclusion are unclear. At least a partial explanation may be found in the history of efforts to deal with the issue of water diversion. For almost a hundred years, the allocation of Great Lakes water was either an international or an interstate concern. The institutions that developed to manage allocations of water, like the International Joint Commission and later the Great Lakes Council of Governors, were by definition tied to the states and provinces. For the greater part of the twentieth century the Tribes in the east and midwest were desperately poor, and essentially powerless. It was only after the 1970s that Tribes and First Nations in the area began to be in a position to assert their always-existing rights. Thus, during the period when the initiatives, which ultimately resulted in the Annex 2001 process, were developing, it seems likely that the claims of the Tribes were simply outside the frame of reference of state and provincial decision-makers. As a result, when the effort to create binding government-to-government agreements began, no reference was made to the tribal role in the Annex 2001 Agreement itself, nor in the mechanism set up to accomplish the task. It appears that it was contemplated that states would represent Tribes whose lands are within their boundaries. This is inconsistent with the sovereign status of the Tribes. In addition, often there is substantial tension between state natural resources agencies and Tribes with whom states share resources. To the extent that the Tribes were included, they were invited to participate as members of the public at large, not as sovereigns who had property interests in the water in question. In particular, while the Water Management Working Group and the Advisory Group included not only federal, state and local officials, but also representatives of particular water use sectors and environmental groups, neither body contained a single tribal representative.

Tribal Response to Annex 2001

Tribal leaders on both sides of the border began to protest the situation soon after the First Draft of the Compact was made public on July 19, 2004. While generally supportive of the goals represented by the document, the tribal response unanimously attacked the exclusion of the Tribes from the process. In addition, Indian commentators generally believed that its provisions were not sufficiently protective of the waters of the Great Lakes. With regard to the flaws in the process, the August 30, 2004 letter of Jane TenEyck, Acting Executive Director of CORA, is typical:

> It is unfeasible to expect that one or two individuals could represent all of the Great Lakes Tribes and First Nations. Instead, CORA has repeatedly requested that the Council give the opportunity for each and every sovereign Tribe within the Great Lakes Basin to participate at the highest decision-making level … The Council's decision was to allow each State to 'deal' with the Tribes that reside within its respective border. While I recognize and appreciate the State

> of Michigan's outreach to the Tribes within its border, it must be conceded that no State has jurisdiction on tribal lands nor to water within Tribal jurisdiction.[39]

The letter of Laura Spurr, Tribal Chairperson of the Huron Band of Potawatomi, dated October 13, 2004, is equally explicit:

> The little consideration given to the Tribes [in the process] occurred in the Great Lakes Basin Water Resources Compact. Section 3.8 calls for 'appropriate consultation' with federally recognized Tribes. The ability to submit comments as a member of the general public concerning new or increased diversions is not an 'appropriate' level of Tribal input … At no time were the Tribes invited to be members of the Working Group as governmental agencies.[40]

The comments of Audry Falcon, Tribal Chief of the Saginaw Chippewa Indian Tribe of Michigan, focus on the fact that Tribes are not merely "interested persons," but governments whose cooperation is needed if the agreements are to be effectively implemented. She also articulates the special relationship that the tribes have with these waters: "Moreover, to exclude the tribes from participating in the creation and implementation of this agreement is in contradiction to the spiritual and cultural responsibility native people inherently have toward the earth and the future generations that will inhabit her."[41]

The value of tribal input in the development of an effective system of protection for the lakes was expressed even more strongly in the comments of Frank Ettawageshik, Tribal Chairman of the Little Traverse Bay Bands of Odawa Indians:[42]

---

39 Letter from Jane TenEyck, Acting Executive Director of CORA, to David Naftzger, Executive Director of the CGLG (2004) (on file with author and with the Great Lakes Council of Governors). In the letter TenEyck notes: "In regard to the process of consultation with the Tribes and first Nations during the time period between 2001 and now, CORA's environmental Coordinator has represented CORA on several conference calls with the stakeholders work group, testified at public hearing and has written several letters with our concerns …" *Id.*

40 Letter from Laura Spurr, Tribal Chairperson of the Nottawaseppi Huron Band of Potawatomi, to David Naftzger, Executive Director, Council of Great Lakes Governors (Oct. 13, 2004) (on file with author). Note: this letter refers to the first draft, which was then in the public comment process. After the comment period, a second and Final Draft was made public.

41 Comments of Audry Falcon, Chief of the Saginaw Chippewa Indian Tribe of Michigan (Sept. 28, 2004) (on file with author).

42 Frank Ettawageshik has been at the forefront in tribal efforts to protect the Great Lakes. He was the driving force behind the November meeting and Declaration of Michigan and Canadian tribes.

> We cannot support these documents [the Agreement and Compact] until Tribes and First Nations in the Great Lakes Basin area have a representative voice along with the States and Provinces. Tribes and First Nations interests must be appropriately heard and our solutions for addressing these interests and the interests of the waters must be incorporated into the final Agreement and Compact … Tribal and First Nations representatives will strengthen the process by ensuring that all of the interested parties are represented and have committed to implementing the protections that are being envisioned. We must never lose sight that our goal is the protection of the Great Lakes for this and the next seven generations.[43]

These and similar comments raised important legal and practical questions about the development and content of the Draft Agreement and Compact. Despite their compelling arguments relating to the legal status of the Tribes as sovereign nations, there was substantial concern within the tribal community that it was too late for any real impact on the Final Drafts. While the Final Drafts could be expected to reflect some changes in response to public comments, the basic structure was unlikely to be altered. Recognition of this reality prompted the Tribes to speak with a united voice.

This united voice emerged during the fall of 2004 as member Tribes discussed the issue at meetings of the Midwest Alliance of Sovereign Tribes and of the National Congress of American Indians (NCAI). This later meeting resulted in a strongly worded Resolution, which provided:

> WHEREAS, Tribes were not included during the development process or offered any meaningful involvement in the compact negotiation process for the Great Lakes Water Resources Compact, the resulting compact fails to reflect Tribal and First Nations interests in the groundwater …
>
> WHEREAS the importance of a compact for the survival and long-term well being of the Great Lakes is recognized by all Tribes and First Nations …
>
> NOW THEREFORE BE IT RESOLVED that the NCAI hereby objects to the compact, as drafted, and requests that Congress not consent to the compact until Tribal and First Nations concerns are properly addressed in the process.[44]

43 Comments of Frank Ettawageshet, Tribal Chairman of the Little Traverse Bay Band of Odawa Indians (Oct. 13, 2004) (on file with author).

44 National Congress of American Indians Resolution #FTL-04018, Tribal Participation in the Great Lakes Resources Compact & Great Lakes Basin Water Resources (adopted at the NCAI Annual Session, Oct. 15, 2004) (on file with author). The NCAI is the largest and older organization of tribal governments in the United States, with over 250 tribal government members from all portions of the United States. The NCAI has

Informal discussions at the NCAI meeting also led tribal leaders to conclude that the Great Lakes Tribes must join with the First Nations to articulate their objections to the Annex 2001 process with a united voice before the Agreement and Compact were adopted in final form, then scheduled for January 2005. Slightly over one month later another meeting was held at Saulte Ste Marie, Michigan. A brief description of the meeting may help to provide a feel for the distinctive approach Tribes and First Nations bring to resource protection issues.

The room itself was set up with concentric circles of chairs (rather than the more common auditorium style), with entrances from all four directions; the keynote speaker was a representative of the Water Walkers.[45] In addition, a pipe ceremony was performed using a pipe that is over 300 years old and had been used in Montreal in 1701.[46] Approximately 160 tribal leaders attended from both sides of the border, representing 120 Tribes and First Nations. Signatories included the Union of Ontario Indians, which represents 42 First Nations, the Association of Iroquois and Allied Indians, representing eight First Nations, and the Ninhawbc-Aski Nation, representing 53 First Nations. In addition, 44 individual tribes from Ontario, New York, Pennsylvania, Ohio, Indiana, Illinois, Michigan, Wisconsin, and Minnesota signed.[47] After every leader talked about the document, each came to the front of the room individually to sign it.[48] It was then smudged with sage and read aloud in Anishnabe, in an on-the-spot translation by the Pipe Carrier Frank Kelley. At the end, the drum played an honor song and virtually everyone danced in honor of what had occurred. All in attendance were given a small tobacco bundle to spread with a prayer in their individual portion of the lakes.[49]

The resulting Tribal and First Nations Great Lakes Water Accord reiterated the concerns of the earlier letters and comments, emphasizing that Tribes and First Nations "continue to exercise cultural and spiritual rights of self determination and property rights within our traditional territories ... we are not political subdivisions

---

recently expanded its influence by agreeing to work with the Assembly of First Nations, a comparable Canadian organization.

45 *See supra* note 2. This was important because, in traditional Chippewa and Ottawa culture, women are responsible for protection of water.

46 This was important because tribes on both sides of the border had not been brought together in one place for a very long time. Interview with Frank Ettawageshik, Sept. 22, 2006.

47 *Id.*; Tribal and First Nations Great Lakes Water Accord, Nov. 23, 2004 [Editor's note: the entire Accord, including signatures, can be found in Hand, *supra* note 1, at 840–47]. *See also* Press Release, Indigenous Nations Unite for Inclusion in Great Lakes Decision-making Process (Nov. 23, 2004) (on file with author).

48 Interview with Frank Ettawageshik, *supra* note 48. Some leaders included their clan sign, as was done in the early treaties.

49 Representatives from the Annex 2001 process were at the meeting as observers.

of the States or Provinces."[50] It concluded, "we are further pledging to work together with each other and with the other governments in the Great Lakes Basin to secure a healthy future for the Great Lakes."[51] In effect, the Tribes and First Nations asserted that, without their participation, there is a gap in the coverage of the Agreement and Compact system.

Almost immediately, an invitation was extended to attend a meeting with the Water Management Working Group.[52] This meeting took place in Chicago on February 1, 2005. At that meeting presentations were made by members of both the Working Group and the various Tribal and First Nations representatives. After discussions of both substantive issues and concerns about the process, the Tribes and First Nations were assured that the draft agreements were "not intended to infringe on aboriginal or treaty rights, or rights held by a Tribe or First Nation based on its status as a Tribe or a First Nation."[53] The meeting ended with a promise that the "Working Group will continue to discuss how best to continue dialogue with representatives of the Tribes and First Nations."[54] Further, the Tribes were assured that the agreements "are a work in progress and that alternatives are still under consideration."[55]

The Final Draft of the Compact, while essentially the same as the earlier drafts, does contain additional language of importance to the Tribes and First Nations. The most important language from the tribal perspective occurs in the expansion of Section 8.1, Effect on Existing Rights. The earlier version provided that the Compact will have no effect on water withdrawals established by state or federal law prior to the effective date of the Compact and that the Compact would not interfere with the common law water rights laws of the Signatory Parties. The final draft adds: "Nothing in this compact is intended to abrogate or derogate from

---

50 Tribal and First Nations Great Lakes Water Accord, *supra* note 47.

51 *Id.*

52 A review of the summaries of all the meetings of the Working Group and its Subcommittees shows that, at the Group's initial meeting on March 15, 2002, both the Canadian Environmental Law Association, Great Lakes United, and CORA told the Group that there should be greater involvement of the Tribes. This was reiterated at the next meeting on April 23, 2004 by the Canadian Environmental Law Association. No further mention of the Tribes occurs, despite numerous discussions about public participation, until more than two years later on November 15, 2004, when the Working Group was provided with a summary of tribal comments on the First Draft of the Agreements. After the Inter-Tribal Accord each meeting devoted some time to discussing how the Tribes should be included in the Agreement. For summaries of the meetings, see Water Management Working Group Meeting Summaries, Great Lakes Water Management Initiative, http://www.cglg.org/projects/water/GroupSummaries.asp.

53 Meeting Summary of Council of Great Lakes Governors Water Management Working Group Meeting with Tribal and First Nations Representatives (Feb. 1, 2005) (on file with the Council of Great Lakes Governors).

54 *Id.*

55 *Id.*

treaty rights or rights held by any Tribe recognized by the federal government of the United States based upon its status as a Tribe recognized by the federal government of the United States."[56]

The Compact also provides for consultation but no enforceable input from the Tribes. In language very similar to that of the parallel section of the First Draft, Compact Article 5, Section 51, Tribal Consultation, provides that, in addition to other opportunities for public participation, "appropriate consultations" will occur on "all Proposals subject to Council or Regional Review." It also provides that notice of proposals and of any meeting or hearing on such proposals shall be given to the Tribes. Finally, "the Parties and the Council shall consider the comments received under this Section before approving, approving with modification or disapproving any Proposal subject to this Compact."[57]

In the two years since the Compact went into effect, most activity has focused on developing the institutions that will implement the two agreements. The Council of Great Lakes Governors continues to serve as the secretariat for the Compact and Agreement regime. In a series of quarterly meetings, basic decisions were made about committee structures and procedures required of applicants seeking approval to remove water from the lakes. In each instance, the Regional Body (made up of states and provinces) met immediately prior to the meeting of the Compact Body. (Several of the meetings were held by conference call, in order to save money.[58]) Additionally, before each meeting proposed documents were provided to Tribes and First Nations, followed by a conference call consultation. In contrast to the intense transparency of the 2001 Annex process, no records have been kept of which Tribes chose to participate

56 Great Lakes–St Lawrence River Basin Resource Compact, *supra* note 35. *See also* Great Lakes–St Lawrence River Basin Sustainable Water Resources Agreement (2005), *available at* http://www.cglg.org/projects/water/docs/12-13-05/Great_Lakes-St_Lawrence_River_Basin_Sustainable_Water_Resources_Agreement.pdf.

57 The text of Article 5 Consultation with Tribes reads as follows:

"In addition to all other opportunities to comment pursuant to Section 6.2, appropriate consultations will occur with federally recognized Tribes in the Originating Party for all proposals subject to Council or Regional Review pursuant to this Compact … such consultations shall be organized in the manner suitable to the individual Proposal and the laws and policies of the Originating party.

All federally recognized Tribes within the Basin shall receive reasonable notice indicating that they have an opportunity to comment in writing to the Council or the Regional Body, or both, and other relevant organizations on whether the Proposal meets the requirements of the Standard of Review and Decision when a Proposal is subject to Regional Review or council approval. The notice from the council shall inform the Tribes of any meeting or hearing … and invite them to attend." Great Lakes–St Lawrence River Basin Resource Compact, *supra* note 35, at Art. 5

58 The use of conference calls comes at a price because they inhibit public participation and hence transparency.

in the calls or what comments were made.[59] The clear impression is that in this context "consultation" means "here is what we are doing, what do you think?" rather than genuinely seeking tribal input into decisions.[60]

The requirement in these agreements that the decision-makers "consult" suffers from the common weakness of such requirements: it lacks clear content articulating the parties' obligations. The concept has a long, if sometimes vague, history in international law, generally relating to a requirement to disclose, and, where natural resources are at issue, to prepare an environmental impact assessment that should be made available to the relevant parties. There is, however, a more useful model, which has developed in Canada, defining the duties owed to First Nations, when governmental decisions may injure or otherwise affect natural resources to which a First Nation has a claim. This body of law was triggered by Section 35(1) of the Canadian Constitution Act, 1982.[61] In the 1980s, the Canadian government began a program of resolving First Nation land claims, with a stated focus of developing a sustainable relationship between the First Nations and the rest of Canada, as represented by the Canadian government. This provision was interpreted early on by the Canadian Supreme Court, in *R. v. Sparrow*, to require that any decision by the government that infringes on tribal rights must be justified, and a key component of this justification is to show that the government has adequately consulted with the affected First Nation.[62] Since *Sparrow*, numerous decisions, both by the lower courts and the Supreme Court, have explored the procedural and substantive content of this duty.[63]

The underlying principle driving this requirement is the recognition that the government ("the Crown") has a fiduciary duty to protect the interests of the First Nations. This is articulated in terms of the charming requirement that government activity must be consistent with the "honor of the Crown." This duty means that government actions must infringe on the rights of First Nations as little as possible and a key component in meeting that obligation is to meaningfully consult with the

59 Telephone interview with Peter Johnson, Deputy Director Great Lakes Council Governors, February 8, 2011.

60 This rather thin process has not, so far, triggered any strong objections from the Tribes. This may partially due to the fact that Council actions so far have been limited to processing issues in setting up the structures rather than ones involving approvals of removal of water from the lakes. Also, Tribal governments, like governments generally, have rather limited resources, with many needs calling for their attention and resources. When there is no crisis to be dealt with, their focus tends to be elsewhere.

61 Section 35(1) provides: "The existing aboriginal and treaty rights of the aboriginal peoples of Canada are hereby recognized and affirmed." Constitution Act, 1982, s.35, being Schedule B to the Canada Act 1982 (UK), 1982, c 11.

62 *R. v Sparrow* (1990), 1 S.C.R. 1075 at 119.

63 *See generally* Dwight G. Newman, The Duty to Consult: New Relationships with Aboriginal Peoples (2009).

affected First Nation. Failure to do so will result in a rejection of the government action by the courts.

In enforcing this right, the courts have not laid out an exhaustive checklist of the government's obligations, but have developed and elaborated on the concept over time by examining the facts and circumstances of each case.[64] According to the Canadian Supreme Court, the government must act "in good faith and with the intention of substantially addressing the concerns of the Aboriginal peoples."[65] Acting with honor demands that the Crown must not engage in "sharp dealing" in interpreting treaty rights.[66] This approach, even more than the specifics discussed below, is needed to govern the relationship between Tribes and the other governments, and the operation of the Compact and Agreement.

As the Supreme Court has developed the contours of the duty to consult, the first duty is to inform the First Nation not only of the facts of the development in question, but also of the potential impact of the decision upon the resource of the First Nation and their use of it.[67] This is part of the broader duty of environmental impact assessment, although not limited to it.

The degree of consultation varies with the circumstances. Where the imposition on Tribal claims is "less serious or relatively minor, it will be no more than a duty to discuss important decisions that will be taken."[68] In most cases, the duty requires something significantly deeper, and includes a duty to accommodate aboriginal rights. "Some cases may even require the full consent of the aboriginal nation."[69]

As the above language suggests, the duty to consult is not purely procedural. "The effect of good faith consultation may be to reveal a duty to accommodate … [It] may require taking steps to avoid irreparable harm or to minimize the effects of infringement."[70] At this point, what began as a procedural right includes genuine, if somewhat vague, substantive rights, which are enforceable in court.

The government's duty of consultation is accompanied by an obligation on the part of First Nations to act reasonably. As the British Columbia Supreme Court noted, "consultation is a two way street."[71] Thus, if the First Nation refuses to take part in the process, a court is unlikely to find that the Crown failed to fulfill its duty.

---

64 *R. v Gladstone*, (1986) 2 S.C.R. 723 at 768.

65 *Delgamuukw v British Columbia* (1997) 3 S.C.R.1010 at 1113.

66 *Haida Nation v British Columbia* (Minister of Forests), [2004] 3 S.C.R. 511, 2004. SCC 73. A major issue faced by the Canadian judiciary in developing this doctrine was whether it applied to Aboriginal rights and land claims that had not yet been adjudicated, a question substantial resolved in the United States.

67 *Id.* at 423.

68 *Delgamuukw*, *supra* note 65, at para 168.

69 *Id.* at para 168, quoted with approval in *Haida Nation*, *supra* note 66, at para 40.

70 *Haida Nation*, *supra* note 66, at para 47.

71 *Cheslatta Carrier Nation v British Columbia* [1998] 3 CNLR 1 (BCSC) at 21. *See also Haida Nation*, *supra* note 66, at para 42 ("As for Aboriginal claimants, they must not frustrate the Crown's reasonable good faith attempts, nor should they take unreasonable

While the line of cases developed by the Canadian courts does not provide a simple template for the operation of the commitment to consult, it does suggest an example of a more appropriate relationship with the Tribes and First Nations in the operations of the Compact and Agreement system. The contrast between the between the generous, honorable approach demanded by the Canadian duty to consult and the reluctant, rather crabbed, approach adopted in the negotiation and implementation of the Compact and Agreement is striking.

The current approach to consultation recognizes the government-to-government nature of the relationship of the Tribes with the states and provinces, and their collective body created by the Compact and Agreement. Yet it reflects no commitment to accommodate the Tribes' objections to diversions or consumptive uses that may be approved under the Compact. Concern that this leaves both the lakes and the Tribes vulnerable is justified. The Compact itself allows for diversions of substantial quantities of water without any requirement of approval by the Council or Regional Body so long as the water is transported in containers smaller than 5.7 gallons,[72] a bow to pressure from the bottled water industry. The inclusion of this large loophole in the protection provided by the agreements was a key substantive issue raised by various Tribal and First Nations representatives during the comment process.[73]

Native American Role in Environmental Protection

The weakness of the consultation mechanisms currently in place, particularly in comparison to the more robust Canadian model, is detrimental to the broader good of protecting the Great Lakes. This is true for a variety of reasons, many of which involve the sort of broad generalizations that should be approached very cautiously.[74] Nevertheless, these assertions do have basis in fact, not merely in stereotype or rhetoric.

---

positions to thwart government from making decisions where, despite meaningful consultation, agreement is not reached.").

72 Great Lakes–St Lawrence River Basin Resource Compact, *supra* note 35, at §4.12 (10) Agreement, Article 207(9).

73 For example, in the Comments on the proposed Great Lake Basin Sustainable Water Resources Agreement by the Great Lakes Indian Fish and Wildlife Commission took the position that "the agreements must not allow through the back door what could not be accomplished through the front, that is, they must not allow in essence bulk removals of water in small bottles." (August 31, 2005) (on file with author).

74 Of relevance here is the fact that indigenous people, when faced with a choice between development and environmental protection do not always choose to manage their resources in a pro-environmental way. *See* Ezra Rosser, *Ahistorical Indians and Reservation Resources*, 40 Envtl. L. 437 (2010) (discussing the complexity of such decisions).

Indian Tribes and First Nations people offer a perspective on protection of the land and water, which is quite distinct from that of the dominant culture.[75] This arises from a variety of sources. For many tribes, culture and spirituality are intertwined and relate to sacred places, which are not buildings such as churches or temples, but specific natural features. This encourages particularly intense efforts to protect such places from exploitation so as to preserve them in their natural condition.

This emphasis on preservation of land and water is also tied to physical well-being, at least for tribal members who live on reservations and take at least part of their livelihood from the land. As a result, problems such as high levels of toxic chemicals in fish, which are consumed in much higher quantities than in other communities, are particularly acute.[76] The immediacy of these impacts creates an intense awareness of such problems and particular enthusiasm for remedying them.

Another cultural characteristic, a long-range perspective on decision-making, is broadly embraced by North American tribes. This is often articulated as a principle that decisions should be taken with a view to protecting the welfare of seven future generations.[77] This idea, which is currently asserted by the environmental community under the label of "intergenerational equity," is often overlooked in governmental and commercial decision-making in favor of short-term (usually economic) benefit.[78]

Finally, Indian tribal governments are political like all governmental entities, but the constituencies they need to please can be quite different from those that drive state and federal politicians. For example, during the Compact and Agreement process, the Tribes have been among the strongest voices opposing the well-financed water-bottling industry. As a result, a tribal voice can be a balancing factor against the compelling demands of the industrial and commercial sectors. Taken together, these attributes suggest that Tribal and First Nation participation is likely to improve the quality of resource decision-making. On a more pragmatic level, Tribes and First Nations, which are not bound by the agreement, could

75 Frank Ettawageshik explains, "The degradation of water in the Great lakes devastates the traditional culture and spirituality of native peoples." E-mail comment from Frank Ettawageshik, Tribal Chairman of the Little Travers Bay Band of Odawa Indians to Michigan Department of Environmental Quality, October 18, 2004 (on file with author and with the Council of Great Lakes Governors). *See generally* Rebecca A. Tsosie, *Tribal Environmental Policy in an Era of Self-Determination: The Role of Ethics, Economics, and Traditional Ecological Knowledge*, 21 VT. L. REV. 225 (1996).

76 *See* John Fesher, *Mercury Tainted Fish Special Concern in Native Communities of Great Lakes Region*, Indigenous Environmental Network, http://www.ienearth.org/news/mercury-tainted-fish-special-concern-in-Native-communities-of-great-lakes-region.html.

77 *See* Tsosie, *supra* note 75, at 285.

78 *See generally* EDITH BROWN WEISS, IN FAIRNESS TO FUTURE GENERATIONS: INTERNATIONAL LAW, COMMON PATRIMONY AND INTERGENERATIONAL EQUITY (1989).

arguably undermine it by diverting water or otherwise exercising their rights in a way contradictory to them.

Conclusion

The Compact and Agreement recognize indigenous rights to the Great Lakes by incorporating a duty to consult with Tribes and First Nations. If that duty is exercised by merely informing native peoples what the issues are without taking into account and accommodating their concerns, the system of protection for the Great Lakes may be less than maximally effective. By contrast, if the duty is given real meaning by genuine and generous consultation, not only will the Council and Regional Body, and the governments they represent, have acted with honor, but they will also have constructed an improved template for managing many similarly shared resources.

Chapter 8
Tribes as Conservation Easement Holders: Is a Partial Property Interest Better than None?

Jessica Owley[1]

The Klamath Tribes (composed of the Modoc, Klamath, and Yahooskin) are among the largest and wealthiest of American Indian nations. The current success of the Klamath is perhaps surprising in light of their unsettled history regarding their land. In the 1860s, the Tribes ceded over 23 million acres to the United States in exchange for a secure reservation and guaranteed hunting, fishing, and gathering rights along with other government-provided benefits. In 1954, the Klamath Tribes lost another 1.8 million acres in the termination process.[2] Beyond the economic impacts of losing natural resources, termination was detrimental to the Tribes' spiritual connection with their ancestral lands, for which they held stewardship obligations.

While the Klamath have been successful in restoring their economy and political structure, they have struggled with regaining control of their traditional lands. The Tribes' traditional lands have been degraded and resources have been depleted. The Tribes have prioritized land reacquisition and ecosystem restoration to overcome the termination-era legacies. The Klamath Tribes view return of their formerly held lands as "an essential element of their restoration as a people, and the reconstruction of their once vital economy."[3] The Klamath Constitution

---

1 Associate Professor, University at Buffalo (SUNY) Law School. Many thanks to Ezra Rosser and Sarah Krakoff for organizing the symposium that led to the book, and for providing excellent editorial assistance and advice. I also benefited greatly from conservations with Beth Rose Middleton, whose recent book Trust in the Land: New Directions in Tribal Conservation (2011) is an invaluable resource for anyone interested in this topic.

2 Klamath Termination Act of 1954, P. L. No. 587, ch. 732, 68 Stat. 718 (1955) (codified at 25 U.S.C. 564). The termination policy did two things detrimental to the long-term protection of Klamath land. First, it removed many of the federal government's responsibilities to the Tribes that had earlier been established by treaty. Second, it took land out of tribal ownership and dispersed it to individual landowners. This land quickly moved out of tribal hands and beyond tribal control.

3 The Klamath Tribes, The Long Struggle Home: The Klamath Tribes; Fight to

references the Tribes' intent to reacquire all tribal land and resources[4] and charges the tribal government with protecting the Tribes' wildlife and natural resources.[5]

An essential part of the Tribes' long-term plan to rebuild the community and restore the environment is reacquiring ceded and terminated lands from the federal government, which currently holds over 690,000 acres of Klamath land as U.S. Forest Service land. The Tribes are working with the federal government to resecure title to these lands. Return of these federally held lands to the Tribes will not reestablish all of the Klamath Tribes' former lands, however. Restoration of Klamath ancestral lands also includes acquiring land now in private hands. In their efforts to assert control over these lands in private hands, the Tribes are engaging in a new strategy. Instead of obtaining fee title to former Klamath lands, the Tribes entered into an agreement with private landowners to hold only a partial interest in the land.

Becky and Taylor Hyde, a ranching couple from Oregon, were determined to demonstrate that sensible management of property could restore even the most degraded habitat. To that end, they bought the Yainix Ranch (a severely degraded property) with the purpose of restoring it. From the beginning, they wanted to protect the property with a conservation easement. Conservation easements create perpetual restrictions on land use with the intent of yielding an environmental purpose. The potential enforcers, or holders, of conservation easements vary slightly by state law, but are generally either non-profit land-conservation organizations or governmental entities.

After considering potential conservation easement holders, the Hydes decided to approach the Klamath Tribes. The Hydes felt that the Klamath Tribes had a genuine interest in preserving the natural resources on the land and had the long-term vision appropriate for conservation easement stewardship. The Yainix Ranch is on land once held by the Tribes, and the Klamath Tribes retain hunting, gathering, and fishing rights on the land. Thus, even though the Tribes had no experience with conservation easements, the landowners asked the Tribes to be part of their land restoration and protection endeavor.

While the Tribes hold the conservation easement, the U.S. Department of Agriculture funded the purchase and management of the conservation easement through the Natural Resources Conservation Service's (NRCS) Farm and Ranchland Protection Program. The state of Oregon also provided financial support through the Oregon Watershed Enhancement Board. Even with this structure, it took a few years of negotiating before the Klamath Tribes agreed to accept the conservation easement.

One of the deciding factors for the Tribes was probably the fact that the Yainix Ranch is on land that the Tribes held prior to the termination process in the 1950s.

Restore Their Land, People and Economic Self-Sufficiency, http://www.klamathtribes.org/information/background/home.html (last visited June 15, 2011).

4 The Klamath Tribes Const. art IV, § B.

5 *Id.* § H.

Protection of the Yainix Ranch is in keeping with the Tribes' stated interest in protecting ancestral lands. The decision to hold a conservation easement instead of seeking fee simple title to this land may be an acknowledgment that it will be difficult to obtain title to the over 1.8 million acres of ancestral lands now in the hands of the federal government and private landowners. Acquiring conservation easements over such land may be a way for the Tribes to ensure appropriate management of the land regardless of whether they eventually acquire fee simple title to it.

The story of the Klamath told here presents a potential model for other tribes seeking to obtain some control over lands outside of their jurisdiction. While the Klamath may prefer obtaining fee simple title and establishing jurisdiction over ancestral lands, conservation easements offer them a way to control land use, protect tribal natural resources (on and off reservation), and develop amicable working relationships with nearby landowners.

This chapter explains how conservation easements work and then explores how and why tribal governments might choose to use them. While conservation easements may present a unique opportunity for extending tribal policies to private land, concerns regarding their structure and enforceability indicate that tribes should enter into these arrangements cautiously.

Introduction

Conservation easement use is growing rapidly, as is the number of organizations looking to the tool to meet land conservation needs. Until recently, tribes had not been involved in conservation easement transactions, but examples are now emerging of tribes taking part in conservation easements in multiple ways. Some tribes are deciding to hold conservation easements, either as a tribe or through tribal corporations and non-profit organizations. Others are choosing to encumber tribal land with conservation easements, giving non-profit organizations the ability to enforce perpetual land-use restrictions on tribal land. Finally, some tribes are using their resources to support and promote conservation easements on other land, hoping the restrictions will benefit tribal land and resources.

This chapter examines the most common way in which tribes have become involved in conservation easement transactions—tribes as conservation easement holders. The chapter first defines conservation easements and provides general contours regarding their formation and use. Conservation easements are a creature of state law, and this discussion necessarily delves into that law before examining other legal foundations for tribes to hold conservation easements. The chapter next explores why tribes decide to hold conservation easements. This section looks at the choice to use conservation easements generally and then situates the decision in the evolution of property law in the United States both on and off tribal land. The availability of the conservation easement tool offers tribes a method for extending tribal environmental values and stewardship traditions beyond the borders of Indian land. However, conservation easements are a uniquely American form of property that emerge from Lockean roots and embrace a libertarian notion of property rights.[6] In that light, tribal embrace of the tool may seem surprising as both the Lockean and libertarian notions of property have done harm to tribal sovereignty and may be at odds with traditional tribal practices.[7]

The chapter concludes by asking whether tribes *should* use conservation easements. Wrapped up in this question is an assessment of the conservation easement tool generally as a vehicle for long-term land protection. I have elsewhere cautioned local governments on their conservation easement use,[8] and many of the same concerns apply to tribes deciding to hold conservation easements. The strength of the conservation easement tool is that it gives government entities the ability to extend their land conservation and environmental stewardship roles beyond their jurisdictional boundaries. Tribes may not have the power to regulate land use in nearby communities, but they can acquire conservation easements over such land and obtain similar results. Thus, despite some discordance owing to the anticommunitarian sentiments at the heart of conservation easements, the conservation easement tool may provide tribes with an avenue for furthering tribal goals of conservation and intergenerational equity.

***How*: the Mechanics of Tribes Holding of Conservation Easements**

Conservation Easement Basics

Conservation easements are non-possessory interests in land with a conservation purpose. That is, they are servitudes restricting a landowner's ability to use her land in an otherwise permissible way with the goal that the restriction will yield an environmental benefit. Conservation easements usually restrict development. Under such an agreement, a landowner's ability to develop her land is restricted beyond what federal, state, and local laws already circumscribe.

---

6 Jessica Owley Lippmann, *The Emergence of Exacted Conservation Easements*, 84 NEBRASKA L. REV. 1043, 1063–68 (2006).

7 To describe "tribal notions of property" is a challenging (if not impossible) task. There is no single tribal notion of property or of environmental stewardship. To discuss tribes in general terms means gliding over the fact that we are talking about different nations, different people, and different traditions. Summarizing tribal notions of property in a book chapter necessarily involves painting tribal traditions with a broad brush and using simplistic examples. However, because there are some similar threads in the land-conservation practices of many tribes, the simple comparisons and summaries included herein still offer good fodder for considering the use of conservation easements by tribes in the United States.

8 Jessica Owley, *Use of Conservation Easements by Local Governments*, *in* GREENING LOCAL GOVERNMENT (Patricia Salkin & Keith Hirokawa eds., forthcoming 2012).

Conservation easements are usually, but not necessarily, perpetual. Under classic property law terms, we conceptualize the landowner burdened by a conservation easement as the owner of the servient estate. In a change from the law of servitudes, however, the owner of the dominant estate is not necessarily a neighbor or even a landowner. State conservation easement statutes enable non-profit organizations and government entities to be the owners (or holders) of the conservation easements regardless of their status as landowners.[9] Holders of conservation easements have the right to enforce the agreements and ensure that landowners comply with the restrictions imposed.[10]

Conservation easement statutes outline the permissible purposes of conservation easements, set the rules regarding who may hold conservation easements, and define other terms and restrictions. Although state laws vary in these requirements, there are many similarities among them.[11] Over 20 states have adopted some form of the Uniform Conservation Easement Act (UCEA) promulgated by the National Conference of Commissioners on Uniform State Laws in 1981.[12]

As their name indicates, conservation easements must have a conservation purpose. The UCEA sets forth the following as a list of acceptable purposes:

> retaining or protecting natural, scenic, or open-space values of real property, assuring its availability for agricultural, forest, recreational, or open-space use, protecting natural resources, maintaining or enhancing air or water quality, or preserving the historical, architectural, archaeological, or cultural aspects of real property.[13]

Conservation easements are governed by state conservation easement statutes—not common law. However, in most states, they are still tied to common law rules regarding servitudes. Most conservation easement statutes indicate that conservation easements should follow the same general rules as traditional easements when it comes to issues like recordation, amendment, and termination.[14] Thus, when examining conservation easements, one must consider the state

9 *See, e.g.*, Uniform Conservation Easement Act § 1(2)(i) [hereinafter UCEA]; Cal. Civ. Code § 815.2; N.Y. Envtl. Conserv. Law § 49-0303(2).

10 In some cases, holders also have affirmative obligations usually relating to maintenance of vegetation, signs, or trails.

11 *Powell on Real Property* contains a short overview of the various state laws, explaining broadly the differences among the state conservation easement statutes. 4-34A Powell on Real Property § 34A.03 (Michael Allen Wolf ed. 2010).

12 *Available at* http://www.law.upenn.edu/bll/archives/ulc/ucea/2007_final.htm. Although the act itself has not been amended, the Executive Committee amended the prefatory notes and comments in 2007 to update the discussion of charitable trusts.

13 UCEA § 1(1).

14 *See, e.g.*, UCEA § 2(a). There is a fair amount of debate within the land trust community as to what this actually means. Some scholars feel that charitable trust doctrines apply to conservation easements in a way that trumps this phrase. When trying to

conservation easement statute as well as state statutory and common law of easements. Additionally, conservation easements often create conservation trusts and the agreements are akin to contracts. To fully understand and evaluate the validity and worth of a conservation easement, one must be well versed in property, contract, and trust law. Where tribes are part of the arrangements, federal Indian law is added to the mix, specifically questions involving jurisdiction and sovereignty.

One way that tribes become involved in conservation easements is by deciding to hold conservation easements on non-tribal land. That is, tribes negotiate restrictions with landowners. In exchange for agreeing to the land restrictions, the landowner generally obtains (1) federal income tax deductions, (2) money, or (3) a land-use permit.[15]

State Conservation Easement Statutes

State conservation easement statutes define permissible holders of conservation easements. Most statutes define two types of holders: non-profit organizations with land-conservation missions (or land trusts) and governmental entities. Two states add tribes to this list. No state explicitly prohibits tribes. Thus, conservation easement statutes fall into one of three groups: (1) those that specifically allow tribes to hold conservation easement, (2) those that impliedly allow tribes to hold conservation easements, and (3) those that impliedly prohibit tribes from holding conservation easements.

Specifically allowed Two states explicitly recognize the rights of tribal governments to hold conservation easements: California and Oregon. California's main conservation easement statute, the California Conservation Easement Act (or CalCEA), was passed in 1979. The statute was amended in 2004, adding federally recognized California Native American tribes to the list of permissible holders.[16] The statute explains that a "federally recognized California Native American tribe or [...] nonfederally recognized California Native American tribe that is on the contact list maintained by the Native American Heritage Commission to protect a California Native American prehistoric archaeological, cultural, spiritual, or

determining the rules regarding amendment, merger, and termination, be sure to investigate the property, contract, and trust law implications in your state.

15 I have only seen examples of tribes holding purchased or donated conservation easements, but they could also hold exacted conservation easements. Additionally, some conservation easements are the result of court settlements and eminent domain proceedings. Although there do not appear to be any tribal holders of such conservation easements, it is an arrangement that could develop.

16 § 815.3(c), added by Stats 2004, c. 905 (S.B.18), § 2.

ceremonial place" can hold a conservation easement as long as that conservation easement is "voluntarily conveyed."[17]

Passed in 1983, Oregon's conservation easement act adopts some of the UCEA's language, but has unique requirements regarding permissible holders:

> (3) "Holder" means:
>
> (a) The state, any county, metropolitan service district, soil and water conservation district, city or park and recreation district or a county service district established under ORS 451.410 to 451.610 to construct, maintain and operate service facilities in Washington or Clackamas Counties for the purposes specified in ORS 451.010 (1)(a) and (b) and in Washington County for the purpose specified in ORS 451.010 (5) acting alone or in cooperation with any federal or state agency, public corporation or political subdivision;
> (b) [a land trust]; or
> (c) An Indian tribe as defined in ORS 97.740.[18]

Subsection (c) was added to the act in 2001. Both California and Oregon acknowledge the validity of conservation easements held by tribes and expand the definition of tribes somewhat beyond federally recognized tribes. This explicit statutory inclusion of tribes as holders means that a conservation easement will not be held invalid solely because a tribe is serving as the holder. Such language may increase the faith landowners or funders will have in tribes as holders. Provisions such as these that bolster confidence in the enforceability of the agreements may increase their use.

Impliedly allowed Many states model their statutes after the Uniform Conservation Easement Act. Commissioners at the National Conference of Commissioners on Uniform State Laws (NCCUSL) wrote the model act in 1981,

17 Cal. Civ. Code § 815.3(c). The meaning of this phrase is unclear. This requirement also applies to state and local government holders but not to land trusts. Arguably, it prevents tribes from holding any conservation easement created by condemnation or judicial decree (as with natural resource damages). One could read it to also prohibit tribes from holding exacted conservation easements. No California court has interpreted this phrase. *See* Jessica Owley, *Enforceability of Exacted Conservation Easements* (forthcoming Vermont L. Rev. 2012), *available at* http://papers.ssrn.com/sol3/papers.cfm?abstract_id=1925065.

18 Or. Rev. Stat. § 271.715(3). Interestingly, ORS § 97.740 is a section of state law regarding Indian graves, but section (4) of that law defines Indian tribe as "any tribe of Indians recognized by the Secretary of the Interior or listed in the Klamath Termination Act, 25 U.S.C. 3564 et seq., or listed in the Western Oregon Indian Termination Act, 25 U.S.C. 3691 et seq., if the traditional cultural area of the tribe includes Oregon lands."

and it has been adopted in whole or part by at least 21 states.[19] The act sets forth two categories of permissible holders:

> (i) a governmental body empowered to hold an interest in real property under the laws of this State or the United States; or
> (ii) charitable corporation, charitable association, or charitable trust, the purposes or powers of which include retaining or protecting the natural, scenic, or open-space values of real property, assuring the availability of real property for agricultural, forest, recreational, or open-space use, protecting natural resources, maintaining or enhancing air or water quality, or preserving the historical, architectural, archaeological, or cultural aspects of real property.[20]

This definition of governmental holder is much broader than seen in either the California or Oregon statutes. Although nothing in the legislative history indicates that the commissioners drafting the UCEA considered the possibility that tribes might choose to hold conservation easements, tribes appear to fit under the definition of governmental holder. To confirm this in each state, one must determine whether the state recognizes a tribe as a "governmental body"[21] and then examine whether a tribe is "empowered to hold an interest in real property under the laws of th[e] state or the United States."[22]

---

19 Uniform Law Commission, Legislative Fact Sheet–Conservation Easement Act, at http://www.nccusl.org/LegislativeFactSheet.aspx?title=Conservation%20Easement%20 Act (last visited June 15, 2011).

20 UCEA § 1(2). Seventeen states use the same definition for governmental holders: Alabama, Alaska, Arizona, Delaware, Georgia, Idaho, Indiana, Kansas, Kentucky, Maine, Minnesota, Mississippi, Oklahoma, South Carolina, South Dakota, Texas, and West Virginia. Louisiana's definition differs only by requiring the interest to be in "immovable property." La. Rev. Stat. Ann. § 9-12721(a). Nevada's statute is slightly simpler, explaining that it is a "governmental body empowered to hold an interest in real property," without mention of state or federal law. Nev. Rev. Stat. § 111.390(2)(a). Pennsylvania refers to the commonwealth instead of the state. 32 Pa. Cons. Stat. § 5051(1). Wisconsin changes "a governmental body" to "any governmental body." Wis. Stat. § 700.4(1)(b)(1).

21 For example, tribes and tribal governments do not appear to meet the definition of "governmental body" under Wisconsin law, which defines governmental body as a "state or local agency, board, commission, committee, council, department or public body corporate and politic created by constitution, statute, ordinance, rule or order[.]" Wis. Stat. § 19.82(1). It makes sense for state definitions of governmental bodies to omit tribes as generally state laws regarding governmental entities will not apply to tribes. It is unclear whether a tribe could successfully argue that it qualifies as a governmental body for conservation easement laws but need not meet other legal requirements for governmental bodies (like open meeting laws).

22 UCEA § 1(2). The Klamath Tribes' constitution recognizes a tribal right to hold interest in real property. However, based on the language of the UCEA, it must be state or federal law that recognizes the right. Tribally owned land falls into three categories: trust lands, restricted fee lands, and non-restricted fee lands. The trust lands are owned

Other state statutes use similar language. For example, in Massachusetts[23] and Montana[24] conservation easements can be held "by any governmental body" and in Colorado[25] and Utah, [26] it is a "governmental entity." In Hawaii, it is even broader as conservation easements can be held by "any public body."[27] It is not clear that conservation easements held by tribes would be valid under these various laws. Some states require governmental holders to have a conservation purpose.[28] Tribes may struggle with this requirement, as it is hard to define the purposes of a tribe in the same narrow confines as seen in the purpose sections of conservation easements.

Impliedly prohibited While many state statutes contain broad language that could encompass tribes, a few states have language that clearly leaves tribes off the list of permissible holders. Where a state law specifically names qualifying governmental entities but does not include tribes on that list, the statute impliedly prohibits tribal holders. For example, New Mexico appears to prohibit tribal holdings because the law prohibits all governmental ownership of conservation easements.[29] While no other statute contains such a broad prohibition—explicitly prohibiting tribal holders—some of the implied language is hard to read in any other way.

For example, in Iowa, the defined category of governmental holder is a specific list of entities: "The department of natural resources, soil and water conservation districts …, the historical division of the department of cultural affairs, the state

---

by the federal government and held in trust for the tribes. For fee lands, the tribe holds the title. Sometimes the land is encumbered by legal restrictions regarding alienation or encumbrances. Non-restricted fee lands enable a tribe to obtain legal title under specific statutory authority. Whether states would require an additional federal law recognizing a tribe's ability to hold conservation easements specifically is uncertain.

23 Mass. Gen laws ch 183 §32.

24 Mont. Code Ann §76-6-201(1).

25 Colo. Rev. Stat. § 38-30.5-104(2).

26 Utah Code Ann. §55-18-3.

27 Haw. Rev. Stat. § 198-3.

28 Neb. Rev. St. §76-2, 11 (2)(a). Some state statutes are inartfully written, and it is not clear whether governmental bodies must have conservation purposes or whether that requirement is only related to non-profit holders. Florida's law states that conservation easements "may be acquired by any governmental body or agency or by a charitable corporation or trust whose purposes include protecting natural, scenic, or open space values of real property," etc. Fla stat. ch. 704.06(3). It is not clear whether the governmental body or agency must be one that has conservation purposes or whether that qualification applies only to charitable corporations or trusts. New Hampshire's and Rhode Islands' laws are similar in that respect. It is not clear whether governmental bodies have to have certain conservation-related purposes or whether all governmental bodies are permissible holders. N.H. Rev. Stat. Ann. § 477:4; R.I. Gen. Law. § 34-39-3.

29 N.Mex.§ 47-12-2(A).

archaeologist …, any county conservation board, and any city or agency of a city."[30] The Arkansas, Missouri, North Carolina, and Ohio lists of permissible governmental holders are similarly specific.[31] Because these lists are specific and do not contain categories that cover tribal governments, tribes are unlikely to be permissible holders under these states' conservation easement acts.

This brief examination of state conservation easement statutes indicates that, where states recognize tribes as governmental entities and acknowledge their right to hold property, tribal conservation easements should be enforceable in state courts. There are, however, several state conservation easement statutes that do not recognize tribes as permissible holders. Thus, if tribes decide to hold conservation easements in those states, they run the risk that the state courts will not uphold the agreements. Few conservation easement disputes reach the courts, but tribes would be appropriately cautious to avoid entering into agreements that do not have the force of state law behind them. However, as with most inquiries into tribal endeavors, state law may not be the right body of law to consider.

Other Sources of Law[32]

Tribal law Typically, transactions involving tribes would be governed at least in part by tribal law. Currently, however, no tribes have conservation easement statutes. A tribe could establish such a statute, perhaps following the experiences of the states or looking to the Uniform Conservation Easement Act. Yet the state statutes establish property rules for land *within* their boundaries. They do not give state governments the ability to create enforceable mechanisms outside their jurisdiction, which is what tribes seek to do where they hold conservation easements. Conservation easements represent an opportunity for governments to influence land use both within and outside their jurisdiction. When outside their jurisdiction, though, government entities must abide by the rules of the jurisdiction they are in. Thus, tribal conservation easement statutes could govern the use of conservation easements on lands where tribes have jurisdiction, but it is not clear whether such agreements would provide an enforcement mechanism for agreements tribes make off-reservation.[33] Federal courts have held that a tribe's

30 IOWA § 457A.1.

31 ARK. CODE. ANN. § 15-20-402(2)(A); MO. REV. STAT. § 67:870; N.C. GEN. STAT. § 121-35(2); OHIO REV. CODE ANN. § 5301.69.

32 Although this chapter only discusses the state law implications of state conservation easement statutes, some states may enable tribes to enter into traditional servitudes and allow enforcement of such agreements under traditional property law. This is likely to be easiest where the land in question physically touches tribal land.

33 Tribal jurisdiction on and off tribal land has had a long and complicated history. In *Brendale v. Confederated Tribes and Bands of the Yakima Indian Nation*, 492 U.S. 408 (1989), the Supreme Court held that tribes have the ability to regulate land use on tribally held land, but only on some of the fee land within a reservation (the fee land on "closed" parts of a reservation).

civil and criminal jurisdictional authority does not extend beyond Indian land, except under specific circumstances. In *Montana v. United States*, 450 U.S. 544 (1981), the Supreme Court outlined the two exceptions to the default presumption that tribes have no jurisdiction over non-members or off-reservation. Under the first *Montana* exception, tribes may "regulate, through taxation, licensing, or other means, the activities of nonmembers who enter consensual relationships with the tribe or its members, through commercial dealing, contracts, leases, or other arrangements."[34] The second *Montana* exception recognizes a tribe's authority "to exercise civil authority over the conduct of non-Indians on fee lands within its reservation when that conduct threatens or has some direct effect on the political integrity, the economic security, or the health or welfare of the tribe."[35] Arguably the first *Montana* exception applies to conservation easements held by tribes. A landowner who donates or sells a conservation easement to a tribe enters into a consensual relationship with the tribe. Conservation easements fall somewhere between a contract and a lease and a federal court should hold that the fist *Montana* exception applies and tribal law (and therefore tribal jurisdiction) governs, especially where the terms of the conservation easement illuminate the tribal role and refer to tribal statutes or regulations.

However, federal courts have been hesitant to recognize the applicability of the *Montana* exceptions, and there appears to be a particular resistance when the regulation involves land held by non-Indians. In *Brendale*, the Court limited the tribe's ability to zone on-reservation fee lands owned by non-members to cover only those lands on the "open" part of the reservation. More recently in *Plains Commerce Bank v. Long Family Land & Cattle Co.*, 544 U.S. 316 (2008), the Court held that sale of on-reservation fee lands was not subject to tribal jurisdiction. In *Plains Commerce Bank*, Justice Roberts (writing for the majority) emphasized that a tribe may have the power to regulate certain activities on such lands, but it does not have the ability to regulate sales of such land.[36] The restrictions in conservation easements look more like zoning than sales, but the nature of a conservation easement means that the restrictions run with the land—that is, new landowners will be bound by the agreement entered into by the previous landowner. Although the decision in *Plains Commerce Bank* describes the dispute as a sale of land from a non-Indian (the Bank) to other non-Indians, the facts of the case indicate that the essence of the dispute centered on an Indian landowner and its dealings with the Bank. Thus, while conservation easements appear to fall comfortably within the first *Montana* exception, the uncertainty in this area of law makes enforceability of a tribal conservation easement statute questionable.[37]

---

34 Montana v. United States, 450 U.S. 544, 565 (1981).

35 *Id.* at 565–66.

36 *Plains Commerce* Bank, 544 U.S. at 334.

37 Additionally, landowners may be hesitant to agree to conservation easements that subject them (and future landowners) to tribal jurisdiction. Landowners may insist that conservation easement be enforceable in state court or through arbitration.

Federal Law

States generally have authority over tribes and tribal members for activities off reservation.[38] However, Congress can legislate otherwise, preempting the application of state law with respect to matters involving the unique relationship between tribes and the federal government.[39] Further, many off-reservation activities by tribes are already grounded in federal law. Federal law might, therefore, provide avenues for enforcement of tribal conservation easements.

Case law seems to indicate that conservation easements established pursuant to a federal plan need not adhere to state conservation easement statutes. For example, in North Dakota, conservation easements may not be perpetual.[40] Yet, the Eighth Circuit upheld perpetual conservation easements held by the federal government.[41] The court held that, where state law is "aberrant or hostile to federal property rights," it is not controlling.[42] The Eighth Circuit found it unnecessary to explore the state law questions because, if they were at all hostile to the federal property rights in the conservation easement, they would not have precluded the conveyance of the disputed property right. The court stated:

> We fully recognize that laws of real property are usually governed by the particular states; yet the reasonable property right conveyed to the United States in this case effectuates an important national concern, the acquisition of necessary land for waterfowl production areas, and should not be defeated by any possible North Dakota law barring the conveyance of this property right. To hold otherwise would be to permit the possibility that states could rely on local property laws to defeat the acquisition of reasonable rights to their citizens' property … and to destroy a national program of acquiring property to aide in the breeding of migratory birds. We, therefore, specifically hold that the property right conveyed to the United States in this case, whether or not deemed a valid easement or other property right under North Dakota law, was a valid conveyance under federal law …[43]

The Supreme Court further supported the idea that federal conservation easements do not need to adhere to state law.[44] In *North Dakota v. United States*, the Court held that North Dakota could not restrict the federal government's ability to acquire conservation easements and prohibited the North Dakota legislature from placing any restrictions on acquisition that directly conflict with federal goals.

---

38 Mescalero Apache Tribe v. Jones, 411 U.S. 145 (1973).

39 *See, e.g.*, The Indian Child Welfare Act of 1978, 25 U.S.C. §§ 1901–1963.

40 N. D.Cent. Code § 47-05-02.1(2) (2011).

41 United States v. Albrecht, 496 F.2d 906 (8th cir. 1974).

42 *Id.* at 911.

43 *Id.*

44 North Dakota v. United States, 460 U.S. 300 (1983).

This indicates that, if the federal government established a program to fund and support tribes' acquisition and administration of conservation easements, there may be no need to turn to state conservation easement statutes for validity. Tribes may seek such an arrangement even in states that allow tribes to hold conservation easements. Tribes may prefer to act under a federal scheme and bring their case in federal court if they are concerned about a hostile state court.[45]

Another way to reach a similar result is to have the conservation easement held by the federal government. When a tribe decides to use conservation easements to achieve its conservation goals, it should consider whether it wants to hold the property interest or it wants the federal government (via the Bureau of Indian Affairs or BIA) to hold the property interest on its behalf.[46] Tribes can hold interests in land without the involvement of the BIA, but the BIA is the designated federal trustee of tribal property. Where the federal government is the holder, not only is there a stronger argument that the holder need not comply with the terms of a state conservation easement statute for validity, but also the government may invoke the Property Clause to enforce the agreement. The Property Clause of the Constitution enables the federal government to make all needful rules regarding federal land.[47] Arguably, this includes rules regarding non-possessory or partial interests as well.[48]

Unique Implications of Tribal Ownership

Where a tribe holds a conservation easement, there are unique issues of enforcement and accountability. While conservation easements give the *holder* a right of enforcement, there are also situations where a *landowner* burdened by a conservation easement would wish to enforce the agreement against the holder. This could happen where the conservation easement includes affirmative obligations on the part of the conservation easement holder (such as trail maintenance or invasive species removal). Most state statutes explicitly recognize the right of landowners to bring actions against conservation easement holders.[49] Where such cases arise, however, the landowner may have a tricky road to navigate in determining where

45 Of course, landowners may prefer state law (and enforcement through state courts).

46 The Secretary of Interior may acquire interests in off-reservation lands—including water and surface rights—"for the purpose of providing land for Indians." Indian Reorganization Act of 1934, 25 U.S.C. § 465 (2006). The process for acquiring such property interests can be onerous and time-consuming. 25 C.F.R. part 151 (2010).

47 U.S. Const. art. IV, § 2, cl.3.

48 Indeed, the regulations regarding land acquisition for Indians recognizes the ability of the federal government to acquire partial property interests. 25 C.F.R. § 151.7.

49 *See, e.g.*, UCEA §3(a)(1). The notes following this section explain, "Owners of interests in real property burdened by easements might wish to sue in cases where the easements also impose duties upon holders and these duties are breached by the holders."

(in which court) to bring the case and establishing that the tribe has waived its sovereign immunity.

The venue of the case will turn on the facts of the situation, but the options are tribal, state, or federal court. Landowners may be resistant to entering into a conservation easement if it appears that the only judicial recourse is tribal court. Non-tribal members (and the federal judiciary) have often expressed hesitancy about tribal courts, and a landowner encumbered by a conservation easement may worry that a tribal adjudication of her claim will be unfair. For similar reasons, a tribe may balk at having state courts preside over conservation easement disputes. Conservation easements that will be (or may become)[50] held by tribes should be clear about the venue for any disputes.

The more complicated issue is whether the tribe can be sued. As with other sovereign governments, tribes can only be sued where they have so consented. A landowner bringing suit against the tribe must show that the tribe has waived its sovereign immunity.[51] Waivers of tribal immunity must be clear.[52] Without a tribal statute regarding conservation easements, the terms of the conservation easement itself must form the basis for waiver.

Potentially more common than landowners suing for enforcement are actions challenging a holder's lack of enforcement. Such cases would arise where a conservation easement holder fails to enforce a conservation easement (whether by choice or inadvertence) or the holder has agreed to terminate or modify a conservation easement in circumstances that others find objectionable. For example, in the Myrtle Grove Controversy, the National Trust agreed to amend a conservation easement in ways that the grantor's descendants (not the underlying landowners), neighbors, environmental organizations, and attorney general felt went against the purposes of the conservation easement and violated the charitable trust created by the conservation easement.[53] In a more recent case, the IRS (Internal Revenue Service) penalized a charitable organization

50 There is an added complication that has yet to arise in practice. Theoretically, a landowner could negotiate a conservation easement with a government agency or non-profit organization that then transfers the conservation easement to a tribe. If the parties did not contemplate the possibility of a tribal holder at the outset of the agreement, the conservation easement deed is unlikely to address issues of venue and sovereign immunity. Where a state government entity held a conservation easement and waived its sovereign immunity regarding the conservation easement, would a tribe's acceptance of transfer constitute a waiver of sovereign immunity? This is a complicated question that may never arise in practice, but with perpetual agreements it is hard to predict the future.

51 *See, e.g.*, Kiowa Tribe v. Mfg. Techs., Inc., 523 U.S. 751, 754 (1998).

52 A tribe can waive its sovereign immunity, C & L Enters., Inc. v. Citizen Band of Potawatomi Indian Tribe, 532 U.S. 411, 418 (2001), or Congress can waive a tribe's immunity, Santa Clara Pueblo v. Martinez, 436 U.S. 49, 58–69 (1978). In either situation, the waiver must be clear.

53 Nancy A. McLaughlin, *Amending Perpetual Conservation Easements: A Case Study of the Myrtle Grove Controversy*, 40 U. Rich. L. Rev. 1031 (2005–2006).

that was not enforcing its conservation easement by stripping it of its charitable tax-exempt status.[54]

While not overwhelming, there are increasing numbers of cases where the actions of conservation easement holders are being challenged. Where the holders are charitable organizations, there are possible repercussions for failing to enforce conservation easements. The organizations may lose their 501(c)(3) status, have to pay fines, or find themselves at the wrong end of an expensive lawsuit (as occurred with the National Trust).[55] Where the conservation easement holder is a governmental entity, there are other methods of compelling enforcement. While the exact mechanisms vary by state, there are usually avenues of enforcement through state and federal administrative procedure acts.[56]

Where the holder of the conservation easement is a tribe, the responses to lack of enforcement are less clear. This is especially true if there is no clear waiver of sovereign immunity. Public outcry and bad press may be persuasive enough, especially where a tribe is eager to build or maintain community relationships and goodwill. In some states, the attorney general (or possibly another entity) may be able to enforce directly against a landowner, but she may be hesitant to do so if it could cause political problems.

At the end of the day, this lack of certainty regarding accountability and enforcement may lead landowners to be cautious about entering into conservation easements with tribes. If a landowner is seeking a tax deduction for donation of a conservation easement, the choice of a tribe as the conservation easement holder could raise questions about long-term viability with the IRS. Despite these abstract concerns, however, there have not been any actual problems with tribal holders of conservation easements. In fact, as with the Hydes and their agreement with the Klamath Tribes, landowners may feel the tribes are the most likely entities to comport with their long-term visions for the land.

---

54 I.R.S. Priv. Ltr. Rul. 201109030 (March 4, 2011).

55 In the *Myrtle Grove* case, the National Trust originally consented to conservation easement amendments that would have conflicted with the conservation easement (and arguably the charitable trust it created). After public protests, the National Trust withdrew its consent for the amendment and was then sued by the landowner for breach of contract. The National Trust settled the case but for a substantial amount and only after extensive judicial proceedings. McLaughlin, *supra* note 53, at 1062.

56 In such cases, persons would sue the agency for failing to enforce the agreement. This would be a complicated arrangement requiring state statutes enabling the suit and a showing of statutory and constitutional standing. It is an inefficient route of enforcing a conservation easement. It is a suit compelling someone else to enforce a law (as opposed to a citizen-suit-style provision that would enable someone with standing to bring suit directly against the landowner, requiring landowner compliance with the terms of the conservation easement). Jessica Owley Lippmann, *Exacted Conservation Easements: The Hard Case of Endangered Species Protection*, 19 J. Envtl. L. & Litig. 293, 345–52 (2004).

Why: The Choice to Hold Conservation Easements

Beyond the complicated discussion of state laws and avenues for enforcing tribal conservation easements lies another important inquiry. Why do tribes choose to hold conservation easements? This section briefly discusses why tribes might consider holding conservation easements on non-tribal lands.[57]

Most conservation easement holders use the tool because they are concerned about environmental amenities and want to protect land. The question here is not why organizations and governments care about land conservation, but why they choose to use the conservation easement tool among the array of tools available. Making that assessment in the present context requires consideration of what tools are available to tribes seeking to conserve land outside their jurisdiction.

Where a tribe chooses to hold conservation easements instead of purchasing fee simple title to the land, cost may be a strong motivator. Usually, purchasing a conservation easement is cheaper than buying fee simple title, and conservation easement holders do not have to pay property taxes. Holding a conservation easement may also be preferable to fee simple ownership because the land management duties remain with the underlying landowner. There is no need for tribal employees to maintain the land, keep out trespassers, or act as landlords. This is particularly salient for conservation easements over working lands, like ranches, forests, and agricultural land. A tribal government may not want to engage in agriculture or forestry. Leaving the landowner in place, while the tribe holds only the development rights, alleviates the need to find tenants and manage leases. These cost factors may be strong motivators for tribes who have less robust tribal governments and lower enrollments. Many tribes—like the Klamath—however, seek to gain fee simple title to land. The choice of a conservation easement may simply be tied to a landowner's unwillingness to sell.

Many argue that conservation easements are more likely to persist than fee simple land ownership. A parcel held in fee can always be sold or conveyed. At least in theory, a conservation easement can be perpetual. A tribe can transfer a conservation easement to a qualified holder if it no longer wants the burden of being a holder, but the restriction on the land remains in place. For this reason, conservation easements are appealing to tribal government officials who worry that subsequent office holders will not share their conservation goals. Conservation

57 Determining why conservation easements holders choose to hold conservation easements necessarily involves broad generalizations and hypotheses regarding motivations that we cannot actually discern without in-depth examinations and interviews with each of the tribes holding conservation easements. While such a project is underway and will enrich understanding of conservation easement use, it is beyond the scope of this chapter. Instead, this chapter presents theories of why tribes hold conservation easements based on the benefits conservation easements can provide to governments, public statements by tribes and others, and a general examination of the tool's benefits.

easements enable current tribal leaders to shape the local landscape in a way not possible through fee simple purchase.

Owning conservation easements instead of fee title may also be more politically appealing. Community members might balk at having large parcels of land under tribal ownership. Perhaps there are concerns about the tribal jurisdiction. Neighboring property owners may be concerned that tribal ownership will mean casino development. Building relationships through conservation easement programs may help demonstrate a tribe's interest in land conservation.

Where tribes hold conservation easements, they have a unique ability to extend their goals of protecting resources beyond their jurisdiction. In cases like the Yainix Ranch, tribes can secure conservation easements over land that they had traditionally held but lost through treaties and termination. Tribes may also seek to use conservation easements to protect off-reservation lands that serve as subsistence resources. This is a way to assert interest in tribal lands not officially recognized as such by state and federal governments.

Protection of land outside of reservations also promotes the ecological health of reservation lands. As Mary Wood has noted, tribes are often searching for ways to protect their natural resources and "extend their environmental prerogatives" beyond reservation boundaries.[58] Preventing development and unsustainable practices on neighboring land can protect environmental benefits on tribal land. Tribes and other governments often fight battles over water quality with their upstream neighbors. Obtaining conservation easements over such land may ensure water quality protection beyond the current methods offered by the Clean Water Act.[59]

Holding Conservation Easements and Traditional Notions of Tribal Property Law

Many scholars studying conservation easements and activists working in the field are unaware of the extent to which tribes use conservation easements.[60] Many concerns regarding conservation easements relate to their use as a conservation tool. Essentially, it is questionable whether static, perpetual, piecemeal agreements

58 Mary Christina Wood & Zachary Welcker, *Tribes as Trustees Again (Part I): The Emerging Tribal Role in the Conservation Trust Movement*, 32 Harv. Envtl. L. Rev. 373, 393 (2008).

59 In a related example, New York City uses conservation easements extensively in the Catskills to protect the New York City watershed. Using conservation easements to protect land and restrict agriculture in riparian areas is a more effective and efficient way to ensure high water quality in the region than outright ownership.

60 *But see,* Wood & Welcker, *supra* note 58; Middleton, *supra* note 1.

make sense for long-term land protection.[61] Some may be particularly surprised by tribal use of the tool because conservation easements embrace and reify Western libertarian notions of property.

While the use of conservation easements largely occurs because well-intentioned individuals and organizations seek to conserve land with any tool available, the use of conservation easements represents an unwelcome shift in property law that continues a move toward valuing individual real property rights over social good. Conservation easements reinforce the "bundle of sticks" metaphor of property implying that all property rights rest with individual landowners who should be compensated for any detraction from those rights or limitations on their actions. This ignores the fundamental role of property as a social construct to meet evolving needs of the community.[62]

Conservation easements reinforce a present libertarian view of property in which the individual landowner has the right to determine what occurs on the land.[63] A person has rights as a landowner, but those rights are necessarily tempered by societal rights. Private property is developed because it meets societal needs. Where property ceases to benefit society, it ceases to serve a viable function and does not merit public enforcement.

Thus, private property exists to further social goals and should be tempered by societal needs. Solidifying the power of individual landowners creates an anticommunitarian view of property and may make needed regulation (and other

---

61 *See, e.g.*, Jessica Owley, *Changing Property in a Changing World: a Call for the End of Perpetual Conservation Easements*, 30 Stan. Envtl L. J. 121 (2011) (also raising concerns regarding accountability and justice).

62 *See generally* Jessica Owley, *The Parcelization of Property Rights* (work in progress).

63 *Id.* There are some in the property rights movement that disagree with this view of conservation easements, arguing instead that conservation easements erode private property rights because they give non-landowners rights perpetual rights in the land. *See, e.g.*, Carol W. LaGrasse, *Land Trusts Threaten Private Property* 5 Positions on Prop. (2000), unpaginated excerpts *available at* Property Rights Foundation of America, http://prfamerica.org/positions/LandTrustsThreatenPP.html; J.B. Love, Conservation Easements From the Landowner's Perspective: Boon or Boondoggle (undated), available from the Davis Mountain Trans-Pecos Heritage Assoc. and summary *available at* http://dmtpha.org/easement.htm (last visited June 22, 2011). Others argue that conservation easements represent an unwanted form of government ownership and regulation. Dana Joel Gattuso, *Conservation Easements: The Good, the Bad, and the Ugly*, National Policy Analysis #569 (May 2008), *available at* http://www.nationalcenter.org/NPA569.html. It does not appear that these organizations oppose non-possessory rights (such as easements and real covenants), but largely object to conservation easements because of the government involvement and funding of the programs. *See also* Laura S. Beliveau, Comment, *The Forest Legacy Program: Using Conservaton Easements to Preserve the Northern Forest,* 20 B.C. Envtl. Aff. L. Rev. 507, 517–18 (1993) (discussing comments filed by property rights advocates arguing against conservation easements (because they show a lack of respect for private property) as part of the U.S.D.A.'s Forest Legacy Program).

land-protection strategies) even more difficult to achieve. The use of conservation easements and other mechanisms where we pay landowners to refrain from harmful activities overlooks the fact that landowners can be prevented from engaging in such activities by common law nuisance concepts or land-use and environmental regulation. We have instead created a market for something that someone should not necessarily be paid for. With conservation easements, we perpetuate the myth that the landowner is the king or queen of a realm where others' rights are always subservient to theirs. We strengthen the resistance to government regulation and suggest that landowners have no responsibility regarding the land.[64]

These significant objections to the use and proliferation of conservation easements served as the background for this investigation into how tribes are becoming involved with conservation easements. While concerns with the tool overall remain, this project reveals not only the attraction of conservation easements for tribes, but also how conservation easements may present a vestige of tribal notions of land conservation and intergenerational equity.

Traditional landholdings were extraordinarily complex, recognizing the shifting rights of individuals and groups in the same parcel of land. The idea of a fee simple landowner was not often a format for tribal property interests. The idea that one person can assert control over a piece of land, sometimes in defiance of group interests or wishes, does not comport with most traditional tribal notions of land use.[65] This indicates why conservation easements may be in conflict with traditional tribal notions of property. Conservation easements put the individual landowner center stage as the decision-maker. The landowner receives compensation for changes to the land. The landowner has the power to bind the rights of future generations regarding the land. Winona LaDuke objects that this Western view of natural resources as inanimate things that man can commodify and manipulate is inherently at odds with the traditional Indian view of land.[66]

There are some aspects of conservation easements, however, that do not seem to be so directly counter to tribal property notions. For example, conservation easements acknowledge that multiple people or groups can hold different interests in the same parcel. The fee landowner may have the right to occupy the land, but someone else may have the right limit the development of the land. Mary Wood

---

64 *See* John D. Echeverria, *Regulating Versus Paying Land Owners to Protect the Environment,* 26 J. Land Resources & Envtl. L. 1, 38–41 (2005–2006).

65 That is not to say that tribes did not recognize individual ownership interests, or that one mode of thinking about property describes all tribal experiences or histories. For example, early laws of the Cherokee Nation recognize the right of individual Cherokees to own land. Stacey L. Leeds, *The Burning of Blackacre: A Step Toward Reclaiming Tribal Property* Law, 10 Kan. J.L. & Pub. Pol'y 491, 493 (2000). Individual ownership of land, however, is not necessarily synonymous with Blackstonian fee simple ownership, and tribes mores and laws were often more restrictive on use and dispersal of land than Anglo property laws.

66 Winona LaDuke, Voices from White Earth 35–37 (1993).

argues that conservation easements are more akin to tribal property notions than it may first appear because both support beneficial uses of natural resources and reject exclusive use of land.[67]

While conservation easements solidify the power of individual landowners, they simultaneously acknowledge the ability of multiple parties to hold rights in the same parcel of land. This aspect of conservation easements may coincide with earlier expressions of tribal rights. Treaty rights, for example, often recognize that tribes have interests related to land that they do not occupy or that is not recognized as tribal land by the federal government. Where treaties recognize tribal rights to hunt, gather, or fish on land that they do not hold, those rights look very similar to easements.[68]

Conservation easements generally appear to reinforce a misguided notion that property law gives individual landowners the ability to put the land to any use they deem beneficial without consultation with or limitation by society. Yet, the availability of conservation easements may present an opportunity for tribes to use Western property law concepts in a beneficial way. With conservation easements, tribes can exert influence and even a type of property interest over lands that they identify as belonging to the tribe even if the federal or state governments do not.

Tribal notions of property and natural resources recognize the need to protect the land for future generations. Conservation easements seek to do that but with a twist. Protecting land for future generations is not necessarily the same as preventing future generations from using the land in ways they so choose.

There is a bit of a conservation conundrum before us. Conservation easements may create cumbersome structures for future generations, but this cumbersome and potentially unjust structure may be necessary to prevent present development and degradation pressures. Inequitably restricting future generations appears to be a price we are willing to pay. Although conservation easements restrict future generations, the real aim appears to be limitations on current use. Embodied in the narrative of conservation easement use is a belief that future generations are going to be better at protecting the land than current generations, because they will see the need for land protection more acutely than do current generations. Thus, what now appear as cumbersome restrictions may not seem so onerous to them. Preventing development and diminishing degradation may provide more future options even if it entails encumbering the land.

In the end, conservation easements may provide tribes with a novel way of protecting land in a country where tribal sovereignty is continually diminishing and tribal land bases have a tendency to shrink rather than expand. From a

67 Wood & Welcker, *supra* note 58, at 379.

68 In particular, they are akin to a category of easements called profits (or profit à prendre). Such easements recognize an individual's or landowner's right to take natural resources such as forest products or wildlife from the burdened land. *See also, id.* at 387 (describing the Supreme Court's treatment of the Stevens Treaties in the Pacific Northwest, which the Court described as reserving "easements").

programmatic standpoint, details regarding jurisdiction and enforceability may hamper the immediate growth in use of the tool. The strength and sensibility of conservation easements will probably vary with the restrictions they entail. Some conservation easements may make more sense ecologically and politically than others. For example, conservation easements protecting open space and watershed health fit the tool better than conservation easements seeking to protect mobile resources (such as elk) or ecosystems likely to change with global warming. Tribes can take advantage of the experience of those who have gone before them in this area, examining the concerns and challenges that other governmental entities and land trusts have faced. In particular, tribes should be cautious regarding how they use conservation easements, ensuring that the tool lines up with their goals.

Tribal Realism and Case Studies

Chapter 9

Natural Allies: Conservationists, Indian Tribes, and Protecting Native North America

Kirsten Matoy Carlson and Robert T. Coulter[1]

Scaly, dark American crocodiles swim amongst the eerie dense vegetation of tangled mangroves. Elegant, snowy egrets stand tall against silvery gray cypress trees looming out of swampy waters. Lean and muscular, coats shining golden in the sun, panthers stalk the sea of grass silently searching for unsuspecting prey.

Few wetlands exhibit abundant flora, fauna, and landscapes like the Florida Everglades. Great egrets, wood storks, alligators, whooping cranes, American peregrine falcons, panthers, and countless other rare species thrive throughout these sawgrass marshes, freshwater prairies, mangrove jungles, coastal estuaries, and forested uplands.

For over two centuries, Seminole Indians have devoted their existence to protecting their traditional lands in the Everglades of south Florida. It was not until the early twentieth century, when damming, dredging, and draining threatened the delicate balance of the Everglades' ecosystem, that conservationists started their efforts to preserve these immense, subtropical wetlands.[2] Relative latecomers, conservationists focused their efforts on the creation of a national park to protect the Everglades.[3]

Conservationists celebrated what they saw as a significant achievement with the creation of Everglades National Park.[4] However, the Park's creation did not halt the environmental destruction. Over the next 50 years, agricultural conversion and

1 Kirsten Matoy Carlson (Cherokee descent) is a staff attorney with the Indian Law Resource Center. Robert T. Coulter (Potawatomi) is founder and Executive Director of the Indian Law Resource Center. The authors would like to thank the Independent Traditional Seminole Nation, the Lannan Foundation, and the Conservation Fund; Curtis Berkey, Dick Ludington, Matthew Sexton, Ken Margolis, R. Michael Wright, Jon Roush, and Lucy Simpson for reading earlier drafts; and Sarah Krakoff and Ezra Rosser for their assistance in editing this piece.

2 Robert H. Keller & Michael F. Turek, American Indians and National Parks 219–220 (1999).

3 *Id.* at 220.

4 *Id.* at 229 (noting that no Indians were invited to or mentioned at the ceremony opening the Park).

real estate development drained 1.5 million acres—over half of the Everglades.[5] By the 1990s, rivers had been channeled into a series of canals, Lake Okeechobee's southern waters were penned up behind dikes, and much of the wetland areas that received runoff from these waters had dried up and disappeared.

No one felt the impact of development in the Everglades more than the Independent Traditional Seminole Nation (Traditional Seminoles), a remote community of approximately 300 traditional Seminoles, living to this day according to the customs and traditions of their ancestors. Unlike their relatives, the Seminole Tribe of Florida and Miccosukee Tribe of Indians, the Traditional Seminoles have no reservation and no casino, and no plans to get either one.[6]

In 1991, the Traditional Seminoles faced a new threat to their long-standing efforts to preserve their lands and subsistence lifestyle. That year, the non-Indian owners of the land where the Seminoles have traditionally held the Green Corn Dance, the sacred ceremony at the center of their religion and culture, intervened in, and compromised, the ceremony. This chapter tells the story of how the Traditional Seminoles succeeded in preserving the Green Corn Dance. Their success entailed enlisting lawyers, non-Indian conservation groups, and philanthropists, and engaging in creative methods for acquiring and preserving access to land. Too often and even when their interests appeared to converge, tribes and conservationists have failed to work together[7] or have openly opposed one another.[8]

---

5 Winona LaDuke, All Our Relations: Native Struggles for Land and Life 30 (1999).

6 The Traditional Seminoles have, since the time of the Seminole Wars, had an exceptionally deep distrust of the United States, especially because of the betrayal of the Seminoles in the removal treaties. Catherine Caufield, *Selling a Piece of Your Mother*, Whole Earth 1 (Fall 1998). Common stories include that Osceola refused to sign any further treaties and even stabbed his knife through the pages of one. The Traditional Seminoles generally regard reservations as areas controlled by the United States with the aim or result of controlling Indian people. They refuse to be involved in any way with things (such as reservations) or activities that involve outside governments (such as the federal government). *Id.* at 1; LaDuke, *supra* note 5, at 37–38. *See also Distribution of Seminole Judgment Funds: Hearing Before the Senate Select Comm. on Indian Affairs*, 95th Cong. 49–50 (1978) (statement of Guy Osceola, Spokesperson, Traditional Seminoles). This, of course, includes casinos, which are heavily regulated. These well-known positions and beliefs were also conveyed to one of the authors personally by the Traditional Seminoles.

7 *See generally* Mark David Spence, Dispossessing the Wilderness: Indian Removal and the Making of the National Parks (1999); Philip Burnham, Indian Country, God's Country: Native Americans and the National Parks (2000); Mac Chapin, *A Challenge to Conservationists*, World Watch (Nov. /Dec. 2004); Mark Dowie, Conservation Refugees: The Hundred-Year Conflict between Global Conservation and Native Peoples (2009).

8 For example, the Sierra Club opposed the transfer of National Park Service lands to the Havasupai Tribe in the 1970s. Keller & Turek, *supra* note 2, at 183. More recently, the Southeast Alaska Conservation Council has launched a campaign opposing federal legislation to finalize the land transfers granted to Sealaska Native Corporation in the

The Traditional Seminoles' story demonstrates how tribes, non-Indian conservation groups, and philanthropists can work together to protect the environment by finding common interests, overcoming their misperceptions of one another, and developing innovative solutions that meet both their needs. The path to protecting the Green Corn Dance was not always a smooth one, but some of the bumps encountered by the Traditional Seminoles might serve as instructive lessons for other indigenous peoples hoping to preserve their traditional lands and cultures and for conservationists hoping to collaborate with them. Those lessons include the importance of finding conservation partners that have similar goals and beliefs, of building solid relationships with those partners, and of considering informal and innovative approaches to conservation.

The Green Corn Dance Project

The Green Corn Dance project started when our old friends and long-standing clients, the Independent Traditional Seminole Nation, called us about the impending loss of the site of their Green Corn Dance. The Traditional Seminoles live in open houses with thatched palm roofs (called chickees), speak the Hitchiti language fluently, grow their own gardens, cook over a communal fire, share resources equally among the people, and make their own decisions. Their existence seems precarious, if not unimaginable, by modern Western standards.[9] Their steadfast adherence to a traditional way of life in the modern world, their rejection of reservation life, and their fierce independence set them apart as a symbol of the strength of American Indian culture. As a matter of principle, they reject state and federal aid (except for medical care). Although they made agreements with the United States in 1842 and 1845 guaranteeing their rights to a large area of land, they are virtually landless.[10] They continue to live in their villages on their

---

Alaska Native Claims Settlement Act. Southeast Alaska Conservation Council, What You Can Do, Sealaska Bill Action, http://seacc.org/what-you-can-do.

9 For a fuller description of the Traditional Seminoles and their way of life, see Caufield, *supra* note 6.

10 Proclamation by President James K. Polk (1845) (on file at Indian Law Resource Center); *Distribution of Seminole Judgment Funds, supra* note 6, at 512. Caufield succinctly explains the map formalizing the agreements between the Seminoles and the United States: "A copy of a map of southern Florida … identifies all the land south of Lake Kissimmee (which lies roughly midway between the north and south of the state) and west of Lake Okeechobee as 'the District set apart for the use and occupancy of the Seminoles.' Another twenty-mile wide swath outside this area is designated as 'neutral ground, reserved from survey and sale.'" In the margin is a memorandum in Polk's handwriting, date May 19, 1845, and signed by him: "Within the red lines is the country assigned the Seminoles by Gen. Worth Aug. 14, 1842, in which for the present they are allowed to live, hunt and plant." This map, and a slew of supporting documents, including an Army memorandum authorizing Gen. Worth to offer the land to the Seminoles, a record of the meeting in which

traditional lands because they have a gentleman's handshake agreement with the family that owns the land.[11] Similar informal agreements have historically given the Traditional Seminoles access to and use of their ceremonial sites.

The Green Corn Dance is an annual religious and cultural ceremony, central to Seminole identity, and the heart and soul of the Traditional Seminole way of life. Traditional Seminole spokesman Danny Billie describes the Green Corn Dance's importance, "It defines who we are and what we are as traditional Indian people."[12] During the ceremony, ancient religious rites and practices are performed, the political affairs of the Nation are discussed, disputes within the Nation are resolved and the communal life and ways of the Seminole people are celebrated and renewed. The ceremony occurs once a year for approximately five days, and must be held on land maintained in its natural state. Without the Green Corn Dance to nurture and sustain it, Seminole culture may disappear.

By 1993, the Traditional Seminoles could no longer access and use the site where they had performed the Green Corn Dance for over 250 years. The encroaching development of sod farms, citrus groves, and cattle farms destroyed many of the natural plants, herbs, and medicines that the Traditional Seminoles required to conduct the Green Corn Dance. The land had lost the natural character that it needed to sustain the ceremony. The Traditional Seminoles would have to find a new site for the Green Corn Dance.

The Traditional Seminoles' long-term goal was to acquire a parcel of land that would be permanently protected as an ecological preserve and new Green Corn Dance grounds. They wanted to create an ecological preserve because maintenance of the land in its natural state is key to the Green Corn Dance. The Traditional Seminoles were looking for an unspoiled area of land approximately 3000 acres in size to serve as a permanent location for the Green Corn Dance. A suitable ceremonial ground would require a relatively secluded parcel of natural, unspoiled land containing cypress swamps, pine forests, a naturally occurring lake or pond and streams or creeks with ample stocks of native fish.

---

the Seminoles and Worth came to their agreement, and a report to Congress from the War Department confirming that the Seminoles had adhered to the conditions of the agreement, form the basis of the Independent Traditional Seminole Nation's claim to five million acres of south Florida—13 percent of the state. Caufield, *supra* note 6, at 10. For a more detailed discussion of Traditional Seminole land rights and copies of the documents, see *Distribution of Seminole Judgment Funds*, *supra* note 6, at 65–87 (Report of the Indian Law Resource Center).

11 Phone interview with Curtis Berkey (Sept. 2009).

12 LaDuke, *supra* note 5, at 43.

Finding Conservation Partners

Almost immediately, we knew, and the Traditional Seminoles knew, that we would need to enlist the help of conservationists and philanthropists to protect the Green Corn Dance. We saw the project as a model for a new vision of what is possible in land conservation: conservation and environmental protection cognizant of the relationship between humans and the Earth and consciously linked to American Indian cultural preservation.

We quickly noticed how similar the Traditional Seminoles' goal was to that of some local conservationists. The Traditional Seminoles' strategy to establish an ecological reserve closely resembled that of private conservation organizations such as the Nature Conservancy, Conservation Fund, 1000 Friends of Florida, and the Audubon Society. These conservation groups were also working to protect Florida wetlands by acquiring lands or conservation easements that would maintain the lands in their natural state.

We knew some conservationists had interests similar to those of the Traditional Seminoles. We needed to find conservationists and donors who would respect the Traditional Seminoles by listening to their concerns and allowing them to direct the project. At the same time, they had to be people that the insular Traditional Seminoles felt they could trust.

The convergence of the interests of the Traditional Seminoles and conservationists was anything but unique. Over 560 Indian tribes and Alaska Native nations own and manage 100 million acres of land rich in natural resources, wildlife, and diverse flora and fauna.[13] As governments with the right to govern themselves and to manage their own property and affairs, Native nations steward these lands and natural resources.[14] While it is impossible to generalize about Indian and Alaska Native nations because each nation has its own unique history, culture, and traditions, many have historical and cultural relationships with their lands and natural resources and wish to protect them. Indian and Alaska Native nations frequently have particular sites on their land or on their former lands that are regarded as sacred, essential to cultural and spiritual practices, and sometimes secret.[15] Many nations also retain interests and rights in lands and natural resources that they no longer own[16]—including legal rights to fisheries, grasslands, waterways, forests, and sacred sites—and see the protection of these lands and resources as a priority. Most of these lands and natural resources remain undeveloped and have tremendous conservation value.[17]

---

13 David H. Getches et al., Cases and Materials on Federal Indian Law 20–21 (6th ed. 2011).

14 Cohen's Handbook of Federal Indian Law §§ 4.01, 4.04, 17.01 (Nell Jessup Newton et al. eds. 2005).

15 *Id.* at § 14.03[2][c][ii][B].

16 *Id.* at § 18.04 (discussing off-reservation hunting, fishing, and gathering rights).

17 Getches et al., *supra* note 13, at 22–24.

Conservationists and those working to protect the environment encounter Indian and Alaska Native nations in many different settings throughout the country. Indian and Alaska Native nations are found in every imaginable geographic setting from the Arctic to the desert Southwest to the Everglades of Florida.[18] Organizations working to preserve biodiversity, critical habitat, and environmental quality, and to protect watersheds and wetlands often find that Native peoples occupy or have rights in the lands and waterways the conservationists seek to protect. To provide just two of many possible examples, Native nations have land holdings or reservations all along the Yukon-to-Yellowstone wildlife corridor, and Alaska Native nations are almost the only inhabitants of the enormous and important Yukon River watershed. Conservationists also routinely encounter Indian and Alaska Native nations and their lands when working to protect endangered species,[19] clean up and restore polluted lands and waters,[20] combat global warming and its effects,[21] create and protect wild lands and other protected areas,[22] and stop or reduce harmful development and unsustainable resource use.[23] In some of these settings, Native peoples have the particular knowledge of wildlife, botany, and other aspects of the ecosystem that is crucial to conserving it.

While not all Indian and Alaska Native nations may be interested in protecting their lands and resources from environmental destruction, many probably are. Many Indian tribes and Alaska Native cultures have deeply embedded traditional norms concerning (in modern terms) conservation and environmental protection. Indian and Alaska Native nations often find themselves objecting to and combating the failed or ineffective conservation management policies of the federal or state

---

18 For a map and discussion of where tribes are located, see *id.*at 10–12.

19 *See, e.g.*, Memorandum of Understanding between the National Wildlife Federation and the InterTribal Bison Cooperative (Jan. 22, 1997), *available at* http://ncseonline.org/nae/docs/nwf.html.

20 *See, e.g.*, Montana Environmental Information Center, MEIC Joins Tribes in Lawsuit Over Zortman-Landusky Cleanup,http://meic.org/mining/hardrock-mining/cyanide_mining/zortman_landusky_mines.

21 *See, e.g.*, National Wildlife Federation, Tribes, Climate Change and Solutions, http://tribalclimate.org/ (documenting tribal climate change conferences held by the National Wildlife Federation).

22 *See, e.g.*, Crown of the Continent, Badger Two Medicine Area, http://www.crownofthecontinent.net/content/badger-two-medicine-area/cotD6F6B9EA2513FD006 (acknowledging collaboration among Blackfeet Nation, conservations, and the U.S. Forest Service to end motorized travel and drilling in the pristine Badger Two Medicine area of the Rocky Mountain Front).

23 *See, e.g.*, Navajo Nation v. U.S. Forest Service, 535 U.S. F.3d 1058 (9th cir. 2008) (en banc), cert denied by 129 S. Ct. 2763 (2009) (environmentalists and Indian tribes litigating to prevent expansion of the Arizona Snowbowl and discretion of the San Francisco Peaks).

governments, particularly regarding wildlife resources and fisheries on which Native peoples depend for sustenance and cultural survival.[24]

Overall, the environmental records of many Native governments may be above average, but there are also plenty of modern examples of Indian and Alaska Native nations engaging in activities that are environmentally harmful or undesirable.[25] Like state, local, and the federal governments, Indian and Alaska Native nations must be responsible for the full range of interests of their communities: jobs, health, education, economic development, cultural development, housing, and more.[26] Most nations cannot base their actions on a single issue or interest. At the same time, Indian and Alaska Native nations are broadly representative governments, speaking for the interests of their entire nations, and they can be tremendously effective as advocates for conservation and environmental protection.[27]

Partnerships with like-minded conservationists can be invaluable to Indian and Alaska Native nations interested in protecting their lands, culture, and natural resources. Native nations deal with all kinds of environmental issues, including, among others, non-point source water pollution, decaying waste handling facilities, noxious and invasive plant species, wildlife habitat loss, mine tailings, military waste, and Superfund sites.[28] As governments, they are responsible for addressing these and other environmental and conservation issues.[29] Indian nations

---

24 *See, e.g.*, Ron Selden, *Fort Belknap Tribes File New Law Suit over Mining Pollution*, Indian Country Today, Feb. 19, 2004, *available at* http://www.indianlaw.org/sites/default/files/resources/FtB%20ICT%20CleanWater20040219.pdf (recounting history of lawsuits filed by the Fort Belknap Indian Community to get the United States and the state of Montana to enforce violations of the Clean Water Act occurring at the Zortman-Landusky Mines).

25 *See, e.g.*, *Hearing on Protecting Long-Term Tribal Energy Jobs and Keeping Arizona Water and Power Costs Affordable: The Current and Future Role of the Navajo Generating Plant Before the Subcomm. on Water and Power and Subcomm. on Indian and Alaska Native Affairs of the House Comm. on Natural Resources*, 112th Cong. (May 24, 2011) (statement of President Ben Shelly, Navajo Nation), *available at* http://naturalresources.house.gov/UploadedFiles/ShellyTestimony05.24.11.pdf; Felicia Fonseca, *Navajo Nation Coal Plant Focus of Congressional Hearing*, The Salt Lake Tribune, May 24, 2011, *available at* http://www.sltrib.com/sltrib/news/51877714-78/plant-coal-hearing-congressional.html.csp.

26 For a full discussion of the powers and authority of Indian tribes, see Cohen's Handbook, *supra* note 14, at § 4.01[2].

27 *See, e.g.*, Zoltan Grossman, *Cowboy and Indian Alliances in the Northern Plains*, 2 Agricultural Hist. 77 (Spring 2003) (discussing Northern Cheyenne Tribe's opposition to coal development and use of the Clean Air Act to limit coal development in southeastern Montana), *available at* http://academic.evergreen.edu/g/grossmaz/cowboysindians.pdf; David Melmer, *Northern Cheyenne Face Decision of Economy or Environment*, Indian Country Today, Oct. 24, 2006.

28 *See generally* William H. Rodgers, Jr, Environmental Law in Indian Country (2005).

29 Cohen's Handbook, *supra* note 14, at §§ 10.01–10.02.

that experienced the allotment of their lands by the federal government may face particular challenges to environmental regulation and protection.[30] Today these nations have been left with reservations or tribal homelands that consist of Indian lands commingled with non-Indian lands.[31] The question of the status of the land is key because it determines who has the authority to regulate the land.[32] Based on the pattern of land holding, Native nations may not be able to regulate or zone all the land or even adjacent parcels on their reservations.[33] In such cases, Indian nations may need to collaborate with conservationists to ensure that the state or local government or the private sector does not frustrate their efforts at environmental protection.

The Traditional Seminoles are an excellent example of a Native nation committed to protecting its environment but also in need of the help of like-minded conservationists. Like many Indian and Alaska Native nations, the Traditional Seminoles see themselves as staunch environmentalists and protectors of the Earth and view environmental protection as integrated with human rights and the well-being of humanity. Traditional Seminole spokesperson, Danny Billie, explained their perspective:

> We are the guardians of the environment. Whatever damages the earth and the water and the air and the animals and whatever, it concerns us … When we speak of the land and of nature and of the animals, you know, we're not just speaking for our own people or for our own children. We're speaking for all the next generation, no matter whether it's black people, white people, Spanish people, Chinese people … That's the Creator's law, the Breathmaker's law.[34]

While the interests of conservationists and the Traditional Seminoles in protecting and preserving the Everglades seemed to intertwine like the dense vegetation of the Everglades, we knew that conservationists in Florida had missed opportunities to develop cooperative efforts with the tribes in the past. For example, rather than contemplate the Seminoles and Miccosukees as potential partners in the creation and management of the Park, National Park Service and Bureau of Indian Affairs officials had sought their removal from it.[35]

---

30 For a description of the allotment policy and its effect on Indian nations, see *id.* at § 1.04.

31 *See generally* Judith V. Royster, *The Legacy of Allotment*, 27 Ariz. St. L. J. 1 (1995).

32 Montana v. United States, 447 U.S. 134, 566 (1980) (holding Crow Tribe lacked regulatory jurisdiction over hunting and fishing by non-Indians on non-Indian owned land within the Crow reservation).

33 Brendale v. Confederated Tribes and Bands of Yakima Indian Nation, 492 U.S. 408 (1989).

34 Caufield, *supra* note 6, at 14.

35 Keller & Turek, *supra* note 2, at 216–32.

Aware that all too often conservationists and Native communities miss opportunities to work together to promote effective conservation—even when their interests converge—we reached out to conservation organizations in south Florida because we felt that their goals aligned with the Traditional Seminoles' desire to create an ecological preserve to protect a new site for their Green Corn Dance. We discovered that conservationists are almost as varied as American Indian and Alaska Native nations. Environmental groups have different priorities in terms of goals, attitudes towards industry and government, and tactics.[36] As with Native nations, these priorities and attitudes are not static; environmental groups and their priorities change over time.

Through our outreach efforts, we encountered conservationists of all kinds and learned that they do not all share the same ideas about nature or the role of humans in it. Curtis Berkey, an Indian Law Resource Center attorney at the time, prepared and disseminated written materials on the Traditional Seminoles and their efforts to protect the Florida Everglades to conservation organizations.[37] His report, *Vanishing Wetlands—Threatened Seminole Indian Culture*, explained the ecological significance of wetlands preservation in south Florida and the manner in which the protection of lands for the Green Corn Dance contributed to the maintenance of a healthy ecosystem.[38] Berkey then called several conservation organizations, including the Nature Conservancy of Florida, the Trust for Public Lands, the Conservation Fund, and the Audubon Society, which were extremely active in south Florida at the time.[39] Many of these groups had tremendous experience in acquiring lands for conservation protection. Although neither the Center nor the Traditional Seminoles had any previous contact with these

36 At least three variants of the modern environmental movement exist: the mainstream, the radicals, and the third wave. R. Michael Wright, A Typology of the Environmental Movement 1 (May 2, 2010) (unpublished manuscript on file with the authors). In short, "[m]ainstream environmentalists believe that progress toward environmental protection can best be achieved through government action, either legislative or judicial; that incremental progress is possible and that issue-by-issue alliances are an effective means to those ends." *Id.* at 1. The radical branch of the environmental movement grew out of the drop-out "alternative lifestyle" environmental ideas of the late 1960s and early 1970s. Radicals tend to display limited confidence in government, forgo mainstream political action in favor of public protests and civil disobedience, and look toward acceptance of personal responsibility and changes in individual lifestyles to protect the environment. *Id.* at 1–2. The third wave of the environmental movement seeks to move beyond confrontation and seek opportunity for industry and environmentalists to work together harmoniously. They see market mechanisms as the tool of choice and seek to bring about change through collaborative projects.

37 Phone interview with Curtis Berkey (Sept. 2009).

38 Curtis Berkey, *Vanishing Wetlands—Threatened Seminole Indian Culture* (1994) (unpublished manuscript on file with Indian Law Resource Center).

39 Phone interview with Curtis Berkey (Sept. 2009).

organizations, we tried to meet with them to engage their assistance in setting up an ecological preserve for the Green Corn Dance project.

It did not take long for us—members of the Traditional Seminole Nation and attorneys at the Center—to encounter conservationists tied to a view of wilderness that excluded humans. This view reflected the view of many early conservationists. For example, John Muir saw the removal of Indians from majestic places, like the Yosemite Valley, as essential to the protection of wild, pristine American landscapes.[40] These conservationists subscribe to the Yellowstone or Fortress model of conservation, which has dominated conservation efforts for the past half-century. Under the Yellowstone model, protection of the environment requires the setting aside of pristine lands, significantly limiting human use and habitation of these lands, and top-down management by Western-trained ecologists and biologists. This conservation model often conflicts with the views of Indian and Alaska Native nations, who see themselves as stewards of the environment rather than antithetical to it.

We experienced this difference in thinking about the environment and how to protect it first-hand.[41] When we approached the Nature Conservancy about setting aside part of the Florida Everglades for the Green Corn Dance Ceremony, we discovered that the Nature Conservancy's policy at the time would not support the setting aside of land for the Traditional Seminoles because of the human presence and activities to be conducted in the area.[42] The Traditional Seminoles' minimal use of the land for five days each year exceeded the Nature Conservancy's then-existing policy on use of protected land.[43]

In our quest to build alliances with conservation groups, we also quickly learned that not all conservationists hold the same views about nature. While some conservationists still see human use as conflicting with protecting nature, others have been rethinking this idea or have abandoned it entirely.[44] Many

40 Burnham, *supra* note 7.

41 The Traditional Seminoles have continued to confront differences in thinking about the environment and how to protect it. In 2006, the property appraiser for Okeechobee County challenged the charitable exemption from ad valorem taxes of the property acquired and set aside for the Green Corn Dance, arguing that the clearing of 20 acres for a ceremonial site was inconsistent with its exemption for the charitable purpose of conservation. Sherman v. Red Bay Stronghold Foundation, No. 4D05-3240 (Fla. Dist. Ct. App. Dec. 6, 2006), *available at* http://caselaw.findlaw.com/fl-district-court-of-appeal/1250242.html.

42 Phone interview with Curtis Berkey (Sept. 2009).

43 *Id.*

44 William Cronon, *The Trouble With Wilderness; or, Getting Back to the Wrong Nature*, 1 Envtl Hist. 7 (1996); Paige West, James Igoe, & Dan Brockington, *Parks and Peoples: The Social Impact of Protected Areas*, 34 Annu. Rev. Anthropol. 251 (2006); Paige West & Dan Brockington, *An Anthropological Perspective on Some Unexpected Consequences of Protected Areas*, 20 Conservation Biology 609 (2006); Jim Igoe, *Measuring the Costs and Benefits of Conservation to Local Communities*, 10 J. Ecological Anthropol. 72 (2006).

conservationists have come to the conclusion that conservation can only be successful if people are involved, especially the local, indigenous people living off the land. They believe that it is often essential to work with Native peoples, particularly those that inhabit or have other substantial rights or interests in protected areas or areas of conservation importance.

To some extent, conservationists have little choice but to interact with Indian and Alaska Native peoples. Despite the once common myth, especially prevalent at the time the conservation movement emerged, that Indians and Alaska Natives are a dying race that will soon disappear entirely,[45] Indian and Alaska Native nations have proven that they are not a temporary phenomenon. Far from disappearing, Native nations and peoples are growing in size and political and legal strength.[46] They are not going away, they speak for themselves, and they can and will manage their own lands and resources.

Conservation giants, like Conservation International, once heavily criticized for their failure to involve local communities,[47] have recently reached the same conclusion. For example, Conservation International have developed formal policies that list increasing partnerships with indigenous peoples as one of their major goals.[48] Other large conservation organizations, such as the National Wildlife Federation and the Sierra Club, now have policies relating to Native communities and resources or designated staff responsible for interacting with Indian and Alaska Native communities.[49]

Early on, we identified such conservationists in Dick Ludington and Matt Sexton of the Conservation Fund, a non-profit environmental organization that partners with the private sector, non-profit organizations, and public agencies to help protect America's outdoors.[50] The Conservation Fund specializes in land acquisitions.[51] We developed a partnership with them, and they took the lead in identifying possible sites for the Green Corn Dance. The Lannan Foundation generously offered to help fund the land acquisitions.

---

45 Fergus M. Bordewich, Killing the White Man's Indian: Reinventing Native Americans at the End of the Twentieth Century 49 (1996); Cohen's Handbook, *supra* note 14, at § 1.04 (noting that the purpose of the assimilation and allotment policies of the late 1900s was to end Indian culture). *See generally* Zane Grey, The Vanishing American (1925).

46 Getches et al., *supra* note 13, at 12–13 (noting dramatic increase in American Indian and Alaska Native population). *See generally* The Harvard Project on American Indian Economic Development, The State of the Native Nations (2007).

47 *See, e.g.*, Chapin, *supra* note 7.

48 Dowie, *supra* note 7, at 62.

49 *See, e.g.*, Sierra Club, Tribal Partnerships, http://www.sierraclub.org/ej/partnerships/tribal/default.aspx; National Wildlife Federation, Tribal Lands Conservation Program Information Sheet (on file with authors).

50 The Conservation Fund America's Partner in Conservation, http://www.conservationfund.org/.

51 Personal communication with Dick Ludington (May 2010).

Building Strong Relationships

Our efforts to protect the Green Corn Dance were successful largely because we were able to identify and develop working relationships with conservationists at the Conservation Fund and the Lannan Foundation.[52] However, those relationships had to be nurtured and developed over time. We had to overcome communications and knowledge gaps to build strong, trusting relationships among all the parties involved. We learned that open-mindedness and a willingness to listen by all parties can help to overcome misperceptions that can hamper or prevent the development of successful working relationships.

When we reached out to conservationists in south Florida, we were fortunate to find conservationists who were open to working with and had similar goals to the Traditional Seminoles. However, even some of these conservationists demonstrated an acute lack of information about Indian and Alaska Native nations, their lands and resources in general, and the Traditional Seminoles in particular. Some had heard of the Miccosukee Tribe or the Seminole Tribe of Florida, but had little experience of working with them. Like most Americans, they had had little, if any, direct contact with Indians and Alaska Natives at all.

Misperceptions about Indians and Alaska Natives and their nations are common because of the lack of direct contact between Natives and most other Americans, and the inadequate information provided about Native communities in public schools, colleges, and universities. It is no wonder that there has been some difficulty: conservationists, for the most part, do not know and have difficulty finding accurate information about contemporary Indian and Alaska Native nations and communities.[53] Most people in the United States accept what is said to be "common knowledge" about Indians and Alaska Natives (often mistakenly called "Eskimos"), unaware that this old body of lore is mostly wrong or misleading at best. Stereotypes abound, usually without ill will, but they are wrong and offensive all the same. Common misperceptions are that tribes are not open to outsiders; that tribal governments are unstable and difficult to work with; that Indians receive preferential treatment, such as hunting rights and not having to pay taxes; and that Indians are lazy or drunk and thus unreliable.[54] Such commonly heard ideas about

---

52 Phone interview with Curtis Berkey (Sept. 2009).

53 Jan Balsom explains: "Environmental organizations need to be educated. We've got an awful lot of 'wannabe' Indian sorts, but they don't truly understand tribal views. They have this magical, mystical view of what should be, not the real world. They need to be humbled a bit, to realize that the tribes have much more of an interest in the well-being of the system than they do … Some groups need to get off their high horse of environmental elitism and deal with the people who are part of the land to begin with, not some yuppified version of what it should be. They need to consider local tribes of the area, a factor they never think about." KELLER & TUREK, *supra* note 2, at 183.

54 *See generally* DEVON A. MIHESUAH, AMERICAN INDIANS: STEREOTYPES AND REALITIES (1996).

Indians and Alaska Natives and their nations are untrue, and yet may have caused some conservationists to avoid working with Native communities.[55]

Other common misperceptions suggest that all Indians and Alaska Natives are environmentalists or that Mother Earth and humanity would be saved if everyone just learned the secrets of the Native way of life.[56] While these seem to portray Indians and Alaska Natives in a more positive light, such romantic visions are also based on stereotypes. These misperceptions may prevent successful relationships from developing between conservationists and Indian and Alaska Native communities because they may lead conservationists to have unrealistic expectations about Native nations and their commitment to the environment.

Throughout the Green Corn Dance project, we heard conservationists, land owners, and state officials express concerns related to these common misperceptions about Indian and Alaska Native communities. Some were curious about how the Traditional Seminoles would use the land and exhibited a deep suspicion that the Traditional Seminoles were not conservationists at all but wanted the land to build a casino or smokeshop. Others were troubled by the secrecy of the Green Corn Dance, elements of which could not be revealed to outsiders. A few expressed frustration about the everyday logistics of working with the Traditional Seminoles, who could be hard to reach because of their limited use of modern technology, including phones, cell phones, and the internet. We had to overcome many of these logistical obstacles and misperceptions to build viable working relationships among the Traditional Seminoles, conservationists, and potential benefactors.

For some, like Matt Sexton of the Conservation Fund, who played a key role in identifying suitable properties for the Traditional Seminoles, working with the Traditional Seminoles involved a leap of faith and a willingness to trust them. In reviewing possible sites, he admitted that he "had a vague idea of what they were looking for" but that he did not know their exact criteria.[57] He explained that "Only their spiritual leaders can make the decision" about possible sites.[58]

Sexton was able to develop a working relationship with the Traditional Seminoles because, instead of coming to the project with his own preconceived ideas about what they wanted and needed in a ceremonial site, he was willing to listen to them. Sexton and his colleague at the Conservation Fund, Dick Ludington, consulted with the Traditional Seminoles about dozens of possible sites, often walking the land with the Traditional Seminoles to see if it would meet their needs.

---

55 Keller & Turek, *supra* note 2, at 183 (describing the National Sierra Club's opposition to a land transfer to the Havasupai Tribe, which resorted to public campaigns calling the land restoration a "land grab" and playing on stereotypes of Indians as greedy, lazy, and stupid).

56 Defending Mother Earth: Native American Perspectives on Environmental Justice xvi (Jace Weaver ed. 1996).

57 Jacques Picard, *Seminoles Want to Hold Green Corn Dance in County*, The Tribune, Sept. 1, 1996, at C2.

58 *Id.*

Through these actions, they gained the trust of the Traditional Seminoles, and early on, were able to build a successful partnership between the Conservation Fund and the Traditional Seminoles.

Despite this growing trust, we quickly learned that many of the existing conservation programs failed to incorporate the needs or concerns of Indian and Alaska Native peoples. Initially, we investigated the possibility of leasing conservation lands owned by the state of Florida through either the Conservation and Recreation Lands (CARL) program or the Save Our Rivers program of the South Florida Water Management District.[59] After careful deliberation, both of these options were rejected because they were not good fits for the Traditional Seminoles. The CARL program did not suit the needs of the Traditional Seminoles because its statutory mandate required that the lands be managed for public outdoor recreation and these lands were rarely leased to one group exclusively. Similarly, the Save Our Rivers program did not lease lands to a single group for exclusive use and occupancy, and the state retained primary management responsibility over the lands. The Traditional Seminoles preferred an area that they exclusively used and controlled, and this did not seem possible under either of Florida's programs.

In evaluating these programs, we realized how easy it is for conservationists, who have goals similar to Indian and Alaska Native nations, to create programs and projects that overlook the unique situation of Native nations, and thus, make it more difficult for conservationists and Indians to engage in collaborative efforts. The state of Florida wanted to conserve lands, and many state and county officials publicly acknowledged that its land conservation goals aligned with those of the Traditional Seminoles,[60] but the state's land conservation programs were not flexible enough to accommodate the needs of Indian nations, like the Traditional Seminoles. Early on, the South Florida Water Management District expressed concerns about tree cutting, liability, hunting rights, and public access on any lands that it could possibly lease to the Nation. While some of these issues probably could have been resolved, they showed how the state's programs were not well suited to accommodating joint tribal–state conservation projects. If the state's programs had been more accommodating, there may have been more opportunities for tribal–state collaboration.

Conservationists were not the only ones that had to take a leap of faith to make the collaboration on the Green Corn Dance project a success. The project also proved to be a journey for the Traditional Seminoles. We learned that tribes can have just as many hesitations and misperceptions about working with conservationists as conservationists can have about working with tribes. At a feast to celebrate the creation of the ecological preserve, Danny Billie expressed the reservations of his own nation in engaging in the project, "We've never done anything like this

59 For more information on the State of Florida's land acquisition programs, see James A. Farr & O. Greg Brock, *Florida's Landmark Programs for Conservation and Recreation Land Acquisition*, http://www.dep.state.fl.us/lands/AcqHistory.htm.

60 Picard, *supra* note 57.

before, and it's been a roller-coaster ride, emotionally, for a lot of us working on this project. It's been hard because we've had to follow our laws, and then, you know, we've had to deal with the outside world's rules and regulations."[61]

Many Indian and Alaska Native nations may hesitate to work with conservationists because they are skeptical of outsiders. Too often, outsiders, including those who believe they have the best interests of Native peoples at heart, have imposed upon or ignored Native communities.[62] Despite their good intentions, they have not always treated Indian and Alaska Native nations with respect or listened carefully to the wishes of the nation. Our experiences with the Traditional Seminoles and other Native nations have indicated that trust, honesty, and respect are key to creating successful alliances between Indian and Alaska Native peoples and conservationists.

We knew that for the Green Corn Dance project to be successful we needed to listen closely to and take direction from the Traditional Seminoles. Early on in the project, we met with the Traditional Seminoles to craft a land management plan for the new Green Corn Dance site. We listened carefully as the Traditional Seminoles expressed frustration and misgivings about conventional conservation plans, which they described as purely science-oriented and overly legalistic. We realized that our challenge was to create a plan that was consistent with Seminole traditions and their religious, ecological, and cultural ethos, yet detailed and specific enough to guide and direct the responsibilities of the entity established to see that the land is properly preserved and cared for. We talked with the Traditional Seminoles at great length about the history of the ceremony, their vision and purpose for the new ecological preserve, and the land use restrictions that would be placed on the land.[63] We also discussed the kind of influence they wanted to have over the management of the land, their relationship with the Board of the non-profit organization that would own the land (including resolution of disputes and how to keep each other informed), who should be on the board, and how they wanted to use the land (residential, ceremonial, other). These conversations guided the creation of the land management plan and the Conservation Fund's efforts as they sought to find a suitable parcel for the ecological preserve.

The Traditional Seminoles expressed their gratitude for our patience, understanding, and respect at a feast to celebrate the creation of the new ecological preserve. Danny Billie acknowledged that the Traditional Seminoles could not have done it on their own. He thanked the Conservation Fund and the Lannan Foundation, which generously gave most of the money used to purchase the site, for the respect and interest they showed in the project. He stated, "The Lannan

61 Caufield, *supra* note 6, at 23.

62 For example, proponents of the allotment policy, which fostered the assimilation of individual Indians, the alienation of tribal property, and the destruction of tribal governments, called themselves "Friends of the Indians." COHEN'S HANDBOOK, *supra* note 14, at § 1.04.

63 Personal communication with Armstrong Wiggins (February 2011).

family has been a special group. They got personally involved. When it was time to come down and walk the land, they came out and walked the land with us."[64] Billie's comments emphasize how outsiders can develop positive relationships with Indian and Alaska Native nations, even isolated, traditional nations like the Traditional Seminoles, by listening to and respecting them.

Finding Innovative Solutions

Another important lesson that we learned during the Green Corn Dance project was that a willingness to use unconventional legal approaches may provide tribes and conservationists with more opportunities to protect the environment and indigenous cultural practices. Once the Traditional Seminoles rejected the State of Florida's land acquisition programs, we considered other possible options for holding the land. Creating a land acquisition strategy raised complicated issues about who would own and manage the land once it was acquired. We realized that the needs of the Traditional Seminoles could not be met by traditional models of land conservation in the United States. Most of the lands set aside for conservation purposes are owned and managed by either private land trusts or state or local agencies. These arrangements are used because most conservation organizations and others in the United States think of lands, resources, and other property in the context of exclusive ownership, either private or governmental.

These traditional models of land conservation proved problematic for the Traditional Seminoles because they do not see land as a commodity or believe that it can be bought or sold. As Guy Osceola explained it, "The Great Spirit put the land here for everyone to live on … It belongs to everybody."[65] While the Traditional Seminoles wanted to play a role in the land's management, they did not want to own the land. Further, we were not certain that they could own land under state law as a tribe not incorporated under state law.[66]

We had to consider alternative forms of land tenure to accommodate the needs of the Traditional Seminoles. We had to formulate and identify the characteristics of an appropriate legal entity to hold title for the long term. We had to find a solution that accommodated both Traditional Seminole laws about owning land and state and federal laws governing land ownership and protection, and we had to formulate an innovative way to conserve the land so that the Traditional Seminoles could play a role in managing the land even though they would not own it.

Working closely with us, the Conservation Fund, and the Lannan Foundation, the Traditional Seminoles decided to create an independent non-profit organization under Florida state law to own and manage the land in conjunction with the Traditional Seminoles. The search for a suitable site for the Green Corn Dance

64 Caufield, *supra* note 6, at 24.

65 *Id.* at 1.

66 Phone interview with Curtis Berkey (Sept. 2009).

proved challenging and time-consuming. First, the search was limited to the few remaining cypress swamps and wetlands in Florida. Second, the Traditional Seminoles needed to find a large parcel of these wetlands—at least 2000 acres—that was still in a natural state. After looking at dozens of possible sites, in 1996, the Conservation Fund identified a property near Okeechobee that the Traditional Seminoles agreed was suitable. We planned to purchase the property but discovered that several restrictive covenants encumbered it and made it inappropriate for the Traditional Seminoles. We spent several months negotiating with the owner to remove the restrictions, but were unable to do so.

With the help of the Conservation Fund, the Traditional Seminoles found another, even more natural, site in October 1997. The Conservation Fund's diligence, persistence, and commitment had finally paid off. The unique 2400 acre tract included a river, grasslands, a cypress swamp, groves of live oaks and pines, and a wet prairie. It was located not far from the Traditional Seminoles' old dance site in Okeechobee County and had barely been developed. Unlike some of the other sites, it had not been "cultivated or planted with grass, and it was not cut up by fences, bridges, dikes, or canals."[67] In December 1997, we purchased 1750 acres of the property with a grant from the Lannan Foundation on behalf of the Independent Traditional Seminole Nation. We later acquired adjacent tracts to supplement this initial parcel and protect close to 2500 acres of Florida wetlands.

After we purchased the land, we created the Red Bay Stronghold Foundation, an independent non-profit organization under Florida state law, to own and manage the land in conjunction with the Traditional Seminoles. The Red Bay Stronghold Foundation differs from other non-profit organizations in its unique relationship with the Traditional Seminoles. Traditional Seminoles are not members of the Foundation's board, but they have final say over who sits on the board. The Foundation consults with the Traditional Seminoles regularly, seeking their input and advice before making any decisions about the land.[68] The Red Bay Stronghold Foundation holds title to the Green Corn Dance ceremonial grounds and "leases" them to the Traditional Seminoles at no cost.

The lease between the Red Bay Stronghold Foundation and the Traditional Seminoles was devised by the Traditional Seminoles and has several unique features. The lease includes several provisions to ensure the conservation of the natural resources on the property in perpetuity. First, it places several restrictions on land use and alienation.[69] For instance, the Traditional Seminoles cannot use the land for any commercial or industrial purposes, and the Foundation cannot sell any part of the land. Second, it establishes specific and unique obligations on both parties.[70] While the Traditional Seminoles have the day-to-day responsibility of

---

67 Caufield, *supra* note 6, at 22.

68 Phone interview with Curtis Berkey (Sept. 2009).

69 Lease Between the Independent Traditional Seminole Nation of Florida and the Red Bay Stronghold Foundation § IV (on file with the Indian Law Resource Center).

70 *Id.* at § III.

managing the land, the Foundation has "proactive fiscal and legal responsibility for (a) maintenance and management of the protected property; and (b) vigilantly protecting the property from damage, pollution, environmental degradation or other harm or loss to the extent reasonably possible with the resources and technology available to the Red Bay Stronghold Foundation."[71] The Foundation also "shall consult and consider the views of the Independent Traditional Seminole Nation of Florida in all matters pertaining to this lease."[72] These unique features allow the Traditional Seminoles to manage the land consistent with their laws and traditions without having to own the land.[73]

Conclusion

In 2002, the Traditional Seminoles, with the generous support of the Lannan Foundation, and the help of the Conservation Fund and the Indian Law Resource Center, established an ecological preserve to protect approximately 2500 acres of wild, undeveloped lands in south Florida. While everyone involved celebrated the creation of an ecological preserve to permanently protect the Green Corn Dance, the Traditional Seminoles (like many conservationists) knew that the conservation work was far from done. Bobbie Billie summed up the feelings of the Nation when he said, "I hope this land will continue the way it is forever. Having a ceremonial ground, though, is just the start. It's just one piece of the earth we're saving. We still have the rest to save."[74]

The creation of an ecological preserve to protect the Green Corn Dance and a portion of the undeveloped lands in south Florida is a moving example of what can be achieved through consistent and determined efforts by Native communities and environmentalists, but as Bobbie Billie pointed out, it is just the beginning of our piece-meal efforts to save the earth. We learned many lessons during the Green Corn Dance. We discovered that successful partnerships most often develop between conservationists and Native nations when they are based on similar interests; respect; open, honest, and frequent communication; and mutual trust. Successful collaborations are built through an often time-consuming process of listening and learning through regular communication. Conservationists and tribes have to be patient, willing to listen to and learn from each other, and open to new and unconventional ways of protecting the environment. We hope conservationists and tribes can learn from our experiences and improve upon them.

71 *Id.* at § III.A.2.

72 *Id.* at § III.A.3.

73 Caufield, *supra* note 6, at 23 ("This is the first instance of a tribe securing a permanent site without the involvement of any government agency and without the taint of buying or owning the land itself.").

74 *Id.* at 24.

Chapter 10

The Role of Indigenous Custom in Environmental Governance: Lessons from the Inter-American Human Rights System

Ghislain Otis[1]

Introduction

As recently proclaimed in the Anchorage Declaration, indigenous peoples view themselves as the guardians of their ancestral lands against environmental degradation.[2] They are also among the communities most vulnerable to the upheavals caused by phenomena such as climate change and deforestation.[3] Today, the international community is increasingly sensitive to the situation of indigenous peoples and is therefore less hesitant to acknowledge the potential contribution of indigenous rights and knowledge systems to environmental protection.[4] The

1 Ghislain Otis PhD, Chaire de recherche du Canada sur la diversité juridique et les peoples autochtones, Faculté de droit, Université d'Ottawa, Canada Research Chair on Legal Diversity and Indigenous Peoples. This chapter is substantially revised version of an article that appeared in French in issue 20.3 of the Journal of Environmental Law and Practice.

2 The declaration was adopted by indigenous leaders from all parts of the world at the Indigenous Peoples' Global Summit on Climate Change. *See International Peoples' Global Summit on Climate Change DECLARATION* (April 24, 2009), http://www.indigenoussummit.com/servlet/content/declaration.html.

3 *See* Bradford W. Morse, *Indigenous Rights as a Mechanism to Promote Environmental Sustainability, in* Reconciling Human Existence with Ecological Integrity: Science, Ethics, Economics and Law 159 (Laura Westra, Klaus Bosselmann & Richard Westra eds. 2008); Arctic Climate Impact Assessment (ACIA), Impacts of a Warming Arctic: Arctic Climate Impact Assessment (2004).

4 *See United Nations Convention on Biological Diversity*, June 5, 1992, 1760 R.T.N.U. 79 (Dec. 29, 1993). This convention recognizes the link between certain traditional uses of land and resources by indigenous peoples and the preservation of biological diversity, but it does not directly protect indigenous customary law regarding such uses. Article 8 (j) of the Convention reads as follows: "Each contracting Party shall, as far as possible and as appropriate: Subject to national legislation, respect, preserve and maintain knowledge, innovations and practices of indigenous and local communities embodying traditional lifestyles relevant for the conservation and sustainable use of biological diversity and

preamble to the UN Declaration on the Rights of Indigenous Peoples solemnly affirms that "respect for indigenous knowledge, cultures and traditional practices contributes to sustainable and equitable development and proper management of the environment."[5] The Declaration also recognizes the unique environmental protection needs of indigenous peoples.[6] Nevertheless, the continued hegemony of States in international normative development, albeit increasingly contested, remains an obstacle to the equitable participation of indigenous peoples in the global process of environmental governance.[7]

The question as to the role of indigenous legal or normative systems in environmental law is ever more relevant, owing to failures in the laws of States and indigenous claims for greater control and protection of their ancestral lands. In the area of environmental law, the dialogue between indigenous and Western legal cultures has become a matter for international debate and, through the use of human rights instruments by indigenous groups to combat the degradation of their environment,[8] has given rise to normative developments. Consequently, the contribution of international human rights law to the creation of a space wherein indigenous custom is used to manage and protect the environment of traditional indigenous lands constitutes a relevant topic for reflection.[9]

The following pages provide an analysis of work completed by the Inter-American Court of Human Rights, the judicial body responsible for interpreting and applying the American Convention on Human Rights[10] (the Convention), the

---

promote their wider application with the approval and involvement of the holders of such knowledge, innovations and practices and encourage the equitable sharing of the benefits arising from the utilization of such knowledge innovations and practices."

5 G.A. Res. 61/295, Annex, U.N. Doc. A/RES/61/295 (Sept. 13, 2007), *available at* United Nations, *United Nations Declaration on the Rights of Indigenous Peoples* (Sept. 13, 2007), http://www.un.org/esa/socdev/unpfii/fr/drip.html [hereinafter *Declaration on the Rights of Indigenous Peoples*]. The adoption of the Declaration has attracted considerable scholarly attention, see in particular Viniyanka Prasad, *The UN Declaration on the Rights of Indigenous Peoples: A Flexible Approach to Addressing the Unique Needs of Varying Populations*, 9 CHI. J. INT'L L. 297 (2008); REFLECTIONS ON THE UN DECLARATION ON THE RIGHTS OF INDIGENOUS PEOPLES (Alexandra Xanthaki & Stephen Allen eds., 2009).

6 For example, article 29 of the *Declaration* states that indigenous peoples "have the right to the conservation and protection of the environment and the productive capacity of their lands or territories and resources."

7 Sophie Thériault, *Sécurité alimentaire et justice environnementale dans l'Arctique canadien: l'impératif d'une participation accrue des Inuit à la gouvernance de l'environnement, in* L'ÉQUITÉ ENVIRONNEMENTALE: CLEF DU DÉVELOPPEMENT DURABLE, LES CAHIERS DE L'INSTITUT EDS 10–28 (2009).

8 Nigel Bankes, *International Human Rights Law and Natural Resources Projects within the Traditional Territories of Indigenous Peoples*, 47 ALBERTA L. REV. 457 (2010).

9 In this chapter, the phrase "indigenous peoples" includes tribal peoples.

10 Organization of American States, American Convention on Human Rights, O.A.S.Treaty Series No. 36, 1144 U.N.T.S. 123 entered into force July 18, 1978, reprinted

main human rights treaty of the Organization of American States (OAS). The OAS is a regional agency within the meaning of Article 52 of the UN Charter,[11] with a membership comprising the 35 sovereign states of the Americas. The Convention entered into force on July 18, 1978, and the Court was established on September 3, 1979. So far, 24 member States of the OAS have ratified the Convention. States not bound by the Convention—including the United States and Canada—are nonetheless bound to respect the OAS Charter.[12] The Charter, for its part, refers to the American Declaration of the Rights and Duties of Man[13] (the Declaration), which protects many of the rights set out in the Convention.[14] The Inter-American Commission on Human Rights, whose mission is to promote and verify compliance with the Declaration, has recognized that the Court's jurisprudence relating to a right also enshrined in the Declaration is relevant to defining the international obligations of all OAS members, including those obligations concerning the rights of indigenous peoples.[15]

---

in Basic Documents Pertaining to Human Rights in the Inter-American System, OEA/Ser.L.V/II.82 doc.6 rev.1 at 25 (1992).

11 U.N. Charter, art. 52 *available at* United Nations, *United Nations Charter* (June 26, 1945), http://www.un.org/fr/documents/charter/pdf/charter.pdf.

12 Organization of American States, Charter of the Organization of American States, Avr. 30, 1948, 2 U.S.T. 2394, 119 U.N.T.S. 3; as amended by the Protocol of Buenos Aires in 1967, Feb. 27, 1967, 21 U.S.T. 607, 721 U.N.T.S. 324; as amended by the Protocol of Cartagena de Indias, Déc. 5, 1985, 25 I.L.M. 527; as amended by the Protocol of Washington, Dec. 14, 1992, 33 I.L.M. 1005; as amended by the Protocol of Managua, June 10, 1993, 33 I.L.M. 1009, *available at* Department of International Law—Organization of American States (Jan. 18, 2011), http://www.oas.org/juridico/english/charter.html [hereinafter *OAS Charter*].

13 Organization of American States, American Declaration of the Rights and Duties of Man, 1949, Doc. off. OEA/Ser.L/V/II.23/doc.21 rev. 6, *available at* Inter-American Commission on Human Rights, American Declaration on the Rights and Duties of Man (1948), http://www.cidh.org/basicos/french/b.declaration.htm.

14 *See* LUDOVIC HENNEBEL, LA CONVENTION AMÉRICAINE DES DROITS DE L'HOMME, MÉCANISMES DE PROTECTION ET ÉTENDUE DES DROITS ET LIBERTÉS 24–36 (2007). *See* articles 3l, 16, 45, 49, 51, 106, 145 of the *OAS Charter*, *supra* notc 12.

15 See the rulings of the Inter-American Commission in the cases Mary and Carrie Dann v. United States, Case 11.140, Inter-Am. Comm'n H.R., Report No. 75/02 (2002), *available at* University of Minnesota (Dec. 27, 2002), http://www1.umn.edu/humanrts/cases/75-02a.html; Maya Indigenous Communities of Belize (Preliminary Report), Inter-Am. Ct. H.R. No. 96/03 (Oct. 24, 2003), *available at* University of Arizona, Maya Indigenous Community (Oct. 24, 2003), http://www.law.arizona.edu/depts/iplp/advocacy/ maya_belize/documents/Belize2003-12prelimrpt1.pdf; The Kichwa Peoples of the Sarayaku community and its members v. Ecuador, Inter-Am. Ct. H.R. Case 167/03 No. 62/04, OEA/Ser.L/V/II.122 Doc. 5 rev. 1 at 308, *available at* University of Minnesota (Oct. 13, 2004), http://www1.umn.edu/humanrts/cases/62-04.html. According to the Commission, the American convention, "in many instances, may be considered to represent an authoritative expression of the fundamental principles set forth in the American Declaration." Grand

The jurisprudence of the Inter-American Court should be a matter of interest to American and Canadian legal scholars in particular, since the Inter-American Commission has heard petitions presented by indigenous communities from the United States and Canada. One such petition sought to hold the United States liable for the degradation of the Arctic environment.[16] Another complaint, brought against Canada by indigenous communities from British Columbia seeking the return and control of ancestral lands, has recently been found by the Commission to be admissible.[17]

This chapter will highlight the functional relationship between the international protection of group rights in traditional lands and resources and the recognition of indigenous custom as a source of environmental law. It will in no way attempt to posit a perfect equation between environmental preservation and sustainable development on the one hand and the protection of the indigenous right to the untrammelled enjoyment of their ancestral lands on the other.[18] When it comes to environmental protection, indigenous collective land tenure under customary law is no more sacred than the Western notion of individual private property rights. In ecological matters, no human beings are above suspicion, and in certain circumstances, indigenous societies, like all others, are capable of degrading the natural environment and wasting its resources.[19] The aim of this article is simply to show how the recognition and guarantee of ancestral land rights empowers indigenous peoples to invoke their own customary norms and institutions, if they

---

Chief Michael Mitchell v. Canada, Inter-Am. Comm. H.R. No. 61/08, Annual Report of the Inter-American Commission on Human Rights: 2008, OEA/Ser.L/V/II. 134/doc. 5 rev. 1 (July 25, 2008) 160, *available at* Interamerican Commission on Human Rights, Grand Chief Michael Mitchell (July 25, 2008), http://www.cidh.org/annualrep/2008eng/Canada12435eng.htm at 64 [hereinafter *Grand Chief Michael Mitchell*].

16 Petition available online at Inuit Circumpolar Conference, Petition to the Inter-American Commission on Human Rights Seeking Relief from Violations Resulting from Global Warming Caused by Acts and Ommissions of the United States (Dec. 7, 2005), http://www.inuitcircumpolar.com/files/uploads/icc-files/FINALPetitionICC.pdf. The Commission has dismissed the petition on the grounds that the petitioners had not proved a causal connection between environmental degradation in the Arctic and the conduct of the United States. See Andrew C. Revkin, *Americas: Inuit Climate Change Petition Rejected*, N.Y. Times, Dec. 16, 2009, at A9; Jessica Gordon, *Inter-American Commission on Human Rights to Hold Hearing After Rejecting Inuit Climate Change Petition*, 7 Sustainable Dev. L. & Pol'y 55 (2007).

17 Hul'qumi'num Treaty Group v. Canada (admissibility), Inter-Am. Ct. H.R. No. 592/07 (Oct. 30, 2009), *available at* Inter-American Commission on Human Rights, Hul'qumi'num Treaty Group (Oct. 30, 2009), http://www.cidh.oas.org/annualrep/2009eng/Canada592.07eng.htm.

18 For a discussion of the link between indigenous rights and environmental protection in international law, see Leena Heinämäki, *Protecting the Rights of Indigenous Peoples—Promoting the Sustainability of the Global Environment?*, 11 Int'l Comm. L. Rev. 3 (2009).

19 *See* Shepard Krech III, The Ecological Indian: Myth and History (1999). For a depiction of traditional societies as being culturally more respectful of the environment, see Sabine Rabourdin, Les sociétés traditionnelles au secours des sociétés modernes (2005).

so desire, to protect the environment and promote sustainable development. In this way, this discussion is part of a scholarly movement exploring the connection between environmental issues and land tenure, which seeks to understand the actual or potential role of traditional land tenure systems in environmental regulation.

Since the subject matter at hand encompasses the rights of indigenous peoples and the status of indigenous custom in international law, it is useful to begin by situating recent developments in the inter-American system within the general context of the evolution of international norms. I will begin by describing the relatively recent transformation of international law from the rigidly State-centric positivist version of the nineteenth century to an order more receptive to normative pluralism and indigenous legal traditions as a material source of human rights in connection with property. In the second section, I will proceed with an analysis of recent jurisprudence of the Inter-American Court dealing with indigenous claims founded on a pluralist and decolonized notion of property. Because this jurisprudence has already been the subject of commentary,[20] my contribution here will focus on an important aspect that has so far been overlooked by writers, that is, the unique role the inter-American system actually assigns to indigenous custom in the management and protection of lands and natural resources.

Indigenous Custom in International Law: From Denial to Recognition

Since the approach to indigenous peoples under colonial international law was largely grounded in the Discovery Doctrine, the definition of the relationship between State law and customary indigenous law was a matter falling under the exclusive jurisdiction of each State. Repressed and marginalized, indigenous custom was considered unfit to contribute to the development of international law. Indigenous groups and their aboriginal legal systems were at the mercy of States and their colonial policies, which were almost invariably racist. The twentieth century, however, saw the gradual expansion of international law to encompass areas such as human rights that had, until then, been solely the concern of fully sovereign States. Decolonization and the resulting cultural diversity of

20 For general accounts of the jurisprudence of the Inter-American Court regarding indigenous peoples' land rights, see Bankes, *supra* note 8, at 478–91. *See also* Enzamaria Tramontana, *The Contribution of the Inter-American Human Rights Bodies to Evolving International Law on Indigenous Rights over Land and Natural Resources*, 17 INT'L J. ON MINORITY & GROUP RTS. 241 (2010); Jo M. Pasqualucci, *International Indigenous Land Rights: A Critique of the Jurisprudence of the Inter-American Court of Human Rights in Light of the United Nations Declaration on the Rights of Indigenous Peoples*, 27 WIS. INT'L L.J. 51 (2009); Lisl Brunner, *The Rise of Peoples' Rights in the Americas: The Saramaka People Decision of the Inter-American Court of Human Rights*, 7 CHINESE J. INT'L L. 699 (2008); Jenniger A. Amiott, *Environment, Equality, and Indigenous Peoples' Land Rights in the Inter-American Human Rights System: Mayagna (Sumo) Indigenous Community of Awas Tingni v. Nicaragua*, 32 ENVTL. L. 873, 902 (2002).

participants in international organizations, the egalitarian and pluralist ideology inherent in human rights, and constant efforts by non-Western societies to curb the historical eurocentrism of international law are all factors that have undermined the hierarchical model of relationships between legal cultures.

The first international norm recognizing indigenous legal systems was formulated in International Labour Organization (ILO) treaties setting out rights specifically adapted to the unique position of indigenous peoples. As the instruments evolved over their successive incarnations, the relationship of customary law and State law, once defined by subordination and domination, became increasingly egalitarian. The international community's first attempt to rein in the absolutism of States in their dealings with indigenous peoples, the Indigenous and Tribal Populations Convention, 1957 (Convention 107),[21] nevertheless restricted the application of custom to residual matters, remaining in line with the objective of the gradual legal acculturation of indigenous peoples. For example, Article 7 of the Convention states that indigenous populations "shall be allowed to retain their own customs and institutions where these are not incompatible with the national legal system or the objectives of integration programmes." Matters to be governed by custom included the regulation of traditional lands, and therefore the protection of these lands and the natural resources they contained.[22]

In every aspect of the legal experience of indigenous peoples, however, the hierarchical superiority of State law remained unchallenged, and the supplanting of customary law by Western law was valid anywhere it was deemed to be furthering the objective of the national integration of indigenous peoples. Accordingly, the Convention approved of customary rules governing the transmission and use of traditional lands only insofar as they were consistent with the Western concept of economic and social development.[23]

In the decades that followed, indigenous issues sparked unprecedented international mobilization and became a matter of global concern. Recognized as such by the UN, the international organization undertook large-scale work eventually leading to the 2007 Declaration.[24] This was also a period of significant

---

21 Indigenous and Tribal Populations Convention (no 107) of 1957, International Labour Organization, June 26 1957, 328 R.T.N.U. 247 (June 2, 1959), available at International Labour Organization, Indigenous and Tribal Populations Convention (2006), http://www.ilo.org/ilolex/cgi-lex/convdf.pl?C107 [hereinafter *Convention 107*].

22 *See Id.* at Articles 11 and 13.

23 *See Id.* at Article 13 (prescribing that indigenous customary tenure "shall be respected, within the framework of national laws and regulations, in so far as they satisfy the needs of these populations and do not hinder their economic and social development").

24 *See* Robert T. Coulter, *The U.N. Declaration on the Rights of Indigenous Peoples: A Historic Change in International Law*, 45 IDAHO L. REV. 539 (2009); Megan Davis, *Indigenous Struggles in Standard-Setting: the United Nations Declaration on the Rights of Indigenous Peoples*, 9 MELBOURNE J. INT'L L. 439 (2008); Alexandra Xanthaki, *Indigenous Rights in International Law Over the Last 10 Years and Future Developments*, 10 MELBOURNE J. INT'L L. 27 (2009).

development within the ILO, which updated its instruments to ensure greater respect for indigenous cultures and identities. In 1989, this resulted in the adoption of the Indigenous and Tribal Peoples Convention (Convention 169),[25] which established a more balanced relationship between indigenous and Western legal cultures. Under this new treaty, the primacy of State law over custom was limited to the area of human rights only. For example, Article 8 recognized that indigenous peoples had "the right to retain their own customs and institutions, where these are not incompatible with fundamental rights defined by the national legal system and with internationally recognised human rights." Custom was still subordinate, but substantially less so.

Under Convention 169, the scope of custom was extended to cover issues regarding the tenure of lands traditionally occupied by indigenous groups.[26] Customary norms ensuring environmental protection in the use of lands and resources by indigenous peoples were given even greater recognition through Article 7, which sets out the right of indigenous peoples to "decide their own priorities for the process of development as it affects their lives, beliefs, institutions and spiritual well-being and the lands they occupy or otherwise use."

The equality of State and indigenous legal cultures was finally affirmed in the Declaration on the Rights of Indigenous Peoples. Article 34 of the Declaration eliminates any reference to the hierarchical supremacy of State law by making customary law subject only to international human rights standards:

> Indigenous peoples have the right to promote, develop and maintain their institutional structures and their distinctive customs, spirituality, traditions, procedures, practices and, in the cases where they exist, juridical systems or customs, in accordance with international human rights standards.

Under the Declaration, States no longer have the power to prevent or limit the application of custom through their internal legal systems or can do so only by invoking international human rights standards. This recognition of the potentially important role of indigenous customary law in the environmental field is confirmed in a number of provisions in the Declaration, including those setting out the right of indigenous peoples to the ownership, possession, and control of their traditional lands and resources, to which the States are enjoined to give recognition "with due respect to the customs, traditions and land tenure systems of the indigenous

25 Indigenous and Tribal Peoples Convention (no 169), June 27, 1989, Bulletin officiel de l'OIT, vol. LXXII, ser. A, no 2 (Sept. 5, 1991), *available at* International Labour Organization, Indigenous and Tribal Populations Declaration (2006), http://www.ilo.org/ilolex/cgi-lex/convdf.pl?C169 [hereinafter *Convention 169*]; *See also* Xanthaki, *supra* note 24, at 67–70.

26 *See Convention 169*, *supra* note 25, at Articles 13, 14, and 17.

peoples concerned."[27] The right of indigenous peoples to maintain their spiritual relationship with their natural environment and "to uphold their responsibilities to future generations in this regard" is also recognized.[28] The right to self-determination set out in Article 3 of the Declaration provides the framework principle within which these rights and customary normative powers are to be exercised. The right to self-determination includes the right to autonomy or self-government in matters relating to lands[29] and the right of indigenous peoples to "maintain and strengthen their distinct political, legal, economic, social and cultural institutions."[30]

The main point of interest in ILO Convention 169 and the UN Declaration, however, is not the formal restrictions they place on a large number of States, since the binding character of the Declaration is in fact contested[31] and few States have ratified the ILO treaties.[32] Rather, it is the gradual emergence of the model they propose in general human rights instruments, which member States have largely ratified, that gives them their normative clout. Indeed, the implementation organs of general international human rights treaties have followed the current favorable trend of supporting indigenous claims and developed general norms to include the protection of indigenous customary rights.

The UN Committee on the Elimination of Racial Discrimination has determined that the concept of non-discrimination includes the obligation of States to recognize and protect collective indigenous land tenure over traditional lands.[33] Because such tenure is frequently based on an indigenous customary system, it would be discriminatory not to give it effect in the law of the State. Thus, the enshrinement of a composite legal system has become a requirement for the equality of indigenous peoples within a State. Other UN bodies have interpreted

---

27 Article 26, *Declaration on the Rights of Indigenous Peoples*, *supra* note 5, at Art. 26.

28 *Id.* at Art. 25.

29 *Id.* at Art. 4.

30 *Id.* at Art. 5.

31 For a general discussion, see Mauro Barelli, *The Role of Soft Law in the International Legal System: The Case of the United Nations Declaration on the Rights of Indigenous Peoples*, 58 INT'L & COMP. L.Q. 957 (2009).

32 *Convention 107* remains in force in 18 states and *Convention 169* has so far been ratified by 22 states.

33 Committee on the Elimination of Racial Discrimination, *General Recommendation XXIII (51) on the Rights of Indigenous Peoples*, adopted Aug. 18, 1997. The Committee relies on article 5 of the *UN Convention on the Elimination of Racial Discrimination* which provides that: "In compliance with the fundamental obligations laid down in article 2 of this Convention, States Parties undertake to prohibit and to eliminate racial discrimination in all its forms and to guarantee the right of everyone, without distinction as to race, colour, or national or ethnic origin, to equality before the law, notably in the enjoyment of the following rights: … (v) The right to own property alone as well as in association with others."

general human rights instruments in a manner that favors the indigenous right to collective control over traditional lands and resources and, consequently, the right to govern those lands in accordance with their legal traditions. Common Article 1 of the 1966 Covenants[34] setting out the right of indigenous peoples to self-determination and permanent sovereignty over their natural resources has been construed this way.[35]

The gradual international recognition of indigenous custom raises the question of its role in environmental regulation. The Inter-American Court of Human Rights, having carried out a remarkable experiment in the cross-fertilization of human rights with the underlying logic of indigenous rights, has provided an innovative answer that is worth our attention here.

The International Recognition of Indigenous Custom as a Foundation for Environmental Regulation: The Role of the Inter-American Court

In practice, the capacity of indigenous peoples to apply their own customary law to matters involving the management, use and protection of the natural resources in their lands depends on their ability to prove that they have collective title to these lands, which is itself based on custom. The Inter-American Court, relying on the principle of the equality of legal cultures and on property rights, has recognized indigenous customary title in and jurisdiction over ancestral lands and resources.

The Inter-American Court has interpreted the American Convention as requiring the integration of indigenous legal traditions into the interpretation and application of international law. In so doing, it has determined that indigenous custom is an actual material source of international law that can contribute directly to the substance of the terms of an international treaty in the same way as Western legal traditions. Indeed, in the seminal case Communidad Mayagna (Sumo) Awas Tingni v. Nicaragua,[36] the Inter-American Court ruled that its interpretation of the rights in the American Convention, and specifically the right of each person to

34 International Covenant on Civil and Political Rights, March 23, 1976, R.T. Can. 1976 No 49, *available at* Office of the United Nations High Commissioner for Human Rights, International Covenant on Civil and Political Rights (2007), http://www2.ohchr.org/french/law/ccpr.htm; International Covenant on Economic, Social and Cultural Rights, Jan. 3, 1976, R.T. Can. 1976 No 27, *available at* Office of the United Nation High Commissioner for Human Rights, International Covenant on Economic, Social and Cultural Rights (2007), http://www2.ohchr.org/french/law/cescr.htm.

35 *See* Erica-Irène A. Daes, *Indigenous Peoples Permanent Sovereignty over Natural Resources*, Final Report, E/CN.4/Sub.2/2004/30/Add.1 (2004).

36 Inter-Am. Ct. H.R. (Ser. C) No. 79 (Aug. 31, 2001), *available at* University of Minnessota, Mayagna (Sumo) v. Nicaragua (Aug. 31, 2001), http://www1.umn.edu/humanrts/iachr/AwasTingnicase.html [hereinafter*Awas Tingni*].

"the use and enjoyment of his property" in Article 21,[37] must be informed by the autonomy and cultural neutrality of international law and not be based solely on the categories of Western law. Thus, by relying on a provision affirming what appears to be an individual right, it has incorporated customary systems of indigenous collective property into the regime of the Convention.[38] The requirement that indigenous legal systems receive equal treatment under international human rights law is plainly expressed in a later judgment of the Court:

> This notion of ownership and possession of land does not necessarily conform to the classic concept of property, but deserves equal protection under Article 21 of the American Convention. Disregard for specific versions of use and enjoyment of property, springing from the culture, uses, customs, and beliefs of each people, would be tantamount to holding that there is only one way of using and disposing of property, which, in turn, would render protection under Article 21 of the Convention illusory for millions of persons.[39]

In Saramaka People v. Suriname,[40] the Court decided that the collective tenure is not limited to the actual lands but also extends to the natural resources the lands contain, provided those resources have a close connection with their traditional indigenous lifestyle and culture.[41] In the view of the Court, the resources protected

37 Article 21 stipulates, "1. Everyone has the right to the use and enjoyment of his property. The law may subordinate such use and enjoyment to the interest of society."

38 *Awas Tingni*, *supra* note 36, at 146, 149.

39 Sawhoyamaxa Indigenous Cmty. v. Paraguay (*merits, reparation and costs*), Inter-Am. Ct. H.R. (Ser. C) No. 146, par. 120 (March 29, 2006), *available at* University of Pretoria, Advanced Human Rights Courses, http://www.corteidh.or.cr/docs/casos/articulos/seriec_146_ing.pdf. *See also* The Case of the Xákmok Kásek Indigenous Community. v. Paraguay *(merits, reparations and costs)*, Judgment of August 24, 2010. Inter-Am. Ct. H.R. (Ser. C) No. 214, par. 87 (Aug. 24, 2010), *available at* Inter-American Court of Human Rights, http://www.corteidh.or.cr/docs/casos/articulos/seriec_214_ing.pdf.

40 Case of the Saramaka People v. Suriname *(preliminary objections, merits, reparations and costs)*, Inter-Am. Ct. H.R. (Ser. C) No. 172 (Nov. 28, 2007), *available at* Inter-American Court of Human Rights, http://www.corteidh.or.cr/docs/casos/articulos/seriec_172_ing.pdf [hereinafter *Saramaka*].

41 The Court explained: "members of tribal and indigenous communities have the right to own the natural resources they have traditionally used within their territory for the same reasons that they have a right to own the land they have traditionally used and occupied for centuries. Without them, the very physical and cultural survival of such peoples is at stake. Hence the need to protect the lands and resources they have traditionally used to prevent their extinction as a people. That is, the aim and purpose of the special measures required on behalf of the members of indigenous and tribal communities is to guarantee that they may continue living their traditional way of life, and that their distinct cultural identity, social structure, economic system, customs, beliefs and traditions are respected, guaranteed and protected by States." *Id.* at 121.

by the Convention are those that are integral to the community's traditional lifestyle and therefore essential to its survival as a culturally distinct society.[42]

For example, the Court found that the exploitation of the forest by the community for subsistence and small trade purposes was part of the traditional Saramaka lifestyle. It therefore affirmed that the Convention protects the community's collective right to use and control this resource to ensure the economic, social, and cultural survival of its identity.[43] Because there was no substantial exploitation of specific metals such as gold in the traditional Saramaka economy, however, the right to the use and enjoyment of property under Article 21 of the Convention does not cover this resource.[44] Presumably, since the lifestyles of a good number of indigenous peoples are traditionally based on hunting, fishing, gathering, and subsistence farming, in many cases the protection of Article 21 will not confer on them the coveted control of the mining, water, oil, gas, or wind resources that are frequently abundant on indigenous lands. It must be pointed out that such a static, backward-looking construction of indigenous identity may make it impossible for indigenous groups to use the Convention, in the interest of promoting their own modern development, as a way of harnessing the economic potential represented by the resources in their lands and thereby reconciling their quest for security of identity with the necessary adaptations to the changes taking place in their societies. In this way, the Inter-American Court, much like the Supreme Court

42 According to the Court, "it follows that the natural resources found on and within indigenous and tribal people's territories that are protected under Article 21 are those natural resources traditionally used and necessary for the very survival, development and continuation of such people's way of life." *Id.* at 122.

43 The Court writes: "This evidence shows that the members of the Saramaka people have traditionally harvested, used, traded and sold timber and non-timber forest products, and continue to do so until the present day. Thus, in accordance with the above analysis regarding the extraction of natural resources that are necessary for the survival of the Saramaka people, and consequently, its members, the State should not have granted logging concessions within Saramaka territory unless and until the three safeguards of effective participation, benefit-sharing, and prior environmental and social impact assessments were complied with." *Id.* at 146.

44 The Court concludes as follows: "According to the evidence submitted before the Court, the members of the Saramaka people have not traditionally used gold as part of their cultural identity or economic system. Despite possible individual exceptions, members of the Saramaka people do not identify themselves with gold nor have demonstrated a particular relationship with this natural resource, other than claiming a general right to 'own everything, from the very top of the trees to the very deepest place that you could go under the ground.'" *Id.* at 155.

of Canada, for example,[45] runs the risk of locking indigenous cultures into a stereotypical, traditionalist mold.[46]

The fact remains, however, that an approach based solely on the Western notion of full individual ownership would not have provided any basis whatsoever for the protection of communal indigenous customary tenure. Only a pluralist model can create the opening needed to finally do away with the long-standing hierarchal model of legal cultures. This stage in the process of the decolonization of international law frees the interpretation of "property" from its Western origins and its a priori assumption of individualism, absolutism, and exclusivity. Moving beyond the modern ownership myth opens up the possibility of communal tenure reflecting culturally distinct phenomena of appropriation.

The international recognition of customary regimes of collective ownership confers legal personality on the community as such. The Inter-American Court understands this very well and has therefore imposed on States the obligation to recognize the legal personality inherent in indigenous peoples who hold collective land tenure.[47] As a legal entity, distinct from its members, a community holding rights in lands and resources can determine the conditions under which these rights may be exercised and enjoyed by its members. In other words, the collective right to land traditionally occupied and possessed by the community is also a "jurisdictional right" that can be set up against the members of the community and the State.

This autonomy inherent in customary collective tenure over lands and resources has been recognized by the Inter-American Court, which considered it at great length in the Saramaka judgment in particular. In that case, the Court was asked to rule on a petition brought by the Inter-American Commission on behalf of tribal Saramaka communities complaining of Suriname's failure to respect the ancestral title of the Saramaka in their traditional lands and its violation of their indigenous rights to the natural resources in these lands. The Commission and the Saramaka argued that the violation was the result of granting forest and mineral concessions to corporations and private individuals without having obtained the

---

45 In a series of decisions, which earned it almost unanimous academic disapproval, the Supreme Court of Canada has confined the scope of aboriginal rights to practices that are a logical evolution of those that were an integral part of the distinctive culture of an aboriginal people at the time of contact. *See* R. v. Van der Peet, 2 S.C.R. 507 (1996); R. v. Sappier; R. v. Gray, 2 S.C.R. 686 (2006). The Court has however not applied this restriction to cases where actual aboriginal ownership of the land based on ancestral occupancy is demonstrated. *See* Delgamuukw v. Colombie-Britannique, 3 S.C.R. 1010 (1997).

46 For a similar critique of this aspect of the ruling in *Saramaka*, see Bankes, *supra* note 8, at 490–91. *See also* Pasqualucci, *supra* note 20, at 80–81.

47 *Saramaka, supra* note 40, at 172. On the issue of the international juridical personality of indigenous peoples, see Howard Berman, *Are Indigenous Populations Entitled to International Juridical Personality?*, 79 Am. Soc'y Int'l L. Proc.189 (1985), Chidi Oguamanam, International Law and Indigenous Knowledge: Intellectual Property, Plant Biodiversity and Traditional Medicine 159–60 (2006).

free, prior, and informed consent of the Saramaka people. The Court was therefore asked to specify the degree of control that a tribal community could exercise over its traditional lands and the resources therein.

After finding that the Saramaka occupied and possessed their lands for centuries, the Court noted the existence of a traditional legal regime governing land tenure.[48] According to the Court, customary collective land tenure gave rise to "the right to manage, distribute, and effectively control such territories, in accordance with their customary laws and traditional collective land tenure system."[49] Thus, not only does custom provide a basis for indigenous property rights in traditional lands, but also it governs activities relating to the occupation, use, and protection of ancestral lands by individuals belonging to the group that holds indigenous tenure.[50] Customary organizations and authorities responsible for indigenous modes of regulation are thus protected, and the autonomy of the group becomes a medium for the expression of indigenous custom in the context of environmental regulation. Indigenous practices compatible with environmental protection and sustainable development, as well those that are less so, fall within customary normative jurisdiction, which the community is free to adapt to current circumstances.

When traditional lands and resources are used by members of the indigenous community, the customary regime is applied pursuant to a collective jurisdiction that can be characterized as "primary," since it is based on an immediate legal relationship between the group and the individual. When the land and resources are used by non-members, custom may be applied pursuant to a "secondary" jurisdiction. Such jurisdiction may be exercised through a contract if, for example, a non-member wishes to access communal lands to extract resources under a specific agreement with the community. The indigenous group can then wield its contractual power to require the third party to comply with customary norms governing the use of the territory and its resources. Such a practice would represent a kind of contractualization of environmental custom.

A non-member wishing to exercise a right to extract resources under a license issued by the State may also be subject to a secondary jurisdiction flowing from the right of indigenous peoples to effective participation in any decision-making process involving ancestral rights on traditional lands. Indeed, in the Saramaka

48 *Saramaka*, *supra* note 40, at 100.

49 *Id.* at 194 (c). *See also* Case of the Saramaka People v. Suriname (*Interpretation of Judgment of Preliminary Objections, Merits, Reparations and Costs*), I/A Ct. H.R. (Ser. C) No. 185, par. 48 (Aug. 12, 2008), *available at* Inter-American Court of Human Rights, Case of the Saramaka People v. Suriname, http://www.corteidh.or.cr/docs/casos/articulos/seriec_185_ing.pdf [hereinafter *Saramaka II*].

50 In *Saramaka II*, the Courts writes, "To the extent that this property corresponds to the members of the Saramaka people, they have the 'right to manage, distribute, and effectively control such territories, in accordance with their customary laws and traditional collective land tenure system.'" *Id.* at 50.

case, the Inter-American Court found that the State was not entirely free to unilaterally authorize the exploration or extraction of natural resources located on indigenous territory if the activity impinged on or risked impinging on the group's traditional lifestyle.[51] Before permitting such activity, the State must first ensure the effective participation of the indigenous group in the decision-making process. The free, prior, and informed consent of the indigenous community is not invariably required, however; on this point the Court distanced itself from those for whom such consent is an integral part of indigenous land title.[52] At a minimum, indigenous participation takes the form of consultation; in the case of large-scale projects likely to substantially affect a significant portion of the land, however, the group's consent must be obtained:

> The Court … considers that, in addition to the consultation that is always required when planning development or investment projects within traditional Saramaka territory, the safeguard of effective participation that is necessary when dealing with major development or investment plans that may have a profound impact on the property rights of the members of the Saramaka people to a large part of their territory must be understood to additionally require the free, prior, and informed consent of the Saramakas, in accordance with their traditions and customs.[53]

Thus, when a development project on ancestral lands—such as building a hydroelectric dam or digging an open-pit mine—presents a risk of serious environmental impact potentially threatening access to a natural resource traditionally used by the community, or a risk of degradation to the natural environment that would seriously compromise traditional subsistence activities, the indigenous or tribal group may either invoke customary prohibitions to block the project or require that developers respect its customary environmental norms as a condition for approval of the project. If it wishes, the indigenous community can even negotiate a legal framework to protect the land and resources, drawing inspiration from the unique customary notion of the relationship between humans and nature. If these efforts fail, it can use its veto to block the project altogether. This co-decision-making dynamic promotes the creation of a mixed regime of indigenous and State environmental protection law growing out of a dialogue between legal cultures in which indigenous custom is, for all practical purposes, on the same footing as State law.

Even where the limited scope of the resource development project means that the group's consent is not required, consultation must nevertheless proceed

---

51 *Saramaka, supra* note 40, at 129.

52 Pasqualucci, *supra* note 20, at 87–91. *See also* Alex Page, *Indigenous Peoples' Free Prior and Informed Consent in the Inter-American Human Rights System*, 4 SUSTAINABLE DEV. L. & POL'Y 16 (2004).

53 *Saramaka, supra* note 40, at 137.

in conformity with indigenous custom, which the State must then bear in mind when coming to a decision and, where necessary, when determining the methods of implementation that are the least prejudicial to indigenous tenure rights and traditional activities. The normative force of custom is weakened here, since the customary legal regime does not have the formal equality required to stop a project from going ahead. It is not entirely without power, however, since the State must nevertheless make every effort to reach an agreement with the indigenous community.[54] It cannot simply make a decision as though customary requirements did not exist because the joint design of a negotiated environmental regime that reflects indigenous norms certainly is strongly favored by the law.

The decision of the Inter-American Court in the Saramaka case provides significant clarification of international law as it concerns indigenous participation in decision-making processes relating to the management and use of their lands and resources.[55] Some international organization guidelines and policies, including Article 32 of the Declaration on the Rights of Indigenous Peoples,[56] remain ambiguous on whether indigenous peoples have veto rights. The Inter-American Court, however, has identified the circumstances in which indigenous peoples should be recognized as having a true co-decision-making power, although it has, it must be admitted, allowed a real uncertainty to persist as to the practical distinction between projects with potential impacts giving rise to the obligation of prior indigenous consent and those without.

Conclusion

This brief overview has demonstrated that the jurisprudence of the Inter-American Court substantially contributes to the recognition of a role for indigenous legal traditions and systems in land management and environmental protection on

---

54 The Court specifies that "consultations must be in good faith, through culturally appropriate procedures and with the objective of reaching an agreement." *Saramaka*, *supra* note 40, at 133.

55 On prior informed consent, see Frédéric Desmarais, *Le consentement préalable, libre et éclairé des peuples autochtones en droit international à la lumière des modèles de l'intégrité culturelle et de l'autodétermination: la nécessaire redéfinition de son cadre conceptuel*, 19 R.Q.D.I. 161 (2006); Melanie Nakagawa, *Overview of Prior Informed Consent from an International Perspective*, 4 Sustainable Dev. L. & Pol'y 4 (2004); Parshuram Tamang, An Overview of the Principle of Free, Prior and Informed Consent and Indigenous Peoples in International and Domestic Law and Practices, Off. Doc. CES UN, 2005, Doc. NU PFII/2004/WS.2/8 (2005).

56 Par. 32(2) of the Declaration reads as follows: "States shall consult and cooperate in good faith with the indigenous peoples concerned through their own representative institutions in order to obtain their free and informed consent prior to the approval of any project affecting their lands or territories and other resources, particularly in connection with the development, utilization or exploitation of mineral, water or other resources."

indigenous territories in the Americas. First, custom is acknowledged through the recognition of indigenous communal rights on traditional lands. Because such customary rights give the community actual jurisdiction over its members, customary environmental norms can be imposed on the community as well as on third parties who wish to access the land and its resources through a contractual agreement with the group. Second, indigenous groups are recognized as having the right to participate in normative, decision-making processes concerning the management and exploitation of resources on their lands. Indigenous participation will contribute to the integration of custom into the normative framework applicable to projects affecting traditional lands.

The Inter-American Court arrived at these results through an interpretive approach drawing on indigenous legal traditions in its definition of property as a concept or category of international law. Indigenous custom has thus become a material source of international law, and this development represents a real weakening of the ethnocentric positivism that has characterized international law since the nineteenth century. The pluralist and egalitarian concept of international law in the Court's decisions has, albeit indirectly, welcomed indigenous peoples to the sphere of international environmental governance by legitimizing the contribution of their legal systems to the definition of international norms liable to influence the resolution of environmental problems.

Of course, collective indigenous property rights on traditional lands protected by the Inter-American system are not absolute. The State has the power to regulate the exercise of these rights or even take them away for compelling and legitimate reasons.[57] Nevertheless, public authorities will be increasingly required to accept the interaction of their official laws with customary indigenous legal orders in the creation of regimes for the management, conservation, and exploitation of the natural resources located on indigenous lands. It is hoped that this cross-fertilization of state law and custom will give birth to a hybrid process, a sort of transcultural public environmental legal regime reflecting both the unique relationship of indigenous peoples with land and resources and the desire for the sustainable economic development of indigenous peoples and the general population.

Care must be taken to remain realistic in our appraisal of the consequences of the decisions of the Inter-American Court, however. The actual, tangible impact of indigenous custom will depend on several factors including, first and foremost, the formal and legally effective demarcation of land held under indigenous tenure. Since this exercise, which potentially involves the rights of third parties, is more often than not complex and very long, the risk that the marginalization of indigenous peoples will persist in the medium term is very real. Governments and indigenous groups will have to think long and hard about the tangible ways, and in particular the technical and financial circumstances, in which traditional structures of governance can be made effective, while bearing in mind cultural changes and

57 *See* Pasqualucci, *supra* note 20, at 82–86.

the consequences of centuries of inequitable dealings with Western institutions. They will also have to conceive of mechanisms to promote cooperation as they coordinate their respective normative actions and defend against the hegemonic temptation of the State.

The End

Index

For Product Safety Concerns and Information please contact our EU representative GPSR@taylorandfrancis.com
Taylor & Francis Verlag GmbH, Kaufingerstraße 24, 80331 München, Germany

www.ingramcontent.com/pod-product-compliance
Ingram Content Group UK Ltd.
Pitfield, Milton Keynes, MK11 3LW, UK
UKHW011003180926
475701UK00004B/543

* 9 7 8 1 1 3 8 2 7 4 6 5 5 *